MENHIRS, DOLMEN

AND

CIRCLES OF STONE:

THE FOLKLORE AND MAGIC

OF

SACRED STONE

MENHIRS, DOLMEN AND CIRCLES OF STONE: THE FOLKLORE AND MAGIC OF SACRED STONE

Gary R. Varner

Algora Publishing
New York

ISBN: 0-87586-349-3 (softcover)
ISBN: 0-87586-350-7 (hardcover)
ISBN: 0-87586-351-5 (ebook)

Library of Congress Cataloging-in-Publication Data

Varner, Gary R.

Menhirs, dolmen, and circles of stone: the folklore and magic of sacred stone / Gary R. Varner.

p. cm.

Includes bibliographical references and index.

ISBN 0-87586-350-7 (alk. paper) — ISBN 0-87586-349-3 (pbk. : alk. paper) — ISBN 0-87586-351-5 (ebook)

1. Rocks—Religious aspects. 2. Megalithic monuments. I. Title.

BL457.S7.V37 2004
203'.7—dc22

2004017625

Printed in the United States

Other Books by This Author:

Sacred Wells: A Study in the History, Meaning, and Mythology of Holy Wells & Waters (2002)

Water of Life — Water of Death: The Folklore and Mythology of Sacred Water (2004)

We implore the pastors to expel from the Church all those whom they may see performing before certain stones things which have no relation with the ceremonies of the Church.

— The Council of Tours, AD 567

...as in remote places and in woodlands there stand certain stones which the people often worship we decree that they all be cast down and concealed.

— Christian decree, Britain, AD 658

...it is perhaps the spirit of evil which exercises its power on us...teaching us, little by little, that safety is not to be sought from God but from a gem.

— Anselmus De Boot, *Gemmarum et lapidum historia*, 1636

The worship of stones was expressly forbidden by the Council of Nantes in the seventh century, and as late as 1672 by an ecclesiastical ordinance, ordering the destruction of circles.

— James Bonwick, *Irish Druids and Old Irish Religions*, 1894

The adoration of sacred stones continued into Christian times and was much opposed by the Church.

— J.A. MacCulloch, *The Religion of the Ancient Celts*, 1911

Among countless stones, one stone becomes sacred — and hence instantly becomes saturated with being — because it constitutes a hierophany, or possesses mana, or again because it commemorates a mythical act...

— Mircea Eliade, *Cosmos and History: The Myth of the Eternal Return*, 1959

It could be that the entire history of the land is recorded within...ritual stones, each of which is a repository of ancient wisdom and a channel for healing energies.

— Paul Broadhurst, *Tintagel and the Arthurian Mythos*, 1992

...throughout history the assumption seems to be the same — that stone can in certain circumstances become more than the stuff of which it is made.

— Lyall Watson, *The Nature of Things*, 1992

The Megalithic faith was a powerful and widespread religion, as compelling as Christianity was later to become.

— Dorothy Carrington, *The Dream-Hunters of Corsica*, 1995

At the most basic level, stone is the fabric of the earth, and as such is a symbol of the everlasting. The anthropomorphic view of the world sees stones and rocks as the bones of Mother Earth. They are the fundamental structure that supports all other aspects of physical existence and contains traces of earlier life-forms.

— Nigel Pennick, *Celtic Sacred Landscapes*, 1996

To my wife Susan, who first thought of this book, and to my grandfather, James Berrian Smith who, along the banks of the Mississippi River, introduced the world of prehistory to me when I was a child.

Acknowledgements

While I have visited many of the sites discussed in this book, by no means have I been able to gain firsthand information about more than a handful — there are many others whom I wish to thank for their research. Aubrey Burl, Sir Peter Buck, Paul Devereux, Lewis Spence, James Mooney and the many folklorist, historians, archaeologists and ethnologists, living and deceased, who have recorded the artifacts, legends and rituals, have given me much to work with and to think about.

A note of thanks goes to Ms. Aloha Montgomery for her research assistance on anomalous falling stones, and the German Externstein (site of the Externsteine rocks). She also kindly provided the photo of the Externsteine which appears in this book. All other photographs, unless otherwise noted, were taken by the author.

Table of Contents

Introduction

Philosopher-historian Mircea Eliade wrote, "a rock reveals itself to be sacred because its very existence is a hierophany: incompressible, invulnerable, it is that which man is not. It resists time; its reality is coupled with perenniality."[1] This is true, as far as Eliade goes. But why are some rocks simply tossed out of the way while others, regardless of their size, are held as sacred, mysterious and imbued with power? The very atmosphere which surrounds some of these stones is permeated with a sense of ancient wisdom and we cannot help but walk quietly, often peeking over our shoulders in the attempt to catch that other being peeking right back at us.

When I see large rock outcroppings, I am always tempted to stop and climb my way to the top — not only to observe the world from the lofty pinnacle but also to determine how these structures were perceived and used by an older people, in the ancient past.

The word "megalith" brings to mind images of Stonehenge and Avebury, two of the most awe-inspiring, ancient and sacred sites in the world. However, I have found over the years, large stones and standing stones in particular were universally viewed as connections to the heavens, to ancestors, to the gods themselves. Even today, we feel dwarfed not only in physical stature but also in our very existence as we stand next to these massive and timeless features of the natural and supernatural world.

---

1. Eliade, Mircea. *Cosmos and History: The Myth of the Eternal Return.* New York: Harper & Row Publishers, 1959, 4.

It is interesting, though, that these feelings of awe are not applied to every large rock outcropping. Only certain features seem to be infused with a sense of sacredness. What is it in these select stones that instill such feelings? This book will examine the universal view of sacredness assigned to some of these stones, the folklore surrounding them and the usage of certain types of stones as charms and amulets.

The properties of stone were recognized as unique early in humankind's rise to civilization. Even when cultures were transitioning their technologies from stone to metal, it was stone that was used for ritual and other important acts. Early 20th-century Egyptologist Wallis Budge wrote, "in a tomb of the VIth Dynasty at Sakkârah, when the Egyptians had a good knowledge of working in metals, we see in a painting on the wall the act of circumcision being performed on a youth by an operator who uses a flint knife." [2]

Like my other books, this one delves into the world of folklore, early religions and the continuation of ancient traditions into contemporary society. It is important that these things are not forgotten but are remembered, enhanced and continued from one generation to another. I also give an overview of archaeological findings on various megalithic objects and sites, which must be considered when speaking about the folklore of these places.

Certain abbreviations have been used in this book to eliminate the associated religious connotations when discussing time. Scientific journals have gradually gotten away from using BC and AD in discussing dates and have switched to BCE (Before Current Era), CE (Current Era) and BP (before present). I have used those terms in this book, as they generally give a broader and more accurate sense of time when discussing prehistoric and historic sites.

For those readers unfamiliar with certain archaeological terminology, the term *menhir* means a single standing stone or a monolith. These stones normally range from 3 feet to more than 20 feet in height. *Dolmen* is a term referring to a large room-shaped structure consisting normally of three upright stones with a stone roof-slab. These structures originally were covered with earth and were used for burial purposes. The majority of dolmen date from the Neolithic and Bronze Ages.

While some people may find the information in this book to be interesting trivia, I believe that it is an important link in our understanding of our place in

---

2. Budge, E.A. Wallis. *Cleopatra's Needles and Other Egyptian Obelisks.* London: Religious Tract Society, 1926, 4.

the world, our place in nature and how we may coexist peacefully among ourselves and within the greater universe. To lose our sense of awe at the mystery of the world around us is to deprive ourselves of our linkage to the very nature of our existence.

Gary R. Varner, Oregon, 2004

Chapter 1. The Folk Nature of Sacred Stones

They may appear to be simply pieces of smooth rock, but they wind up as "worry stones" in the suit pockets of Wall Street investors and university presidents. Contemporary worry stones are not so different from those smooth stones known as wašicun tunkan, the Oglala guardian spirit named after a deceased person or supernatural being that fills the stone with power, or the "thunder-stones" used during the Roman and Middle Ages. Thunder-stones were believed to protect the man on the street from lightning, and ships at sea from sinking, while bringing victory in court and in battle. Little do the keepers of worry stones today realize that they are practicing one of the ancient traditions of transferring their problems to an inanimate object. The recognition of stones as objects of power continues uninterrupted from the dawn of humankind into the 21st century.

Larger rocks, too, as they occurred in nature and in manmade patterns of standing stones, have exercised a commanding pull on human consciousness since the dawn of time. Religious fanatics during the early days of Christianity and later, during the Reformation, destroyed many standing stones. Over time, they had been sought after for their powers of fertility and healing, but in certain periods, for instance between 1646 and 1649, many traditional festivals and customs (such as observing the patterns[3] at holy wells) were forbidden, and monuments related to them were destroyed. Some were preserved, however, usually due to their remote location, or through "Christianization," or out of fear

3. "Patterns" is a term used to describe the various ritual activity still observed at many holy wells. Such activities included "circumambulating" around the well on your knees three to nine times, many times while saying particular prayers.

of disturbing the "devils" that were associated with them. Many that were pulled down were broken up to be used in the masonry for churches and homes. The practice of incorporating prehistoric monuments into church structures accomplished the Christianization of a region more easily, by preserving part of the Pagan "cult" and letting it continue as a Christian one. One such preserved stone, now in the churchyard of La Pierre de Saint Martin, in France, has become festooned with strips of cloth left by pilgrims — much in the same way that many holy wells are decorated in Europe. France also has many megalithic sites whose place names associate them with witchcraft, such as La Pierre de Sabbat, La Pierre Sanglante and La Cuisine des Sorciers.

Stones are eternal. The mythos surrounding standing stones in particular has been described as one that "offers an image of a reality that survives the passing of time...the stone symbolized the essential being: the soul or spirit of animate life that was not subject to decay, but endured beyond and beneath all appearances."[4] The timelessness of stones is a great part of their appeal and contributes to the feeling of sacredness that pervades many of the locations in which they are found.

To many Native American cultures, stones were the First People and are very much alive. Indeed, some tribes believed that they descended from stones. Rocks and stones were considered *Wakan*, a term given to "spirit"[5] among the Lakota, as stones, like supernatural beings, are very hard to understand. The Rock, in Lakota belief, was also called Inyan, "the primal source of all things."[6] Native Americans, and many other peoples, believed that rocks were the source of life as well as a doorway to the Other World. Dakota Indian Alvina Alberts, born in 1912 and an expert on Dakota folklore, stated that the Dakota "came from the water, and a stone impregnated a woman, and from there we grew."[7] Another Sioux legend tells a different story. Rising floodwater turned people to stone, rather than stone to people:

---

4. Baring, Anne and Jules Cashford. *The Myth of the Goddess: Evolution of an Image.* London: Arkana/Penguin Books, 1993, 96.

5. Walker, James R. *Lakota Belief and Ritual.* Lincoln: University of Nebraska Press, 1991, 70.

6. *Ibid.*, 50.

7. Nixon, Lance, interviewer. *Native American Folklore Interviews Collection* OGL #1260, June 25, 1992: Alvina Alberts. Grand Forks: Elwyn B. Robinson Department of Special Collections, Chester Fritz Library, University of North Dakota.

> In the time of the great freshet (flood), which took place many centuries ago and destroyed all the nations of the earth, all the tribes of the red men assembled on the Coteau du Prairie to get out of the way of the waters. After they had all gathered here from all parts, the water continued to rise, until at length it covered them all in a mass, and their flesh was converted into red pipe stone.
>
> While they were all drowning...a young woman, K-wap-tah-w (a virgin), caught hold of the foot of a very large bird that was flying over, and was carried to the top of a high cliff, not far off, that was above water. Here she had twins, and their father was the war-eagle, and her children have since peopled the earth.
>
> The pipe stone, which is the flesh of their ancestors, is smoked by them as the symbol of peace...[8]

Another legend says that the Great Spirit threw a piece of red pipe stone at a snake and when the stone hit the ground, it became man.

Among the Khoi Khoi in South Africa, the great rain god Tsui'goab was the creator and the Supreme Being, making the first humans from rock. [9] In some Polynesian tales, rocks are living beings, and they have sex and make families the same way other creatures do. Such beliefs were still prevalent in rural 16th-century Europe. In fact, this belief could still be found in England during the early decades of the 20th century. Folklorist Charlotte Burne wrote, "One may still meet with agricultural labourers who believe that *stones grow.* Suffolk farmers have been heard to state that the earth produces them spontaneously, and a piece of 'pudding-stone,' or conglomerate, has been pointed out as a *mother stone,* the parent of small pebbles." [10] Small pebbles, then, were simply the young off-spring of the larger rocks. Hawaiians believed that solid rocks were male and porous ones, female. [11]

Before discussing the folklore of standing stones, we will delve into the magical use of much smaller stones.

---

8. Johnson, W. Fletcher. *Life of Sitting Bull and History of the Indian War of 1890-'91.* Edgewood Publishing Company Publishers, 1891, 214-215.

9. Andrews, Tamra. *A Dictionary of Nature Myths.* Oxford: Oxford University Press, 1998, 211.

10. Burne, Charlotte Sophia. *The Handbook of Folklore.* London: Senate 1996, 23-24 (originally published 1914).

11. Andrews. *op cit.* 164.

Stones Used in Magic: Healing and Charms

The supernatural powers believed to be inherent in stones have caused them to be used as charms for thousands of years. They were worn to protect against the anger of certain gods, to profit in business transactions, to keep diseases and evil at bay, to heal and to gather the energy needed to acquire abundance. It was a common practice in Great Britain to scrape dust and particles from ancient stones, including Stonehenge, and mix the dust with water to drink as a remedy for various illnesses.

Charmed stones were used by the mightiest of rulers to the commonest of the common. Two fourteen-stone chains have been attributed to Naram-Sin, a famous conqueror and ruler of the Akkadian Empire, and to the king of Babylon and lawgiver Hammurabi. These two chains were composed of lapis lazuli, green obsidian and jasper. [12] While the purpose of the chains is not known, it is believed that they were considered to possess powers to enhance the abilities of the two kings to rule.

The Pima Indians who lived between the Santa Cruz and San Pablo Rivers, in Arizona, reportedly used stone tablets, which they had found in ruins left by earlier peoples, in healing rituals. Frustratingly little information remains to suggest where these tablets came from or how they were used. [13] Other stone tablets have been found in many of the Adena mounds in American Midwest — some of which supposedly have Roman and Arabic figures or letters similar to Phoenician characters. Researchers have theorized that the true purpose of these tablets was to stamp cult designs on bodies being buried or newly initiated members of the tribe or for stamping designs on textiles. [14] They also may represent religious items of an unknown purpose.

The belief in the magical protective powers of stones continues, among some people, into the present day. Rumor has it that the Iraqi leader Saddam Hussein put his faith in a magical stone for protection. Iraqi lore says that Hussein once placed the stone on the back of a cow, fired a shot at the cow, and

---

12. Thomsen, Marie-Louise. "Witchcraft and Magic in Ancient Mesopotamia," in *Witchcraft and Magic in Europe: Biblical and Pagan Societies.* Edited by Bengt Ankarloo and Stuart Clark. Philadelphia: University of Pennsylvania Press, 2001, 60.

13. Spier, Leslie. *Yuman Tribes of the Gila River.* New York: Dover Publications Inc., 1978, 283 (originally published 1933).

14. Silverberg, Robert. *Mound Builders of Ancient America: The Archaeology of a Myth.* Greenwich: New York Graphic Society Ltd., 1968, 249.

watched as the bullet swerved around the animal, leaving it unscathed. [15] While many Americans scoff at such a belief, none can dispute the fact that he survived several attempts by American forces to kill him with "bunker busters" and suffered only a bump on his head when captured.

Many odd beliefs have survived into modern times, despite all society's effort to introduce science and rationalism. In Utah, at least through the 1950s, wearing pale blue stones around the neck was believed to relieve headaches. Some also believed that these stones could prevent or stop bleeding. It was a practice in the Ozark Mountains (in Missouri and Arkansas), at least until the 1920s, to sew small stones into children's clothes to protect them from common childhood diseases.

In various locations throughout the world, the "evil eye" was warded off by taking stones found on river and creek banks, drilling holes in them, and placing them on strings around the neck of children. Amber was worn around the neck in many areas of the world including Spain, Kentucky, Utah, Illinois, Ohio and the Pacific Southwest as a protection against heart disease and as an aid in curing such physical ailments as colds, flu, convulsions, goiter, whooping cough, teething, lung ailments, sore throat, poisons, eye ailments, neck swelling and to prevent sexual desire. Necklaces of chalcedony (a broad class of mineral that includes carnelian, agate and jasper) were worn around the neck to ward off or bring recovery from insanity.

The belief that certain stones hold supernatural powers seems to date back to the Stone Age. A belief in the transference of diseases or evil to stones, or, through stones to other persons, is found in ethnological and folklore accounts worldwide. At one time it was customary for people living in the Indonesian Babar Archipelago to strike themselves with stones and throw them away, in the belief that they could transfer their fatigue to the stones.

Stones of different types were used universally to combat illness. Fever was believed to be transferable to agate — place an agate on the individual's head and the fever would move to the stone, and leave the patient relieved. A Scottish treatment for fever states that the person should hold three stones from a streambed in his hands and mouth while lying quietly. Lewis Spence noted in his book, *The Magic Arts in Celtic Britain*, "the number of miraculous stones existing, or formerly existing, in Scotland and Ireland 'defies description.'"

---

15. Hider, James. "Even on the run, Hussein has Iraqis under his 'spell,'" in *The Christian Science Monitor*, August 6, 2003.

Infertility has always been one of the most troubling conditions that can befall a family — there is mystery in its cause, and certainly a mystery in how it might be overcome. Stones were often looked to for help. In Burgos, Spain, a fountain dedicated to Saint Casilda was reported to have the power to make a woman fertile; and if a stone was thrown into the waters, a baby boy was assured. If a girl was desired, then tiles were tossed into the fountain. In Armenia, it is said that barren women would visit the rocky cleft in the mountain pass at Varanta. Legends said that if she was to have a child, the stone would open wide enough to let her pass, but she would not get through if she was not going to have a baby. [16]

Near the Yorkshire village of Ratho, seven miles from Edinburgh, women used the Witch's Stone, a large sloping boulder (now destroyed) with ancient marks cut into it, to encourage fertility; they would slide down the stone, in the belief that this would assist them in conceiving. A similar stone used in the same way is located in Kings Park, Edinburgh. The stones were highly polished by the many women who had slid down them over the years.

A similar tradition was practiced across the English Channel, in Brittany, where, according to Michell, "the grand menhir brisé was not just a possible lunar foresight but an actual resort, annually on the first of May, for women in search of offspring, which they hoped to achieve by bare-arsed slidings along its fragments." [17]

The obelisk of Begig, located southwest of Madînat al-Fayyûm Egypt, was also popular place of visitation for barren women. If they touched it, they believed, it would ensure their ability to bear strong and healthy children.

This practice was also part of California Indian traditions. A large "fertility stone" in an ancient Maidu village located in present day Roseville, California has carvings of breasts and a vulva which the Maidu girls would rub to ensure their fertility. These massive fertility stones were believed to house the spirits of ancestors, who would help the girl become pregnant. In some cultures, these spirits would impregnate the girl so that the spirit could be reborn once again. Similar legends occur in Sioux lore, wherein the mother of Stone Boy (a Lakota cultural hero said to have been "miraculously born") swallows a pebble and becomes pregnant, and in the Aztec myth of the birth of the god Quetzalcoatl. Interestingly, folk notions regarding humankind's origin from stone appear to be

16. Lalayan, E. "Veranda: Family Customs," in *Ethnographic Review* #2 (1897), 186.
17. Michell, John. *Megalithomania.* Ithaca: Cornell University Press, 1982, 89.

Maidu Fertility Stone

repeated in stories about the origin of the gods, themselves. According to legend, Chimalma, while she was sweeping one day, found a piece of jade and swallowed it — and became pregnant, giving birth to Quetzalcoatl, as a result. "The Mexicans," wrote 19th-century US Cavalry officer John G. Bourke, "were accustomed to say that at one time all men have been stones, and at last they would all return to stones," upon death. [18] Similar beliefs have been recorded in Oceania where it was said that rocks gave birth to all things in the world. In Africa, according to John Mbiti, "the Akamba have a rock in the western central part of their country, at Nzaui, which has a hole supposed to be the one through which God brought out the first man and wife."[19]

Archaeologist Campbell Grant wrote, "in many parts of the West, isolated boulders are covered with the distinctive pit-and-groove markings. Such carved boulders are especially abundant in northern California, and in the Pomo territory were known as 'baby rocks' and were used ceremonially by women

18. Bourke, John G. *Apache Medicine-Men.* New York: Dover Publications, Inc., 1993, 141.
19. Mbiti, John S. *African Religions and Philosophy.* Garden City: Anchor Books 1970, 121

wanting children."[20] McGowan notes that these rocks in the Pomo territory were frequented by childless couples, who would "grind off a bit of the rock in one of the cupules and make a paste of the dust. A design was drawn on the abdomen of the woman and some of the paste inserted into her vagina. Intercourse at this time ensured that she would become pregnant."[21]

The Kawaiisu Indians of California's Great Basin area also utilized a special rock for this purpose. It is a small standing rock, about three feet tall, and due to its shape it is known as "one who is a little pregnant." Women seeking to bear children would come, break off small pieces of the rock, and swallow them.

A fertility amulet, also known as a pregnancy stone, was commonly used in Italy. As Walton McDaniel recorded in 1948 in the *Journal of the History of Medicine*:

> [The amulet was] in the shape of a womb...a limonitic concretion or brown hematite, which, on being shaken, produces a sound...the prospective mother wears it nine months, fastened to the right arm, but then, at the arrival of the first pains of partition, she transfers it to the right thigh. Women hire the use of these stones from a midwife, if they do not possess one of their own as a family heirloom. Although these amuletic objects might seem to be somewhat pagan, grateful mothers do not hesitate to deposit them as tokens of success, as ex-votos in a Christian Church.[22]

A folktale of the Yupa Indians of Venezuela speaks of a Yupa woman who "found a stone from which she made a phallus. By having relations with this stone she finally got herself with child and bore a daughter."[23] Women in New Zealand would visit a boulder at Kawhia, called Uenuku-tuwhartu, which was credited with having the power to cure infertility. One side of the boulder was regarded as the male side and the other the female side; the woman would clasp one side or the other, depending on the desired gender for the hoped-for child.

Certain standing stones in Hawaii and Fiji, from six to eight feet in height, were regarded as having phallic powers and thus became fertility shrines. Andersen writes that two such pillars near Puna, Hawaii, had been used in ritual ceremonies since the earliest occupation of the islands. Those in Fiji, according to early ethnologist, were regarded as "consecrated stones" and were periodically

---

20. Grant, Campbell. *Rock Art of the American Indian.* New York: Promontory Press, 1967, 31.

21. McGowan, Charlotte. *Ceremonial Fertility Sites in Southern California: San Diego Museum of Man Papers No. 14.* San Diego: San Diego Museum of Man, 1982, 14.

22. McDaniel, Walton Brooks. "The Medical and Magical Significance in Ancient Medicine of Things Connected with Reproduction and Its Organs," in *Journal of the History of Medicine, 3 (1948)*, page 543.

23. Wilbert, Johannes. *Yupa Folktales.* Los Angeles: Latin American Center, University of Los Angeles, 1974, 92.

given offerings of food. These were described "as like a round black milestone, slightly inclined, with a liku tied around the middle. The liku is a band with a close-set fringe...and its presence accentuates the phallic character of the stone."[24]

In some areas around the world, difficulties in childbirth were avoided by wearing, or keeping close, stones the color of the sea, such as beryl. Stones with holes in them were especially prized and it was believed that suspending one over a woman in labor would give her a much easier childbirth and protect mother and infant against evil. In Roman times, it was believed that a stone used to kill a powerful animal (or a strong man) also had the power to make childbirth easier. The stone was thrown over the house where the woman lay in labor.[25]

For those worried about the inability to conceive, one possible solution was to collect stones from the property of couples who had many children; bringing such stones to one's own household was thought to bring fertility with them. This belief was still present in 1950s Arkansas.[26] In ancient Egypt, it was a practice to make scratch marks on stones in the belief that by doing so, pregnancy would be induced.[27] Other stones were used in Greece, Albania and Germany to ensure that the mother would have an abundant supply of milk for the baby.

Conversely, rock crystal was used by the Apache Indians attempting to prevent pregnancy. According to ethnologist Morris Opler, "rock crystal is used as a medicine when a woman does not want a child. The rock is ground up fine, and some of the powder is put in a drink. There are prayers and a ceremony connected with this, but I do not know them."[28] Bourke notes that a "medicine arrow" worn as an amulet by Apache medicine-women was broken or ground into fine powder and given to women during gestation. Whether to aid the pregnancy or to abort it, he does not say.[29] The medicine arrow was reportedly taken from the top of a mountain at the foot of a tree that had been struck by lightning.

24. Andersen, Johannes C. *Myths and Legends of the Polynesians.* Rutland: Charles E. Tuttle Company, 1969, 413.

25. De Lys, Claudia. *A Treasury of American Superstitions.* New York: The Philosophical Library, 1948, 216.

26. Parler, Mary Celestia. *Folk Beliefs from Arkansas, Vol 3.* Fayetteville: University of Arkansas, 1962, 9.

27. Leland, Charles G. "Marks on Ancient Monuments" in *Folk-Lore*, 8 (1897), page 86.

28. Lalayan. *op. cit.*, 186.

29. Bourke, *op. cit.*, 18-19.

Ethnographic evidence indicates that Comanche shamans used stones at least into the 1970s, if not later, in healing rituals. Ethnologist David E. Jones wrote that a medicine woman he had studied "applied the stone peyote drum 'bosses' to the patient's face so that, through her powers, the positive qualities of these stones — firmness and stability — could be injected into the patient's contorted face to heal him." [30]

The Powers of Holed Stones

It is an ancient and almost universal custom to attribute special properties to stones that are naturally pierced with holes. The Radfords noted, "in almost every country of the world the same superstition prevailed, though there could have been no collusion of the peoples, and no knowledge the one of the other of the superstition. It is, again, the instance of some curious instinct and fear of men of all colours and races leading them to one general belief or trust in an unseen power." [31]

Passing through large, pierced stones is a ritual commonly seen throughout the world's folk medicine traditions. In Greece and Scotland, women desiring children would wade into the sea and then pass through large water-worn holes in nearby rocks. This practice is known from the Middle East to the Orient, with some similarities found in the United States and elsewhere. It is seen as an act of passing through dimensions, in an attempt to "pass on" or transfer illnesses and to obtain power and health. "Pregnant women of Kilghane in County Cork," wrote Aubrey Burl, "passed clothing through such a hole to ensure an easy childbirth."[32] Other traditions included men and women clasping hands through stone holes to swear their troth. It has been suggested that "the wedding ring...may represent the ultimate reduction of the original idea, where finally only a finger is passed through." [33]

There is evidence too that prehistoric people would pass the bones of their dead through holed stones which were erected in the entryways of chambered

30. Jones, David E. *Sanapia: Comanche Medicine Woman.* New York: Holt, Rinehart and Winston Case Studies in Cultural Anthropology, 1972, 96.

31. Radford, Edwin and Mona A. *Encyclopaedia of Superstitions.* New York: The Philosophical Library, 1949, 149.

32. Burl, Aubrey. *Prehistoric Averbury.* New Haven: Yale University Press, 1979, 36.

33. Hand, Wayland D. *Magical Medicine.* Berkeley: University of California Press, 1980, 148.

tombs, which were regarded as portals to the otherworld. Carved standing stones were erected as recently as 750 years ago at Tiya, in Ethiopia, to mark burial sites. The buried section of the stones usually had holes in them to symbolize the passage of the soul from life to death.

A kind of inverse of that ritual, one that focused on life instead of death, was acted out in modern times in Saintongue, France. Folklorist Wayman D. Hand noted that the women of this village "passed their newborn infants through holes in dolmens to guard them against evil, present and future." [34]

Putting parts of oneself through certain monuments was thought to prevent illness and evil and also to allow an individual to obtain forgiveness of sins. A stone scroll at Chela, Morocco, is placed about three feet from the ground so that visitors may easily insert their hands in a hole situated in its center. By doing so, they believe, they will have their sins forgiven.

In the Scottish fishing village of Applecross, a stone circle with a holed stone in the center was used as the community meeting place for both Christian worship and "ritual of a pagan nature." They would place their heads through the hole in the hopes of obtaining good omens. [35] The locals used the holed stone so often for prophetic purposes that the Presbytery in 1656 condemned the users.

Small stones with naturally occurring holes in them have been especially prized for their purported magical properties and in many cases, they were believed to be linked directly to the Goddess. In North Carolina, at least through the 1920s, holed stones were worn by pregnant women to ease childbirth and in Northumberland up to the early 20th century holy, or holed, stones were placed around a horse's neck to protect it from disease. It was a common belief in the Ozarks that stones with naturally occurring holes could ward off witches and evil spirits. It was also believed that such a stone tied to the bedpost would prevent nightmares.

On the Isle of Sheppey, in Britain, it was the custom to hang "such a stone, or even a beach stone, round the neck of every child until it reached its first birthday, but never afterwards," [36] for continued protection from disease.

The Lakota Indian myth about Wohpe, who is an Earth Mother figure, and Okaga, the South Wind, speaks of Wohpe giving a magical holed stone to Okaga: "Here is a stone. Take and keep it. When you see it, think of me. It will

---

34. *Ibid.*
35. Lamont-Brown, Raymond. *Scottish Folklore.* Edinburgh: Birlinn Limited, 1996, 54.
36. Radford *op. cit.* 228.

keep you warm and if you wish a fire, rub it and fire will come from it. When you wish to forget me, throw it from you and you will remember me no more." [37] In another version of this story it is Waziyata, the North Wind, who gives Okaga a small black stone that will accomplish whatever task he wishes and will protect him when danger is near.

One of the most famous holed stone is that of Men-an-Tol, near the healing well of St. Madron's in Cornwall, England. At least through the 18th century, and most probably well beyond that time, persons with back and limb pains would crawl through the hole in hopes of a cure. Children with rickets were also passed through the stone. For relief from pain, the individual had to pass through the hole either three or nine time, against the sun — or "widdershins." Children with rickets could only be cured if they were passed through to an adult of the opposite sex. Local folklore states that the Men-an-Tol had a protective Faery or Pixy in residence and it was this creature who would cure those who passed through the stone hole. In addition to cures, the benevolent Faery would also undo the work of evil Faeries and reverse a changeling into its human baby form. The November 28, 1868 issue of *Notes and Queries* reported that as late as 1749 offerings were being left at this holed stone. "Two pins," the article relates, were found on the top edge of the stone, "carefully lay'd across each other." Such pin offerings were commonly left at holy wells to appease the resident Faery, so we may assume similar beliefs were involved at Men-an-Tol.

Another important holed stone is the Tolvan Stone, also in Cornwall. At the Tolvan Stone, children were passed through the hole nine times, back and forth. To ensure that a cure had been obtained, it was imperative that, on the ninth pass, the child go round on the side where a grassy mound was located. The last part of the ritual was to lay the child to sleep on the mound with a six-pence under his or her head.

Smaller naturally holed stones were hung in stables, cowsheds and homes to keep them safe "from witches, and were believed to protect horses and cattle from being ridden at night to the sabbats...."[38] This practice was used widely from Scotland through Cornwall to keep frogs and other pests from entering homes.

---

37. Walker, James R., ed by Elaine A. Jahner. *Lakota Myth*. Lincoln: University of Nebraska Press, 1983, 68.

38. Merrifield, Ralph. *The Archaeology of Ritual and Magic*. New York: New Amsterdam Books, 1987, 162.

Holed stones and holy wells are two of the features that have had the most universal and timeless following of humankind's ancient popular customs. Patterns of related beliefs can be found from India to Indiana, and the fact that they are so widespread indicates that a belief system existed which surely pre-dates the erection of the huge megaliths.

New mothers in Armenia who had difficulty breastfeeding frequented certain holy stones that were naturally shaped like breasts. According to Lalayan, the women would be taken to these sites, where they would drink the water that dripped from the stone and wash their own breasts with the water. Afterwards, they would pray and light candles in front of the stones. [39]

Healing Stones

Stones were used to treat a variety of complaints and illnesses including mumps, insanity, rheumatism, consumption, and, of course, warts. Warts evidently have been a bane of humankind from the very beginning — and they were treated both at holy wells and at sacred rocks. For the most part, warts were treated via the transference method, by rubbing them with a pin and tossing the pin into a holy well, or rubbing them with rock and tossing the rock away. One ritual recorded in Ohio involved counting the number of warts and collecting the same number of small stones in a small bag. Then the instructions said to "go to the intersection of a road, throw the bag over your left shoulder, and return home by another way. The person who picks up the bag of stones will get your warts."[40] Other varieties of this tradition say that the warts are to be rubbed with the stones first and that the bag should be tied with a red bow.

Another cure, also from Ohio, says to rub warts with a stone and bury it at the first crossroads encountered. This method was apparently imported by settlers from Great Britain and Western Europe, where it was commonly used, as well. We see in these two examples that road intersections, or crossroads, are important for the cure to work. Why this should be held to be so important for the treatment of warts in particular is unknown, but the crossroads are indic-

39. Opler, Morris Edward. *An Apache Life-Way: The Economic, Social, and Religious Institutions of the Chiricahua Indians.* Chicago: University of Chicago Press, 1941, 405.

40. Puckett, Newbell Niles. *Popular Beliefs and Superstitions: A Compendium of American Folklore from the Ohio Collection of Newbell Niles Puckett*, ed. by Wayland D. Hand. Boston: G K Hall & Co, 1981, 498.

ative of a much more magical power. Symbolically, the crossroads represent the meeting place of time and space where magic takes place and where demons also meet. It is a dangerous place.

A Scottish antidote called for the warts to be washed in water collected in natural basins found in "old layer stones." These "layer stones" are assumed to be sedimentary rocks. After washing, the warts would disappear.

Mumps were given a special treatment. According to writer Lady Wilde, nine black stones had to be gathered before sunrise and the patient brought to a holy well with a rope around his neck. It was imperative that no one speak during the journey to the holy well. Once there, the patient was to "cast three stones in the name of God, three in the name of Christ, and three in the name of Mary. Repeat this process for three mornings and the disease will be cured." [41]

Bothered by insomnia? Among the so-called "Pennsylvania Dutch," during the first two decades of the 20th century, it was recommended that to put a small round stone found lying on a fencepost under your pillow — sleep was sure to follow. [42] One wonders whether, as good neighbors, people were in the habit of placing round stones on fence posts just in case a needy person might pass by. A "sleeping stone" and a "waking stone" were also used in the 19th century. Reportedly, if a small number of sleeping stone were hung around a person's neck, the person would sleep straight through for three days and nights. The waking stone, on the other hand, would keep an individual awake without any ill effects and was said to be excellent for night watchmen.

Nine stones taken from a stream treated could be applied to bring down swelling of any kind, and this was used for stings, as well. A different stone was taken each day for nine days and returned to the stream after its use. Similar treatments were common in both Chile and ancient Rome. The number nine is frequently associated with healing and divination lore around the world. Nine was connected with potent magic. Hopper noted that the number nine "invokes the favor of the triple triad of the angels and at the same time enlists the power of the devil." [43]

---

41. Wilde, Lady. *Irish Cures, Mystic Charms & Superstitions*. New York: Sterling Publishing Co., Inc., 1991, 24.

42. Fogel, Edwin Miller. "Beliefs and Superstitions of the Pennsylvania Germans" in *Americana Germanica* (Philadelphia), 18 (1915), 268.

43. Hopper, Vincent Foster. *Medieval Number Symbolism: Its Sources, Meaning, and Influence on Thought and Expression*. Mineola: Dover Publications, Inc. 2000, 123.

Likewise, the number three has held a special value in various rituals. Three is one of the most powerful numbers of religio-magic traditions. In the British Isles, it was common to use three stones in healing rituals. William Black noted in particular that wise-woman Margaret Sandieson took but "thrie small stones and twitched her head thrie tymes with everie one of them"[44] when she treated an ill woman. A similar method was also used in Scotland.

Storaker reported a cure for illness that involved having a woman healer heat three small stones, drop them into water and then have the patient drink the water. [45]

Bonwick noted that in Ireland, "down to a late period," people would pour water on the surface of stone "temples" and drink it, "that the draught might cure their diseases. Molly Grime, a rude stone figure, kept in Glentham church, was annually washed with water from Newell well...babies were sprinkled at cairns in Western or South Scotland down to the seventeenth century. Some stones were kissed by the faithful, like the Druid's Stone in front of Chartres Cathedral, once carefully kept in the crypt." [46]

Stonehenge may be perhaps the largest "healing stone" in the world. Geoffrey of Monmouth wrote in the 12th century that the megaliths had gained a reputation for the healing of many diseases. Again, the combination of water and stone becomes evident as Geoffrey notes that the stones were washed and the water used in baths for the ill. The healing attributed to Stonehenge was accepted well into the 17th and 18th centuries. Similarly, the "12 o'clock" stone, a large standing stone in Cornwall, was reputed to cure children of rickets — as long as they were not illegitimate or the offspring of "dissolute" parents.

Other healing stones from the past include the Red Stone in Perthshire, which was used to cure distemper; the Lee Stone, owned by the Earl of Douglas, that kept plague away (it was lent out — as long as a hefty sum was paid as a security deposit for the stone's return); the Murrain Stone that was, into the 1890s, dipped into water to be given to cattle in order to cure murrain (a term given for any infectious disease of cattle) and hydrophobia; and a charm stone from Ireland that was renowned for healing wounds — as long as it never

44. Black, William George. "Folk Medicine: A Chapter in the History of Culture." London: *Publications of the Folk-Lore Society #12, 1883*, 118.

45. Storaker, Joh. Th. "Sygdom og Forgjo/relse I den Norske Folketro." *Norsk Folkeminnelag* No. 20. Oslo, 1932, 32.

46. Bonwick, James. *Irish Druids and Old Irish Religions.* New York: Barnes and Noble Books 1894, 217.

touched English soil. The last was taken by basket from patient to patient and rubbed on the wound to effect healing.

THUNDERSTONES

Thunderstones are stones found throughout the Old World that people associated with lightning strikes. These turn out to have been Stone Age[47] tools, such as hand axes. Some accounts state that they are always black in color with white streaks running through them — as, apparently, some axes were. They were deemed to have great power for healing and giving strength. They were used in the treatment of jaundice, lameness, cataracts, convulsions, consumption, goiter, and snakebite, in childbirth and, carried on the person, to relieve rheumatism. Neolithic stone axes must, indeed, have mystified people who came along later; they did not look like something that would have occurred in nature, and it would be impossible to explain how they came to litter the landscape. Inevitably, they were endowed with supernatural powers that even aristocratic churchmen would extol:

> He who carries one will not be struck by lightning, nor will houses if the stone is there; the passenger on a ship traveling by sea or river will not be sunk by storm or struck by lightning; it gives victory in law-suits and battles, and guarantees sweet sleep and pleasant dreams.
>
> — Marbodaeus, Bishop of Rennes, 12th century. [48]

The uses for these stone-axe "thunderbolts" in the Old World were numerous; they were tossed into wells to ensure a continuous supply of good water; they were placed in cattle troughs to protect cattle from disease; and water in which the stone had been boiled was used as a treatment of rheumatism.

These artifacts were probably seen as supernatural objects as long ago as the Iron Age, when memories of stone tools had already faded away. [49] In France, prehistoric stone axes were referred to as "witches fingers," lending them an

---

47. These "thunderstones," or hand axes, were created at least 500,000 years ago and continued to be used in parts of Africa until approximately 50,000 years BCE. The "Stone Age" generally is defined as beginning approximately 2.5 million years ago and lasting in some parts of the world yet today. See the appendix for a time-line that illustrates the prehistoric periods and associated megaliths.

48. Merrifield, *op. cit.*, 11.

49. *Ibid.*, 15.

obviously sinister quality. Small projectile points that were found during the Middle Ages were similarly viewed as supernatural in origin; people called them "elfshot" — on the premise that they were arrow points made and fired by elves.

Folklore in Surinam says that, should one bathe in water containing a black thunderstone, enormous strength would be obtained. In fact, it is said that a man may become so strong that he can kill another with one blow — if the stone is dark enough. The darker the stone, the more potent it becomes. [50]

The Lore of Mystical Stones

Stones, in themselves steeped in myth and hidden meaning, are inextricably linked to sacred water. Ancient standing stones and sacred waters have a common ancestry. Their existence is intricately interwoven.

"Rain rocks" utilized by Native American shamans were intended to control the weather, especially rain and snow, and they were prized as well for their ritual ties to the Grizzly Bear. Standing stones erected by ancient Britons are perched high above important water sites in Ireland, such as the five-stone circle at Uragh, County Kerry, situated above the Cloonee Lough Upper and Lough Inchiquin. Large rock outcroppings decorated with carvings and painting rise high above similarly hallowed water sources in the American West.

Individuals still feel an inspiration to create rock monuments on or near water. A rather mysterious creation of several dozen rock cairns was recently found along a sand bar on the American River in the middle of Sacramento, California. Obviously, these cairns are not an ancient construction — as the ebb and flow of the river in flood conditions would have destroyed them. Who created them, and why, is unknown but we can presume there was a certain primeval urge to create a special, physical link between the human and the spirit world, associated with the nature of water and stone.

Also in California, at Panther Meadows, mid-way up Mt. Shasta's 14,000-foot slope, rock cairns are in use even now by Native Americans who still regard the site as a spiritual center. Rock cairns have been used since time began, around the world, to mark migration trails of game, places of death or burial, landing sites for seamen, water sources and holy sites. The Cree say that when

50. Penard, A.P. and T.E. Penard. "Popular Notions Pertaining to Primitive Stone Artifacts in Surinam," in *Journal of American Folklore*, 30 (1917), 260.

Contemporary Cairns on the American River

someone creates a small cairn out of a few rocks, "it grows, no one knows how, rock by rock." [51]

In Finland, the Stone of Pain was situated at the confluence of three rivers and the spirit of pain was believed to reside there. Pilgrims would visit the spot to request relief from their painful physical conditions. The combined power of the three rivers and the stone were construed as creating an ideal source for healing. "Stones of Pain" were actually cup stones that are widely found in Finland and around the world. These "cups" were shallow depressions carved into stone and were referred to as "Stones of Pain" as they were believed to drive away illness and pain. The Stone of Pain mentioned above was a specific cup marked stone located in a particularly important area.

Water is associated with ancient stone circles, too, such as those found on or near Pobull Fhinn on Loch Langass in the Hebrides, Uneval, Kintraw, Argyll,

---

51. Kehoe, Alice B. and Thomas F. Kehoe. *Solstice-Aligned Boulder Configurations in Saskatchewan.* Canadian Ethnology Service Paper No. 48. Ottawa: National Museums of Canada, 1979, 37.

Kockadoon, Co. Mayo, and Killadangan, Co. Mayo (all in the British Isles), among the hundreds situated around the world.

Sacred stones in association with specific holy wells are also common. One such well-stone combination is found at Whitstone, England. Whitstone is a name derived from a white rock located on the south side of the nearby Whitstone church. R.A. Courtney, a noted pre-World War I antiquarian, wrote, "The Church is dedicated to St. Nicholas, and in the churchyard is a well commonly known as St. Anne's well. It is said to never have been known to fail; and it would show that the Church is but the successor of the sacred white stone; the water from the well being used for baptisms. It may be remarked that the saint of the Church is a male, the well a female; and, if my theory is correct, the stone represented the lingam, the well the yoni."[52]

Another megalith with a long history of ritual connected with it is the dolmen called La Pierre à Berthe, located in a field next to the village cemetery of Pontchâteau, in Brittany, France. According to Aubrey Burl, it was believed that the dolmen would cure gout if one approached it on one's knees. "Up to the 19th century," wrote Burl, "pilgrims would go from the fountain by the church to make their devotions at the stone." [53] The fountain, or well, connection to the standing stone had an important part in the perceived cure received at the dolmen. Unfortunately, the dolmen was blown up in 1850 by a treasure seeker.

As the Hupa Indians of Northern California ritually washed certain standing stones called "story people" in the belief that this could change the weather,[54] so the fishermen on the Isle of Skye washed certain stones to improve the weather conditions. W. Winwood Reade, in his classic book *The Veil of Isis, or Mysteries of the Druids*, wrote, "in a little island near Skye is a chapel dedicated to St. Columbus; on an altar is a round blue stone which is always moist. Fishermen, detained by contrary winds, bathe this stone in water, expecting thereby to obtain favorable winds; it is likewise applied to the sides of people troubled by stitches, and it is held so holy, that decisive oaths are sworn upon it." [55]

---

52. Courtney, R.A. *Cornwall's Holy Wells: Their Pagan Origins*. Penzance: Oakmagic Publications, 1997, 30.

53. Burl, Aubrey. *Megalithic Brittany*. New York: Thames and Hudson Inc., 1985, 102.

54. These stones were situated in rows. Heizer wrote, "when frosts come in the fall...a man or a virgin takes a basket of water with incense root and washes all these stones, praying...that gentle rain may come and that the frost may go away" (see "Sacred Rain Rocks of Northern California ").

55. Reade, W. Winwood. *The Veil of Isis, or Mysteries of the Druids*. North Hollywood: Newcastle Publishing Company, 1992, 228.

An account of a "Pagan idol" from the Irish island of Inniskea, off the coast of Mayo, wrapped in flannel, was given in the *Notes and Queries* issue of Saturday, February 7, 1852:

A stone carefully wrapped up in flannel is brought out at certain periods to be adored; and when a storm arises, this god is supplicated to send a wreck on their coast.

Though nominally Roman Catholics, these islanders have no priest resident among them; they know nothing of the tenets of that church, and their worship consists in occasional meetings at their chief's house, with visits to a holy well called Derivla. The absence of religion is supplied by the open practice of pagan idolatry. In the south island a stone idol called in the Irish Neevougi, has been from time immemorial religiously preserved and worshipped. This god resembles in appearance a thick roll of homespun flannel, which arises from the custom of dedicating to it a dress of that material whenever its aid is sought; this is sewed on by an old woman, its priestess. Of the early history of this idol no authentic information can be procured, but its power is believed to be immense; they pray to it in time of sickness, it is invoked when a storm is desired to dash some hapless ship upon their coast, and again it is solicited to calm the waves to admit of the islanders fishing or visiting the main land. [56]

Can we make a connection with this flannel cloth made by a priestess to adorn a sacred stone and the strips of cloth that still adorn wells and trees that are held sacred ? The association of the stone and the holy well is, again, indicative of many sites throughout the British Isles. The stone is also anciently associated with sacred wells and this account may record one of the truly authentic Pagan practices that survived in Ireland into the 19th century.

"Rain rocks" were utilized by shamans as tools to control rain and weather. Rain rocks in Northern California were inscribed with meandering lines, grooves, cupules and carvings of bear claws and paw prints.

The Shasta Indians in the Klamath River area carved long parallel grooves on rain rocks to make the snow fall, and cupolas to produce rain. To stop rain, they covered the rain rock with powdered incense-root. According to rock art researcher Campbell Grant, the Hupa Indians of California "had a sacred rain rock called *mi*. By this rock lived a spirit who could bring frost, prolong the rainy season, or cause drought if he was displeased." [57] The Hupa would cook food

56. Tennent, Sir J. Emerson. *Notes and Queries*, Vol. V, No. 119, Saturday, February 7, 1852, 121.

Bear paw prints carved onto a Maidu sacred stone

next to the rain rock and provide a feast for the spirit to ensure that the spirit would continue to help them. "If the end of a rainy spell was needed," continues Grant, "powdered incense-root was sprinkled on the rock." [58]

Rain rocks were fairly universal among early cultures. In Australia's Northern Territory, it was "essential" for certain types of rocks to be scratched to ensure rain.[59] Although they are rarely found in Southern California, a five-foot rain rock marked with hundreds of small, drilled holes has been discovered on the slopes of Palomar Mountain in northern San Diego County. The site was a proto-historic Luiseño village, known as Molpa. [60] Just below the rain rock is a small spring, which was a steady source of water.

57. Grant, op. cit., 31.

58. *Ibid.*

59. Mulvaney, D.J. *The Prehistory of Australia.* New York: Frederick A. Praeger, Publishers, 1969, 172.

60. True, D.L., C.W. Meighan & Harvey Crew. *Archaeological Investigations at Molpa, San Diego County, California.* University of California Publications in Anthropology, Volume 11, Berkeley: University of California Press, 1974.

Because the decoration or alteration of rock material is difficult to date, we cannot determine when the use of "rain rocks" began. We do know that the Tolowa, Karok and Hupa tribes on the North Coast of California used rain rocks to control the weather at least from 1600 CE, and the practice continued into the early 1800s — and may in fact continue today. [61]

The use of special stones to create rain appears to be a fairly universal practice. Rain-stones were used by the Samoan Islanders, Australian aborigines, by people in Central Africa, Japan, and Great Britain, as well as in North America. In most cases these stones were dipped into or sprinkled with water by priests or shamans and were treated to elaborate rituals. Sir James Frazer wrote that in northwestern Australia, "the rain-maker repairs to a piece of ground which is set apart for the purpose of rain-making. There he builds a heap of stones or sand, places on the top of it his magic stone, and walks or dances round the pile chanting his incantations for hours, till sheer exhaustion obliges him to desist, when his place is taken by an assistant. Water is sprinkled on the stone and huge fires are kindled. No layman may approach the sacred spot while the mystic ceremony is being performed." [62] In North America, the Apache Indians in Arizona would carry water from specific springs and throw it on the top of a certain rock. "After that," Frazer continues, "they imagine that the clouds would soon gather, and that rain would begin to fall." [63] Rain-stones were used in similar ways during times of draught in ancient Rome as well. The stone called lapis manalis was kept near the Temple of Mars and "dragged into Rome, and this was supposed to bring down rain immediately." [64] Just what is the power in these stones that is believed to cause rain? In most instances, the stone was thought to contain the spirit of divinity or act as a conduit to the divine, who could be supplicated via the stone.

A Chinese tale recorded by Pu Songling, in the 17th century, tells of a "Rare Stone from Heaven." The stone, described as "one foot in diameter, exquisite from all angles with picturesque ridges and peaks," had the ability to forecast rain. According to the tale, "whenever it was about to rain, clouds would emerge

---

61. Clewlow, Jr., C. William & Mary Ellen Wheeling. *Rock Art: An Introductory Recording Manual for California and the Great Basin.* Los Angeles: Institute of Archaeology, University of California, 1978, 21-22.

62. Frazer, Sir James. *The Golden Bough: A Study in Magic and Religion.* Hertfordshire: Wordsworth Editions Ltd., 1993, 76.

63. *Ibid.*

64. *Ibid.*, 78.

Maidu "water rock." Note the water ripples coming from the rocks surface.

from each of its holes, which looked from the distance like new cotton stuffed in its openings." Many sought to get their hands on this stone, and all experienced disaster when they tried to possess it. [65]

65. Songling, Pu. *Selected Tales of Liaozhai.* Beijing: Panda Books, 1981, 133.

Stones were used in many parts of the world to control not only rain, but wind. In New Guinea, a "wind stone" was struck with a stick; the strength of the wind would vary depending on how hard the stone was struck. "In Scotland," says Frazer, "witches used to raise the wind by dipping a rag in water and beating it thrice on a stone, saying:

> "I knok this rag upon this stone
> "To raise the wind in the divellis name,
> "It shall not lye till I please againe." [66]

Frazer also notes that at Victoria, British Columbia, "there are a number of large stones not far from what is called the Battery. Each of them represents a certain wind. When an Indian wants any particular wind he goes and moves the corresponding stone a little; were he to move it too much, the wind would blow very hard." [67]

Both in the United States and Britain individual stones in association with water traditionally are said to cure illnesses. If you suffer from cramps while swimming you should pick up a few stones, spit on them and throw them into the water. A Norwegian technique to cure an illness is to take a stone from a hill, one from a field and a third from a crossroad (without touching them with your bare hand, though), heat them and drop them into water. The individual then must sit over the water, with a blanket covering his head. [68] In Ireland, unusually shaped stones found near holy wells are believed to be imbued with healing power. When an individual was too ill to visit the well, one of these stones would be borrowed in hopes of procuring a cure.

Stones also were seen as containing spirits and could be the homes of Rock Babies, Faeries and other citizens of the Underworld. Relating folk beliefs in Norway, Storaker wrote, in 1928:

> It was once believed that one could see the soul of a person as a small flame burning with a clear light. Such a light is often seen from stones. But usually, such a light from the stones is believed to be lit by the spirits living in the stone, and it is burning during the night. When the spirits of the stones appear like that, they are given the names of goblins, gnomes or subterraneans. The light looks like the light that is often seen at mounds, and which is called mound-light or spirit-light. [69]

---

66. Frazer, Sir James. *The Magic Art and the Evolution of Kings, Vol. 1.* London: Macmillan & Co Ltd., 1955, 322.

67. *Ibid.*

68. Storaker, Joh. Th. "Sygdom og Forgjo/relse I den Norske Folketero" in *Norsk Folkeminnelag No. 20.* Oslo, 1932, 31.

Apparently, even Storaker was not quite sure how rational he wanted to be in reporting on this "spirit-light" or "mound-light." He speaks about the lights without apparent question or irony, even while he treats the original premise of souls appearing as flames in stone as simple wives-tales. Storaker also noted that, "occasionally one would see a light burning in some stone, especially at the darkest time of the year. The light came from some creatures that had lived in the stones." If the location was examined carefully, Storaker wrote, sometimes a small, round stone would be found which could be used by a "wise woman" to cure an illness. [70]

Similar tales are also found in Wales. On Innis-na-Gore, in the early 20th century, was a large rock around which a "mysterious light" would suddenly appear in the night. The property owner decided to blow the rock up in an attempt to determine the source of the light. What he found, according to the story, was a Druid "enchantment," that is, a Druid waiting to be released from the stone. The story states that a local priest did away with the object before release could be obtained.

In his work, *Celtic Folklore*, John Rhys speaks of a stone that gave light. He repeats a bit of folklore about a shepherd boy who became lost in the mist on a mountain while tending his flock. He met an "old fat man" who was really a Faery. The two walked on until they came to an oval stone, which the old man lifted up and tapped three times with his walking-stick. Upon the last tap, the stone produced light that varied in brightness from white, to gray to blue. The Faery, with his glowing stone, led the boy on and on until they came to the Land of Enchantment, where the boy stayed a year and a day among the Faery-folk.

Spirits who inhabited stone were a subject in folktales in Belgium, as well. Spence noted a "particularly fearsome ghost story...in which it is related how certain spirits had become enclosed in a pillar in an ancient abbey..." [71] And fearsome "eating ghosts" that would eat the soul of a passerby were believed to inhabit certain long stones in the Banks Islands in the Caribbean. Likewise, the Faery were said to inhabit, or "ensoul," the standing stones of Brittany. It is likely that the Faery were also assumed to be the spirits of dead ancestors awaiting their next incarnation. Icelandic folklore speaks of trapping ghosts under rocks,

69. Storaker, Joh. Th. "Naturrigerne I den Norske Folketro" in *Norsk Folkeminnelag No 18*. Oslo, 1928, 12.

70. *Ibid.*, 14.

71. Spence, Lewis. *Legends and Romances of Brittany*. Mineola: Dover Publications, Inc., 1997, 52.

where they remain until someone removes the stone. (This is certainly one method to "ensoul" the stone.[72]) A ritual still conducted every year in Shebbear, Devon, is called "Turning the Devil's Boulder." To ensure that the village remains protected, the villagers meet after nightfall each November 5th with crowbars to turn over a large boulder that reportedly had trapped the Devil. The ritual is believed to be an ancient one. It is obvious that the boulder did not originate in the area, as no similar type of stone exists there; it appears to have been transported over some distance for some ritualistic purpose — or the stone was naturally dislodged from its original resting space and moved by glacial action.[73]

The concept that human spirits existed in stone is one that has had currency from the Mesolithic Azilian culture to a contemporary Mesolithic society — the Australian Arunta people. Between these two cultures it was believed that the spirits of the dead could be preserved in decorated stones.

In Europe, the Mesolithic (or middle Stone Age) era extended roughly from 10,000 to 4,000 years ago, ending with the introduction and wide spread practice of agriculture. The Azilian culture was spread across northern Spain, England, France, Belgium, Holland, and Switzerland. A hunter-fisher society, the Azilian left little evidence of their religious traditions except river cobbles that they engraved or painted with circles, points, line and human figures.

We do not know specifically what these cobbles meant to the Azilian; to some scholars, the markings on them suggest they represent an early form of markers, or possibly a notation of lunar cycles; but the similarities to the Aruntas' stones are too striking to ignore. Every Arunta tribe has a storehouse that protects their "churingas," painted pebbles, referred to as their "far distant ones." [74] The "far distant ones" are the male and female spirits of their ancestors, carefully arranged in the cave storehouses of the tribe. "The churinga," according to Maringer, "is regarded as the embodiment of the dead person whose spirit and qualities are transferred to the present possessor."[75] In a cave in Switzerland, 133 Azilian stones were found broken. If these were "ancestor stones," researchers

72. Simpson, Jacqueline. *Icelandic Folktales and Legends.* Berkeley: University of California Press, 1972, 135.

73. Glacial action is probably responsible for many of the odd stones found around the world that appear out of geologic context; however, that does not mean that these stones were not later altered or used in ritual or religious observances or in the practice of folk medicine.

74. Spence, Lewis. *The Magic Arts in Celtic Britain.* Mineola: Dover Publications, Inc., 1999, 88.

75. Maringer, Johannes. *The Gods of Prehistoric Man.* London: The Phoenix Press 2002, 128.

conjecture they were intentionally broken by an enemy group who, in effect, destroyed the souls of a tribe's ancestor population — an act of spiritual genocide. If they were a kind of cultural or economic archive, this act of vandalism may have represented the destruction of a people's most sophisticated attainment.

A secret society existing on New Britain, New Guinea would award each newly initiated member a stone in the shape of a human or animal. The stone was believed to absorb the soul of the member and if the stone was broken, the individual was certain to die. [76]

The souls of the departed were also believed to enter stones in Hawaii. MacGregor noted the following in his 1932 ethnographic field notes:

> When a person died and his spirit entered a stone, he was a tupu'a. People went to them and laid their troubles before them and they were assisted. [77]

Since its founding, the Christian Church has condemned "stone worship" — not simply because stones were stones, but because the particular stones represented other gods and supernatural powers, competitors to the God who had decreed "Thou shalt have no other gods before me."

As MacKenzie wrote, "the original Zeus was evidently worshipped as a stone pillar — the pillar which enclosed his spirit, or the spirit of his earthly representative, the priest king." [78] Likewise, the Earth Goddess was represented by a standing stone which was visited at certain times of the year, during certain phases of the moon, by women "who prayed for offspring."

Standing stones and stone circles, however, have a long tradition of being associated not only with gods but also with the Faery and the devil. Lewis Spence wrote in his 1945 publication, *The Magic Arts in Celtic Britain*, "standing stones in Brittany and other parts of that country are associated with fairies, who are thought of as inhabiting or 'ensouling' them." [79] Spence notes that the fairy probably represented "the spirits of dead chieftains once worshipped ancestrally." [80] In some cultures, the Faery are spirits waiting to be reborn. In Scotland, it was said that the devil would appear in the center of any stone circle if one walked around the circle three times "against the sun" at midnight.

---

76. Frazer, *op. cit.* 680.

77. http://www.hawaii.edu/oceanic/rotuma/os/MacGregor/McReligionStones.

78. MacKenzie, Donald A. *Crete & Pre-Hellenic Myths and Legends.* London: Senate, 1995, 184.

79. Maringer *op. cit.*

80. Spence, *The Magic Arts in Celtic Britain*, 88.

The Tolcarne Troll, a little old man dressed in a tight leather jerkin and hood, is reported to live inside the rock in an outcropping of greenstone on a hill above a church in Newlyn, Cornwall. Local tradition places his origin to the Phoenicians. Other names for him include "The Wandering One" and "Odin the Wanderer." [81]

Native American lore is also rich in tales of divine stones. Walker recorded the following account from an old Lakota shaman: "Tunkan is the spirit which fell from the sky. It is a stone. It knows all things which are secret. It can tell where things are when they are lost or stolen..." When children vanished, "the mysterious stones were consulted to learn what had become of the child." [82] The Lakota utilized special shamans, called Rock Dreamers, to communicate with the Tunkan spirit. In the best case, the stone would tell the shaman where lost objects were, or, if they had been stolen, the identity of the individual who stole them. Some shamans use clear, round stones that are normally found on anthills to locate the bodies of the dead or to determine if an individual is still alive. The shaman asks the spirit of the stone to locate the person so that the family will be able to find them, or come to terms with the death. Rock dreamers were believed to take on some of the characteristics of stone, as well, such as being impervious to bullets. Because of this protection, the Rock dreamers were responsible for "war medicine."

Perhaps the most unusual magical stone is the Blaxhall Stone situated on the Stone Farm in Suffolk, England. The Blaxhall Stone grows. Reportedly, a hundred years ago it was the size of a small loaf of bread, and today it weighs in at five tons. It is said to still be growing... Growing stones are also part of Hawaiian lore. According to folklorist Martha Beckwith porous pebbles found on the beach of Koloa on the island of Hawaii "were supposed to grow from a tiny pebble to a good-sized rock and to reproduce themselves if watered once a week."[83]

While stone worship is clearly out, stone lore has been used in Christian theology as examples of recommended Christian behavior. The 13th century Aberdeen Bestiary, written and illustrated in England around 1200 CE, speaks of

81. Evans-Wentz, W. Y. *The Fairy-Faith in Celtic Countries.* Mineola: Dover Publications, Inc. 2002, 176.

82. Walker, 1991, *op. cit.*, 112.

83. Beckwith, Martha. *Hawaiian Mythology.* Honolulu: University of Hawaii Press 1970, 88.

"terrobolem" and how these stone indicate that man and woman should remain aloof from one another:

> On a certain mountain in the east, there are fire-bearing stones which are called in Greek terrobolem; they are male and female. When they are far from each other, the fire within them does not ignite. But when by chance the female draws near to the male, the fire is at once kindled, with the result that everything around the mountain burns.
>
> For this reason, men of God, you who follow this way of life, stay well clear of women, lest when you and they approach each other, the twin flame be kindled in you both and consume the good that Christ has bestowed upon you. For there are angels of Satan, always on the offensive against the righteous; not only holy men but chaste women too. [84]

Saints and Stones

Catholic saints in some cases became associated with traditional holy wells, and in a similar way, certain sacred and healing stones have also become assimilated into Church lore and have become associated with particular saints. One example is St. Fillan, who was a 7th century follower of St. Columba (known primarily for his holy well in Scotland). Into the 18th century, invalids would throw white stones on the saint's cairn as part of a ritual performed in their search of healing. This particular well also was said to move on its own and to cure insanity and other illnesses. The well is still frequented today. Those seeking a cure walk around the well three times and then throw a pebble into the well.

St. Fillan was the son of a princess of Ulster, who later became St. Kentigerna. His father was Prince Federach. Fillan was born with a stone in his mouth, a freak event which enraged (or horrified) his father. Prince Federach grabbed the infant and tossed him into a nearby lake (again the association between saints, water and sacred stones). A local Christian bishop just happened to be nearby (aren't they always, in these tales?) and rescued the baby. Out of gratitude, Fillan's mother became a Christian. [85] In time, Fillan and his mother became missionaries and traveled to Scotland where he established a priory in Auchtertyre at what is now Kirkton's Farm. One of the miracles for which St. Fillan became known was his ability to have his left arm and hand

84. McLaren, Colin, translator. *The Aberdeen Beastiary*. Aberdeen: Aberdeen University Library MS 24, 1995.

85. http://www.simegen.com/writers/nessie/stones.htm.

light up in the dark so he could read at night. Because of this, his arm has been preserved as one of the relics of that age in Glen Dochart, Scotland. (We do not know if it continues to serve as a flashlight or not.)

The most famous relics of St. Fillan are eight healing stones left to the monks at his priory. Like many talismans around the world, the stones are representative of body parts and are used by pilgrims to effect healing of the head (and sight, hearing, headaches, etc.), stomach, back and limbs. These eight stones are kept in an old mill at the priory site where, each Christmas Eve, they are given a new bed of straw and reeds from the river. Pilgrims are allowed to pick up the stones and rub them on afflicted body parts in hopes that St. Fillan's healing powers will work for them as well.

Another curious tale is that of St. Piran. St. Piran was a busy man in his early years, having founded six monasteries in Ireland, and a church in Cardiff, Wales. Legend has it that St. Piran, in advanced age, was captured by local Irish pagans who were jealous of his ability to heal; they tied him to a millstone and tossed him into the ocean, in a horrendous storm. Much to the pagans' amazement, the millstone floated and Piran used it to sail to Cornwall, where he founded a small oratory.

This legend of the floating stone is similar to many told in Ireland. One tale recounts how St. Boec sailed to Brittany from Carn parish in County Wexford on a stone. When the saint landed, near Penmarch, the stone sailed back to Ireland. Supposedly, a piece of the floating stone still rests in a cemetery in Brittany and bears the imprint of the saint's head. It is said that individuals seeking a cure for fever can find it by placing their heads on this stone. [86]

Twelfth-century traveler and writer Gerald of Wales wrote of the church of St. Michael, located on an island off Cork, Ireland, that had a special stone located next to the church door. In a hollow cavity in the stone, according to Gerald, "is found every morning through the merits of the saints of the place as much wine as is necessary for the celebration of as many Masses as there are priests to say Mass on that day there." [87]

86. Logan, Patrick. *The Holy Wells of Ireland.* Buckinghamshire: Colin Smythe, 1980, 105.

87. Gerald of Wales. *The History and Topogaphy of Ireland.* London: Penguin Books, 1982, 80.

Stones that Move and Fall from the Sky

Folklore is rife with stories about stones that move of their own volition. Britain has 39 standing stones or stone circles that reportedly move at certain times. Patrick Logan, in his book *The Holy Wells of Ireland*, relates the tale of a heavy altar slab located near Tobar na Mult in County Kerry:

> The story is that an enemy (Cromwellian) once used an ox cart to take it away from the well. When the cart had got as far as Bullock Hill, it stopped and the oxen refused to move it any further, so it was left on the spot until the next morning. Then, to the surprise of some people, the stone was found to have moved back to its original place near the well. [88]

Other Irish "homing stones" are reported to exist at Gorman, near Malin Head in County Donegal, Kilultagh, County Roscommon, Aghabulloge parish and Loch Hyne, County Cork and Aghinagh parish, also in County Cork. The homing stone at Aghinagh Parish is a large, flat stone (probably an ancient food grinding stone, judging from a worn hollow area in the center), located near the Tobar a'Noonan well. Logan wrote, "the stone, which is very large and heavy, was removed and built into a wall, but was found back at the well in the morning." [89]

Another homing stone is at St. Olan's Well, Dromatimore, County Cork. This mysterious stone is an oval quartzite that rests on a monolith inscribed in the (Celtic) ogham alphabet. It was said to cure a variety of "feminine aliments" and, if worn on the head and carried around the local church three times, cured migraines. According to one authority, "it had the gift of locomotion in that, if removed to any distance, it unfailingly returned to its original position." [90]

Cornish wells in particular appear to have been credited with some inherent protective force which keeps their structures intact. An item in the *Notes and Queries* cited above reported that the writer learned "from a native of the parish that some of the stones of the well [of St. Nun's] have been, at various times, carted away to serve meaner purposes, but that they have been, by some mysterious agency, brought back again during the night."

Carn Cabal, or "Cabal's Cairn" is the site of another returning stone, this one in Wales. Cabal was supposedly King Arthur's dog. During a boar hunt, Cabal left a footprint in one of the stones. Arthur piled stones on top of the print,

88. Logan, *op. cit.* 102.
89. *Ibid.* 103.
90. Evans, E. Estyn. *Irish Folk Ways*. Mineola: Dover Books 2000, 301.

turning it into a cairn. Legend has it that people stop by the site and take the stone away, but are only able to keep it for a day and a night and then it returns, mysteriously, to the cairn.

While not moving on its own accord, the Basin Stone near Arperfeelie, on the Black Isle of Taendore, Yorkshire, was able to complain of being moved. Lore tells that in the early 1800s a farmer took the basin stone home with him. That night, the stone began to emit "strange noises" which became louder and louder. On the third night, a "thunderous voice" ordered the farmer to return the stone to its original resting place. After he had done so, the noises stopped. The Basin Stone was used by the local women, who would bathe in the waters collected in the basin "immediately before sunrise" to ensure fertility.

An almost identical story is that of the Whispering Knights capstone in the Cotswolds. According to legend, a farmer took the stone to be used as a bridge over a stream. Once the stone was in place, the farmer was awakened that night by "strange noises" and the next morning the stone was found lying on the bank of the stream. The farmer quickly returned it to its original location.[91]

A legend from Brittany tells of St. Baldred's Boat. St. Baldred was the second Bishop of Glasgow and during his lifetime a large rock jutting out of the sea wrecked numerous boats. To help the mariners, St. Baldred rowed out to the rock and climbed to the top; at his nod, the rock rose from the waters and drifted over to the nearest shore, where it remains today.

Archeologists have been mystified by the ancient stone city of Nan Matol, built of enormous, many-ton prismatic basalt blocks on top of a coral reef by ancient inhabitants of the Micronesian Island of Ponapé. That a primitive people could have imported such stones and constructed an elaborate city almost defies belief. Many tales have sprung up to account for this. One legend says that two young wizards set out to build a worship center dedicated to the gods, demons and spirits of the Ponapeans but their efforts were thwarted by the wind and surf until they cast a spell that made the blocks of stone fly through the air and land in the positions that created the city.[92]

Back in France, folklorist Lewis Spence noted in his book *Legends and Romances of Brittany*, "certain sacred stones go once a year or once a century to 'wash' themselves in the sea or in the river, returning to their ancient seats after

91. Turner, Mark. *Folklore & Mysteries of the Cotswolds.* London: Robert Hale Limited, 1993, 100.

92. de Camp, L. Sprague and Catherine C. de Camp. *Ancient Ruins: The Past Uncovered.* New York: Barnes & Noble Books 1992, 233.

their ablutions."[93] In addition, Spence tells us, the individual stones of the dolmen at Essé have the ability to change their locations at will. In Britain, Arthur's stone, a prehistoric dolmen in West Glamorgan on the road to Swansea, is also said to go to the sea to wash or drink at Mid-Summer's Eve and All-Hallows Eve. Other walking and drinking stones are those at Carnac, the Four Stones, Radnor, Stanton Drew and the Rollright Stones among others. Similar stories can be found around the world, including Holland, where the stone at Westerklief, a very large boulder, was said to turn around if it heard the church bells chime. Mothers told their children not to make ugly faces, because "when the dog barks, the bell tolls and the stone turns around your mouth will stay that way..." The stone circle known as the Greywethers in Devon is said to move at certain times when the light of the rising sun falls upon the stones.

According to legend, the stone circle called the "Nine Stones" danced every day at noon — especially unusual, as such legends generally indicate a movement that occurs at night.

The English legend of the Crowza Stones tells of Sts. Just and Keverne who, following a feast, argued over a chalice. St. Just had stolen the chalice from St. Keverne and, as he was fleeing, St. Keverne gathered several "Ironstone" pebbles and began to throw them at St. Just. At that moment, Just threw the chalice down and ran off. St. Keverne "threw all the remaining stones after the vanishing figure of St. Just, one by one, and a curse with each." [94] According to legend, the stones remained where they had fallen but they are so heavy only a saint can lift them. The legend says that the stones have sometimes been removed during the day, "but they always return to their places by night." [95]

A Cherokee legend from Tennessee speaks of the Spear-Finger, a huge evil woman with a lethal index finger whose skin was like stone. She "had great powers over stone and she could easily lift and carry immense rocks and could bond them together by merely striking one stone against another. To get across the rough country more easily, she built a great rock bridge through the air from the Tree Rock, on the Hiwassee [River], over to Whiteside Mountain, on the Blue Ridge." [96] Rocky promontories supposed to be pieces of this great bridge can still be seen today.

---

93. Spence, Lewis. *Legends and Romances of Brittany*, 53.
94. Briggs, Katharine. *British Folktales.* New York: Pantheon Books, 1977, 252.
95. *Ibid.*
96. Atalie, Princess. *The Earth Speaks.* New York: Fleming H. Revell Company, 1940, 148.

The Cheesewring cairn, similar to those created in the arctic by the Inuit people, is a pile of flat stones; it is actually reported to be a natural formation. One legend has it that the top stone will turn around when it hears a cock crow.[97]

Polynesian legends speak of Leplafeke — a stone who was unhappy with the amount of fish he was offered during a fish drive. Ethnologist Gordon MacGregor made the following field notes in 1932:

> There is a rock on the sea side of the island of Solkope which is the tupua' Leplafeke. This rock once lived on the island of Haua in Oinafa, but during a great fish drive of Oinafa Leplafeke's share of the catch was given away. The rock became angry at this and started to walk around Rotuma to get away from Haua. When he came to Solkope he thought he would either have to go around the island or go in the bush at the other end. But passing between Sarii [?] and Solkope on the sea side he found a good place, and stayed there to hide from Oinafa. [98]

Chinese folklorist Jin Shoushen wrote of three sacred Black Rocks that had attained sainthood, one for ten thousand years, one for five thousand and one for one thousand. Liu Bowen, a military advisor during China's Ming Dynasty, set out to make the three sacred rocks move from their location in the Shangfang Mountains to Beijing so that they would help control the marauding dragons and tigers in the area. After the three rocks failed to respond to incense and offerings, Liu, with the help of heavenly troops, was only able to get the third Black Rock to walk towards the city. The rock "trundled on till he had lumbered over Lu Gou Qiao" — a city called the Scorpions Tail. Here the Black Rock was stung by the scorpion and stopped dead in its tracks, where it remains today. [99]

In the Near East, historian Franz Cumont noted, "Hippolytus also tells us that in Syrian mysteries it was taught that the stones (beth-el's) were animated." [100] And, we may ask, where did the belief in animated stones originate? Nineteenth-century writer John Nimmo theorized that it was the belief that the deity lived in the stone pillars at Beth-el: "Some have stated, that from this pillar arose all those strange accounts of the Bethyllis, or animated stones, so prevalent in antiquity. The Deity was pleased to appear to Jacob, and to designate himself as

---

97. Bord, Janet and Colin. *Mysterious Britain: Ancient Secrets of Britain and Ireland.* London: Thorsons, 1972, 13

98. http://www.hawaii.edu/oceanic/rotuma/os/MacGregor/McReligionStones.html.

99. Shoushen, Jin. *Beijing Legends.* Beijing: Panda Books, 1982, 18-23.

100. Cumont, Franz. *Oriental Religions in Roman Paganism.* New York: Dover Publications, 1956, 244.

the God of Beth-el, which caused the Israelites to hold this pillar in great esteem, and perhaps might be the origin of all those fables." [101]

Nimmo also wrote that perhaps these pillars "might contribute much to the advancement of idolatry in the first ages. Men," he wrote, "after adoring the Almighty by these pillars, would next adore them as representatives of him; and, lastly, would look upon them as gods themselves."

Stones that move are not confined to folklore. In fact, there are some stones that are factually known to move, such as those of Racetrack Playa, Death Valley, California. Some of these stones, weighing up to three-quarters of a ton, have been recorded to move several hundred feet in a single action. Some have moved up to two miles in total distance. While they are under observation by State Park officials and university scientists, no one has seen them move; but their tracks are left on the flat desert hardpan. Dr. Robert P. Sharp, a geologist in the Division of Geological and Planetary Sciences at the California Institute of Technology in Pasadena, California has studied these stones for years. At one time, Dr. Sharp encircled 30 of the stones with iron stakes; according to him, 28 of the 30 broke free of the stakes. Dr. Sharp also reported that seven of the stones monitored have simply disappeared over time. [102] While scientists have not been able to determine why or how they move, they note that in rainy conditions the ground surface there becomes extremely slick, and the wind can rip between the surrounding dolomite ridges at over 70 miles an hour. Sharp has stated that the stones only move on stormy nights. The National Park Service has been studying these rocks for some time and admits that some of the boulders even appear to move uphill; they, too, think stormy weather may be cause of the movement. Still, that seems to be an incomplete and not entirely satisfactory explanation. [103] Lyall Watson, who once measured a traveling stone's track for 180 feet across the playa, notes, "the problem is that none of the restless rocks, not even smaller rounded ones, ever rolls and many of them tend to travel in different directions."[104]

---

101. Nimmo, John. *Identity of the Religions Called Druidical and Hebrew: Demonstrated From the Nature and Objects of their Worship.* London: University of London Literary and Philosophical Society 1829, 22-23

102. To see photos of some of these moving stones in action, see http://www.angelfire.com/hi/funnyspring/movroc.html and the following citation.

103. http://wrgis.wr.usgs.gov/docs/usgsnps/deva/ftrac2.html.

104. Watson, Lyall. *The Nature of Things: The Secret Life of Inanimate Objects.* Rochester: Destiny books, 1992, 33.

Some stones not only move but also fall out of the sky! Charles Fort was famous for documenting such strange sky-falls of fish, frozen frogs, live snakes and small and large stones in his *Book of the Damned.* But such strange events continue. Stone falls have been reported worldwide ranging from small pebbles falling on building roofs to a cow killed by a large rock in 1972 in Venezuela. Witnesses reported a bright light and loud noise just before the cow was struck. The *New York Times* reported on March 12, 1922 that large smooth "rocks that had been falling 'from the clouds,' for three weeks, at Chico, a town in an 'earthquake region' in California."

Fort wrote about the Chico rock fall in his 1923 book, *New Lands*:

> In the *San Francisco Chronicle*, in issues dating from the 12th to the 18th of March — clippings sent to me by Mr. Maynard Shipley, writer and lecturer upon scientific subjects, if there be such subjects — the accounts are of stones that, for four months, had been falling intermittently from the sky, almost always upon the roofs of two adjoining warehouses, in Chico, but, upon one occasion, falling three blocks away: "a downpour of oval-shaped stones"; "a heavy shower of warm rocks." *San Francisco Call*, March 16 — "warm rocks." It is said that crowds gathered, and that upon the 17th of March a "deluge" of rocks fell upon a crowd, injuring one person. The police "combed" all surroundings: the only explanation that they could think of was that somebody was firing stones from a catapult. One person was suspected by them, but, upon the 14th of March, a rock fell when he was known not to be in the neighborhood.[105]

Other notable stone falls include two extreme examples from Australia. According to the Associated Australian Press, David MacLagen, a scientist with the Australian Radiation Laboratory, was killed in 1981 when a giant boulder fell from the sky and crushed him. According to reports, while he was investigating a uranium deposit near Nabariek, he ventured toward a sacred Aborigine site called the "Green Ant Dreaming Place," when the rock killed him and pinned another scientist, William Karkin, for five hours. Twenty-four years prior to MacLagen's death, a farm worker at Pumphrey, Western Australia was pinned down for five days while stones rained down around him.[106]

Stone falls have been recorded back to Biblical days. In Joshua 10:11, the Israelites are attacking the Amorite army when the following takes place:

> And as they fled before Israel, while they were going down the ascent of Beth-hor'on, the LORD threw down great stones from heaven upon them as far as Aze'kah, and they died; there were more who died because of the hailstones than the men of Israel killed with the sword.

---

105. Fort, *Charles. New Lands.* New York: Boni & Liveright, 1923, 244.
106. *Daily Express*, March 22, 1957.

Another remarkable stone fall recorded in ancient times occurred in the 6th century BCE after the Roman army defeated the Sabines. According to Livy, in his history of Rome:

> After the defeat of the Sabines, when king Tullus [672-640 B.C.] and the entire Roman state were at a high pitch of glory and prosperity, it was reported to the king and senators that there had been a rain of stones on the Alban Mount. As this could scarce be credited, envoys were dispatched to study the prodigy, and in their sight there fell from the heavens, like hailstones which the wind piles in drifts upon the ground, a shower of pebbles.

According to Livy's account, whenever such a fall occurred the Romans would decree nine days of religious observance, as they believed that the stone falls were due to neglected rituals. Thus, one can conclude that these unusual events occurred more than once.

Kunz relates a tale originally published in 1860 about a small magic stone and its ability to return:

A common belief was that spirits good or bad dwelt in the stones, and in case a great misfortune befell a family, this was sometimes laid to the charge of such a sprit. The father of [one such] family having died, his widow commanded her son to throw away their magic stone. This he did, but the spirit was not to be denied, for shortly afterward this very stone was found to have returned to its accustomed place, and had even brought two companion stones with it! [107]

Stories such as these are rare in Native American lore, but the Kawaiisu Indians do have a story that concerns a "flying" stone and the mythic figure of Coyote. In the story, Coyote, while on a walk, notices a couple of women grinding seeds on a milling stone. The women ask Coyote to help them with their task. As he starts to grind the seeds, the milling stone rises into the air; the more he attempts to hold it down, the more it floats up and down — until it falls on his head. [108] The two women turn out to be witches.

Navel Stones — Stones of the Center of the World

Navel stones, also called omphalos stones, were seen as ties to the Gods and the supernatural forces of nature. These stones, like the one at the Temple of

107. Kunz, George Frederick. *The Curious Lore of Precious Stones.* New York: Dover Publications, Inc., 1971, 266.

108. Zigmond, Maurice L. *Kawaiisu Mythology: An Oral Tradition of South-Central California.* Ballena Press Anthropological Papers No. 18. Menlo Park: Ballena Press, 1980, 137.

Delphi in Greece, were oracular in nature. They became known as "Navel stones" because they were located at the center of the world, the navel of the Earth. (They are found in various locations around the world, because they represent each culture's spiritual — if not geographical — center.) The ompahlos is the center of the universe, a place of refuge and a symbol of all birth and renewal. It is also the place of communication between worlds and dimensions.

Like the cosmic tree or cosmic mountain, the omphalos is held to be the cosmic center and acts as the balancing point of the world. Mount Tabor in Palestine derives its name from the same root as the Hebrew "tabor," which means "navel," — and Mount Gerizim, in Samaria, was referred to in the Old Testament as the navel of the Earth. Alexander the Great commissioned a temple to be built on Mount Gerizim in the 4th century BCE. According to Leonard Greenspoon, Mount Gerizim "was the intended focus for priests, cult, and worship" in ancient Samaria. [109] The Hebraic "dwelling place of deity," called beth-el, was a stone kept in the temple at Jerusalem.

While Mounts Gerizim and Tabor are regarded as sacred centers, or ompahloses, they are atypical. The most famous navel stone is the omphalos at Delphi. According to legend, the god Zeus placed the egg-shaped stone at Apollo's shrine. The stone was located next to the tripod where the priestess of Delphi delivered her prophesies. The Greeks, in declaring this stone the navel of the world, "connected the stone with the body of the goddess Gaia, who was seen as the Earth itself." [110] Devereux tells us that Zeus "sent out two eagles from the extremities of the Earth; where their flight paths crossed was the center point where the stone was to be erected." [111] Delphi was actually the home of two of these stones. One was decorated with a coiled serpent and the palm of Delos that was Apollo's symbol. Another omphalos was located on Crete and it was regarded as the umbilical cord of Zeus, which had fallen to the Earth after his birth. These two navel stones linked Zeus and Gaia together as the dual aspect of fertility and creative force.

---

109. Greenspoon, Leonard J. "Between Alexandria and Antioch: Jews and Judaism in the Hellenistic Period," in *The Oxford History of the Biblical World*, ed. by Michael D. Coogan. Oxford: Oxford University Press, 1998, 459.

110. Molyneaux, Brian Leigh. *The Sacred Earth.* Boston: Little, Brown and Company, 1995, 24.

111. Devereux, Paul. *Symbolic Landscapes.* Glastonbury: Gothic Image Publications, 1992, 56-57.

The concept of a sacred center is found universally. The Hopi spiritual center is the Sipapu, located on the Little Colorado River at the bottom of the Grand Canyon. The Sipapu is not a rock or stone but an ancient geyser that has thrust up from the bottom of the Grand Canyon to form a large bubble of mud and rock — it is here that the ancestors of the Hopi climbed from the last world to the current one. The Sipapu is shaped like other traditional omphalos stones, however: it is egg shaped, denoting birth, rebirth and fertility.

One rather neglected and ignored omphalos is located at Glastonbury Abby, site of the revered Chalice Well. Behind the Abbot's kitchen sits an egg-shaped sandstone, approximately three feet long, two feet wide and two feet high. This particular omphalos contains an "eyestone" — a cavity located in the center of the stone. One theory of the "eyestone" is that it was a carved basin used to hold offerings. [112]

A second stone is located halfway up the Tor, just outside Glastonbury. At the beginning of the pathway is a large, elongated white boulder called "The Living Rock." This rock vibrates to the touch and is said to become energized at dawn and sunset each day. The Living Rock marks the entranceway to the Underworld. Visitors to the Tor are sometimes encouraged by local guides to touch the Living Rock — without being warned first that it is regarded as the entranceway to the Underworld Kingdom of Gwynn ap Nudd! Luckily, the entranceway generally remains closed. The Tor was undoubtedly a place of ritual long before the Christian presence.

It is interesting to note that Silbury Hill, not far from Glastonbury and directly south of the Avebury complex, was in ancient days regarded as the omphalos of Britain. This man-made earthen mound is the largest in the world and represented the belly of the Goddess," the literal "navel" of the world. An ancient path snakes around to the top of the mound in the exact form of the serpent on the omphalos of Delphi.

The Stone of Divisions (also called the Stone of Density) located at Uisnech is another navel stone," and is regarded as the center of Ireland. It was here that the archdruid Midhe lit the first fire of the new year," a fire taken across Ireland to light every bonfire in the country. Uisnech was the central point of the five regions of Ireland and, in fact, the name Midhe is more specifi-

112. Griffyn, Sally. *Sacred Journeys: Stone Circles & Pagan Paths.* London: Kyle Cathie Limited 2000, 141.

The Living Rock

cally a term given to mean "middle" or "neck," referring more to the place than to a person.

That these sacred stones were an important part of shamanic ritual cannot be doubted. They may have acted as the doorway to the spirit world as well as a point of connection between the spiritual and physical planes. Could it be that the omphalos has become transmorphed into our foundation stones in large buildings that have their own contemporary rituals associated with them," local politicians and businessmen standing nearby with shiny shovels, installing a time capsule to be opened in the distant future? These stones continue symbolically to provide an opening into both the future and the past, for when the time capsule is buried it is destined for a future time but allows those who open it to view past events.

But more than an entryway to symbolic time travel, the omphalos is also an entryway to paradise. Every account of the earthly paradise indicates that it is/was located at the center of the world, or at least the center of the world, as the individual culture viewed it. According to Eliade, "the map of Babylon shows the city at the center of a vast circular territory bordered by a river, precisely as the Sumerians envisioned paradise."[113] In a similar fashion, the universe was created

113. Eliade, Mircea. *Cosmos and History: The Myth of the Eternal Return.* New York: Harper & Row Publishers, 1959, 10.

from a central point and spread outward, as did the creation of humankind and the human occupation of the Earth. "The omphalos," writes Devereux, "is the mythic point where the figuratively vertical axis of mind intersects the figuratively horizontal plane of the material world, contained within the round of mundane time."[114] It is this intersection that creates the veil between two worlds — our physical world and that of the Otherworld.

Given the universal application of these beliefs in the omphalos, it is worth taking a more analytical look at them. Certainly they are symbolic, but they also figure importantly into the rituals of shamanic people around the glove. They are the focal point used by shamans in their visionary trips to the Otherworld and they represent the idea of a passageway between dimensions. Not only have people believed that solid rock allows Faery creatures and the "Rock Babies" of Native American lore to go back and forth between two worlds, but some legends indicate that a few humans have also traversed between the worlds through rock openings.

One Kawaiisu myth ("A Visit to the Underworld") contains an interesting illustration of these portals. Recorded by Murice L. Zigmond from a Kawaiisu informant, the story tells of a man who entered an opening in a rock to find himself in an Otherworld where the spirits of deer killed in the hunt go after death. The story, as reported by Zigmond, says, "the man saw water that was like a window. He could see the mountains through it. But it wasn't water. He passed through it and did not get wet. When he was outside, he looked back and saw the 'water' again." He was cautioned not to tell anyone for three days (again the importance of the number three) where he had been. [115]

Other important religious shrines still used today, including the Ka'abah at Mecca and the "Holy of Holies (or Foundation Stone of the Earth) in the Temple at the center of Jerusalem, are examples of omphaloses. The Temple of Jerusalem, according to Clifford, was anciently regarded as "the source of order in the world."[116] The stone at Mecca is probably meteoric, as was the original navel stone at Delphi.

According to Devereux, the Etruscans, and then Romans, established an omphalos in every town and city, the very act being a "geometric act of great power."[117] The Etruscans also viewed the navel stone, or omphalos, as the

114. Devereux, *Symbolic Landscapes*, 1992, op. cit. 92.

115. Zigmond, *op. cit.*, 177.

116. Clifford, Richard J. *The Cosmic Mountain in Canaan and the Old Testament.* Harvard Semitic Monographs Volume 4. Cambridge: Harvard University Press, 1972, 179.

doorway to the Otherworld. The center of each Etruscan town, the mysterious entryway was covered with a great stone — referred to by the Romans as the "stone of souls." This stone was removed on important days of the dead to allow the spirits of the dead to once again journey to the world of the living. The "stone of souls" was always located at the crossing point between the two main streets of the city.[118] The Etruscan belief in a universe of order and regulation was illustrated with the placement of a world axis in every Etruscan town. The omphalos established world order and the balance of time and dimension — as well as offering a portal to the spirit world.

Imprinted Stones

As will be discussed later, many sacred stones located around the world appear to have the footprints of royal or sainted persons in them, or footprints of supernatural beings such as faeries and rock- and water-babies. The human-footprint motif is common in American Indian rock art. A site in Colbert County, Alabama contains carvings of four- and six-toed feet, serpents, and meandering lines.

It is interesting to note that the footprint is a common woodland theme, but the number of toes is usually abnormal. Many times the feet are shown larger or smaller than a normal human foot, as well. It is not clear whether these prints were meant to depict the tracks of Water Babies or Rock Babies but the association with serpents and meandering lines would indicate an affinity to water symbolism. Serpents are also an ancient symbol of life.

"Water Babies" or "Rock Babies" are described as small, dwarf-like men in traditional Indian dress with long hair. The Water Babies were regarded as unusually potent spirit helpers that lived along streams and water holes. Likewise, the Rock Babies lived in or near rock features and were able to pass through solid rock. Both the Rock Baby and the Water Baby were believed to enhance the power of the shaman.

In the Owens Valley of California and Nevada is a place called Red Canyon. Here, an unusual stone slab is found which is covered with small, engraved human-like footprints said to be those of the Water Baby. Next to the

117. Devereux, Paul. *Earth Memory: Sacred Sites—Doorways into Earth's Mysteries.* St. Paul: Llewellyn Publications, 1992, 194.

118. *Ibid.*, 199.

Water Baby tracks are engraved bear tracks, which appear to be walking in the same direction. Similar, infant-size footprints have been found painted on rock shelters in Baja California. There are also stones that have the prints of hands, heads and bodies as part of their features.

Several years ago, I happened upon a rock carving in Southern California. A large slab had been formed into a huge four-toed print of some gigantic animal, probably a bear (as can be seen in the photograph, one of the toes has been broken off). I have not seen anything comparable in any other Native American site. This item was found not far from an important rock art site used in fertility and puberty rituals.

Rock carving of a four-toed foot

Kawaiisu Indians in the California Great Basin tell of Coyote climbing to the top of a mountain, where he begins to play his flute made from elderberry wood. As he plays, he notices that clouds begin to appear and start to move toward him. He stops playing his flute, and the clouds stop. He again takes up his flute and becomes so engrossed in his music that he fails to realize that the clouds have gathered above him. As it begins to snow, Coyote becomes worried and tries to run back to his home. Finally, he becomes weary and the snow overtakes him. He falls upon a large rock, where he dies. The legends say that his impression, including his hands, feet and scrotum, can still be seen on the rock.[119]

Similar tales are commonly found within Native Californian mythology and are associated with rock art sites. A boulder located near Perris, California, known as Takwish's Genitals, is one such site. The boulder has the imprinted genitals of a spirit helper who supposedly leaned against the stone — an act of entering the stone in symbolic intercourse. In fact, bedrock mortars (stones used to grind food and other organic materials such as dye) are said to be the result of male spirits copulating with the stone, which is a metaphor for the shaman entering an altered state and merging with the stone during a vision quest.

The impressions of St. Patrick's knees are said to be found at Portpatrick on the island of St. Kilda, as are the knees and elbow imprints of St. Newlyna in Cornwall. Similar to Hawaiian lore, large mortar hole depressions said to be the knee-marks of St. Gwyndaf Hên, found on a flat stone in the river-bed of River Ceri, "appear to nurture the growth of new pebbles from the mother rock".[120]

The Sacred Dome of the Rock in Jerusalem is holy not only to Jews but also to Christians and Moslems. The rock itself is said to have formed the center of Solomon's Temple but also is said to bear the hoof prints of Mohammed's winged horse, Al-Burak ("Lightning"). Legend has it that as the horse leapt into the air from the rock, taking Mohammed to Paradise, his hoofs were imprinted on the stone.[121]

Other imprinted stones found around the world have impressions attributed not to saints, tricksters, or spirit helpers but to the devil. One of these is the Devil's Fist-print in Iceland. According to the story, the devil was indentured to one Saemundur — a local priest. The priest had ordered the devil to muck out his cow shed by licking the muck off the pavement, which was situated by the church. The priest told the devil that he was too slow, and slapped the devil in the head. The devil got angry and slammed his fist down on the stone, which still bears his print. Before he left, the devil also scraped his tongue

119. Zigmond, *op. cit.* 127.

120. Pennick, Nigel. *Celtic Sacred Landscapes.* London: Thames and Hudson, 1996, 41.

121. Brockman, Norbert C. *Encyclopedia of Sacred Places.* New York: Oxford University Press, 1997, 129.

against a stone and the tongue mark is also preserved — five inches deep in stone. [122]

TALKING STONES

There are many stories about rocks and stones that emit noise and actually "speak." The Stone of Destiny, or Stone of Scone, is one of these. It cries out, they say, when a legitimate monarch stands upon it. (One can easily imagine that today's monarchs see no need to test it, or themselves.) Other stones, as noted previously, make strange noises when moved from their original locations and will continue to do so until returned. A speaking stone at County Waterford, called Cloch Labrhais, was said to follow any response to those seeking their future by saying, "the truth is often bitter." [123]

Up through the 19th century, girls who had questions to ask visited the Whispering Knights dolmen. They would put their ears in the hollows of the stone, and even climb up on the dolmen, to hear the whispered answers of the megalith. As will be discussed later, the Whispering Knights dolmen is part of the Rollright Stones in Oxfordshire, which have had a history of odd happenings. Research in the 1980s by the Dragon Project[124] did detect ticking and humming sounds coming from the stone during the full moon. [125]

"Ringing" and "humming" sounds have been heard at Stonehenge and ancient cairns in the Wicklow Hills, Ireland. Devereux describes a strange occurrence at the Blind Fiddler standing stone near Penzance: "At the precise moment the sun set [during a midsummer solstice], [we heard] a sudden muffled thunderclap, audible but emanating from beneath the earth."[126] Should we infer that some stones interact with the sun and moonlight at certain times, perhaps due to changes in temperature or other subtle effects, to produce various sounds?

---

122. Simpson, Jacqueline, trns. *Legends of Icelandic Magicians.* Cambridge: D.S. Brewer Ltd for The Folklore Society, 1975, 23.

123. Pepper, Elizabeth & John Wilcock. *Magical and Mystical Sites: Europe and the British Isles.* Grand Rapids: Phanes Press 2000, 262.

124. The Dragon Project was formed in a London pub in 1977 by an eclectic group of people including dowsers, archaeologists, chemists, physicists, and others to study and monitor suspected energy currents at megalithic sites in England. Much of their work centers on "psychic energy."

125. Devereux, Paul. *Places of Power.* London: Bladford, 1990, 73.

126. *Ibid.* 174.

Might this be another example of a natural phenomenon that could only be interpreted as a supernatural occurrence in earlier ages?

California seems to have a number of "musical" or "ringing" stones. Not far from the maze rock near Hemet, California is a large boulder, which, if struck, produces a variety of musical notes. Depending on where the stone is struck a different tone can be achieved. Devereux discussed such rocks, noting that, "there is some ethnography to indicate they were used in rituals such as girls' puberty rites when elders would sing in accompaniment with the sounds produced by the rock."[127]

And then there is the Bell Rock, which originally was located in a canyon in Orange County, California. County historian Terry E. Stephenson described the stone:

> In a boulder-strewn hillock, covered over with oaks, is the Bell Rock, known to Indians before the Spaniards of Franciscan days gave the canyon its name, La Cañada de Campana — the Canyon of the Bell.
>
> Around this granite boulder native Indians gathered in ancient times. With stone pestles they pounded upon it and the canyon rang with the clear tones of this primitive bell.[128]

The seven- by three-foot stone, weighing seven tons, was moved in 1936 to the Bowers Museum in Santa Ana, California. It is believed to have been an important sacred stone to the Luiseño tribe.

It appears significant that both of these "ringing" stones were located near two rare maze rocks. Evidently, the mazes and the ringing stones were integral parts of the rituals conducted at these sites. It is unfortunate that more ethnographic information has not been obtained and preserved over the years.

It is also possible that some of the great megalithic sites that were built by humans were designed with the intention of being acoustically awe-inspiring. The passage tombs of Newgrange and certain other Neolithic sites have a resonant frequency of 110 hz, which is the frequency of the male baritone voice, and they produce some very amazing acoustic phenomenon. Mark Pilkington, in an article appearing in the November 6, 2003 issue of *The Guardian*, reported "experiments in a replica of the Newgrange passage...showed that if a site was smoky or misty, standing sound waves would become visible as they vibrated particles in

---

127. Devereux, Paul. *Mysterious Ancient America.* London: Vega 2002, 129.

128. Knight, Lavinia C. "Bell Rock and Indian Maze Rock of Orange County" in *Pacific Coast Archaeological Society Quarterly* Vol. 15, No. 2, April, 1979, 25.

the air. Could this visualizing effect account for the zigzag and concentric ring markings on the chamber walls?"[129] A similar acoustic phenomenon occurs at Avebury and Stonehenge as well as other ancient sites around the world, including Chichen Itzá in Yucatan, Mexico. The ball court at Chichen Itzá is a perfect example of such a site: an individual may stand at one end of the site and whisper to an individual at the other end, who will hear clearly what has been said. It seems probable that the priests used this phenomenon to impart the messages of the gods to the worshippers.

One of the twin statues at Thebes, called the statue of Memnon (actually a 50-foot statue of Amenhotep that was built around 1500 BCE), was heard centuries ago making peculiar noises at sunrise which were described as sounding like the breaking of a string on a lyre, or a high pitched note. Such notables as Strabo, Germanicus, Juvenal, Pausanias and the Emperor Hadrian reportedly heard the noises coming from the statue. For some strange reason, the noises stopped in 196 CE. Writer Rupert T. Gould in his book *Enigmas* gave the most plausible explanation for the noise:

> ...it is difficult to avoid drawing the conclusion that the sound was caused by the sun's rays warming the cleft and truncated lower half of the statue; that it was produced by the unequal expansion of the two portions of this fractured monolith — causing them to move, fractionally, one against the other. [130]

And then, there are stones that don't like foul language! The Deity Stone, a heavy stone block just outside the Druids Stone Circle near Gwynedd, Wales, reportedly would strike down anyone who would curse near it. One unlucky man decided to defy the warnings and, so the story goes, late one night he went near the stone and cursed at the top of his lungs. His body was discovered the next day at the foot of the stone.

Humans and Trolls Turned to Stone

Throughout folklore, stories about humans, animals and creatures of the underworld being turned to stone are commonly found. Many times, this was seen as being God's (or the gods') punishment for misdeeds or was a result of being caught in some place that was less than hospitable. As discussed else-

129. Pilkington, Mark. "Early Rock: Were some ancient sites designed to be acoustically, as well as visually, awe-inspiring?" in *The Guardian*, Thursday, November 6, 2003.

130. Gould, Rupert T. *Enigmas*. New York: University Books, 1965, 34.

where, the Merry Maiden's Stone Circle is one example where religious persuasion used folklore to convince people to act in an acceptable Christian manner. The standing stones in the circle, as well as three larger standing stones located some ways away, called the Blind Fiddler and the Pipers, were once girls and musicians — they were turned to stone for dancing on the Sabbath. Other Sabbath breakers included the five farmers at Duddo, in Northumberland, who decided that they would rather work their radish fields than attend church. Like the Merry Maidens, they were turned to stone in swift punishment and serve as an example to their countrymen still today.

In Iceland, they say that Night Trolls are turned to stone if they are caught in daylight — as are any animals that are bred by the Trolls.

The Rollright Stones, in legend, were once a king and his men and a few conspirators who were turned to stone by the local witch, who objected to them crossing her land. In Cumbria, it was the witch who was turned to stone. Long Meg and her Daughters is a large stone circle which folklore says was a group of witches who were dancing when Michael Scott, a known wizard, happened upon them. He promptly turned them to stone. Like other mystical stone groupings, it is said that no one may count the actual number of stones in this circle. One of the standing stones at Long Meg is decorated with cup and ring marks as well as a spiral, which is similar to carvings made at passage graves such as Newgrange in Ireland. These symbols will be discussed later. Another stone circle in Cumbria, called Carles or Castlerigg, has a similar legend saying that the stones were once men, who were punished for breaking some taboo. The famous Callanish Stones on the Island of Lewis are said to be giants who were turned to stone by St. Kiaran when they refused to help him build a chapel.

Perhaps the saddest bit of lore is that of Stanton Drew, a large multi-ring complex in Somerset. Legends say that the stones are members of a wedding party who were turned to stone for carrying their celebrations over into the Sabbath. The vast majority of these legends illustrate the fear that the Christian Church had at one time, especially in Britain, of people continuing their Pagan ways and not observing the Sabbath. Like the Merry Maidens legend, some of these are perhaps due to renewed fervor of the Protestants during the Reformation and their fanatical efforts to strike the fear of God into the hearts and minds of humankind.

In Incan mythology, four pair of brothers and sisters were created by the celestial god Viracocha to civilize the people and to divide them into ten communities. However, the brothers began to fight amongst themselves and one was imprisoned in a cave; two others were turned to stone. The last brother, along with the women, founded the city of "World Pole" in the name of Viracocha and the Sun God Inti.

More recent transformation stories include the tale of the Carreg y Lleidr Stone in Wales. An 1802 account reported, "the country people report that a thief who had stolen some books from a neighboring church was in this place turned to stone with the sack containing his theft laying over his shoulder." [131]

American Indians and Hawaiians both have stories of beautiful women being turned to stone. The Dakota-Sioux legend of Standing Rock tells of an Arikara Indian girl who marries a man from the Dakota-Sioux. After she has a child with him, he takes another wife. The girl is so distraught that she refuses to break camp with the rest of the people, and they leave her behind. Soon, her husband becomes worried and sends his two brothers back to look for her. They find her — but she has turned to stone. The legend says that the people made a travois[132] and placed her stone form on it. The pony pulling the travois, and the travois itself, were decorated in beautiful colors and streamers of brightly colored cloth. The stone was considered holy and the tribe took it with them everywhere they traveled. Today, it is in front of the Standing Rock Indian Agency in South Dakota.[133] The Gabrielino Indians of Southern California have similar legends. Two geographic points in the hills west of Riverside, one called Tehovan, near Redlands, and the other Sokava, "were great rocks 'who had once been people.'" [134]

In Hawaiian legend, the beautiful dancing girl Hopoe is devoured by lava sent by the jealous god Pele. Hopoe had taught Pele's younger sister, Hiiaka, to dance and to make flower leis. The two girls came to love each other, which made Pele angry and jealous. While Hopoe was covered in lava, she was not destroyed but her human spirit was taken and replaced with goblin power. She became a balanced stone, which swayed in the breeze or rocked at the touch of a hand. An earthquake eventually destroyed the stone in the 1800s. [135]

---

131. Alexander, Marc. *A Companion to the Folklore, Myths & Customs of Britain.* Gloucestershire: Sutton Publishing Limited 2002, 44.

132. A travois is a kind of wheel-less cart to be dragged by a dog or horse. It is made of two poles that cross in front, over the shoulders of the animal, and are joined in the rear by a net to hold cargo.

133. Edmonds, Margot and Ella E. Clark. *Voices of the Winds: Native American Legends.* New York: Facts on File, 1989, 212-213.

134. Johnston, Bernice Eastman. *California's Gabrielino Indians.* Los Angeles: Southwest Museum, 1962, 20.

Faeries, Gorics and Other Spirits of the Stone

As previously mentioned, Faeries and other strange otherworldly creatures reportedly live in and around many of the megalithic features of the world. The Rock Babies of Native American traditions live in the stone itself and traverse between the underworld and the physical world through the cracks and fissures in the rock face. Faeries are reported to periodically dance in stone circles and their spirits as well live within certain rocks.

In Brittany the Nains, gargoyle-like creatures said to be black, with a menacing countenance and with clawed, hoofed feet, haunt the ancient dolmens and dance around them in the midnight blackness. Any human who should happen to stumble upon them and join in the dancing would die within the year.[136] Spence theorizes that the Nains were probably respected in the dim past; they were said to have held full rituals on the first Wednesday in May. This date suggests they would fall into Beltaine activities that were so important to the Celts and other Pagan groups. Like many Pagan traditions, the Christian church may have altered the idea of the Nain from their original form to that of a demon in their efforts to absorb the Pagan populations into Christianity. [137] The Nain were also said to be forgers: they would create items that looked like legitimate coins but, after a time, would revert to their natural states as beans, leaves or other worthless objects. (It is conceivable that such a notion was used by more than one self-serving individual to account for "lost" money.)

Other, superficially more pleasant yet treacherous beings called Tylwyth Teg lived in caves in Wales. These were small, pretty people dressed in white, who loved to sing and dance. Normally seen only at night, they would, if they saw a baby left unattended in the daytime, switch the infant with a hunchback or other deformed child-like being or object. They also would tempt travelers to join in their dance, and then play tricks on them. Other groups of the Tylwyth Teg reportedly lived at the bottom of certain lakes. Evans-Wentz, in his book *The Fairy-Faith in Celtic Countries*, written in 1911, quotes J. Morris Jones, a professor of Welsh at University College:

> ...the Tylwyth Teg were a kind of spirit race having human characteristics, who could at will suddenly appear and suddenly disappear. They were generally sup-

135. Westervelt, William D. *Hawaiian Legends of Volcanoes.* Tokyo: Charles E. Tuttle Company, 1963, 87-95.

136. Spence, *Legends and Romances of Brittany, op. cit.* 97.

137. *Ibid.*

> posed to live underground, and to come forth on moonlight nights, dressed in gaudy colours (chiefly in red), to dance in circles in grassy fields. ...I think the Tylwyth Teg were generally looked upon as kind and good-natured, though revengeful if not well treated.[138]

Spence wrote that the Tylwyth Teg were ruled by the lord of the underworld, Gwen ap Nud, and that they were either elemental spirits or the spirits of the dead. [139]

Gorics are another very unpleasant being, from one to three feet in height, said to reside in abandoned megaliths and in the foundations of other ancient structures. Carnac, an awe-inspiring megalithic site in Brittany, used to be called "Ty C'harriquet," or "the House of the Gorics." Local traditions said that the Gorics erected the megaliths. The Gorics, like the Nains and the Faeries, danced around the stones and would attempt to lure unsuspecting travelers into their festivities, keeping them going until they would finally collapse, exhausted and unable to move, accompanied with the laughter of the Gorics. All of these creatures guarded vast treasures, although we will never know what they did with such wealth.[140] Charles J. Billson, in his 1911 essay, *Vestiges of Paganism in Leicestershire*, noted that the Holy Stone, also known as the Hostone or Hellstone, was believed to be inhabited by Faery. He wrote, "a man once heard a deep groan coming from the stone, and ran away, terrified lest he should see one of its unearthly inhabitants." [141] Billson also states that a farmer once broke off a large chunk of the stone and took it home, and died suddenly not long thereafter. [142]

The Gruagach, while not a spirit of the stone or living in them, is similar to the Indian Rock Baby. The name means "the long-haired one" and it was often depicted in folk tales as a sorcerer and valiant warrior. In the Western Islands of Scotland, it was placated with milk poured into a hollow stone called the Gruagach Stone. Milk was often used in various cultures as an offering to gods and goddesses associated with cattle and agriculture.

All of these tales indicate that the deities and creatures of old continued to survive in the public memory, although somewhat changed from their original demeanor, into our contemporary societies. The fascination of present day cultures with gargoyles and Green Men is evidence that, even now, people prefer to

---

138. Evans-Wentz, *op. cit.* 142.

139. Spence, *The Magic Arts in Celtic Britain, op. cit.* 86.

140. Spence, *Legends and Romances of Brittany, op. cit.* 99.

141. Billson, Charles J. *Vestiges of Paganism in Leicestershire.* Loughborough: Heart of Albion Press, 1994, 13.

142. *Ibid.*, 16.

believe in such stories rather than grappling to understand scientific explanations or to recognize and admit the darker capabilities of their fellow humans. Some say that these symbols are so compelling because they are "hard wired" in the human psyche, and continue to tie us to the original feelings of awe and wonder vis-à-vis the overwhelming and inexplicable forces of the natural world.

TREASURE!

Sacred stones have long had an association with buried treasure. This is a worldwide belief that, perhaps, dates back to when rich offerings were given up to sacred rivers, lakes and forests. It also appears to be associated with legends of Faery and Trolls and other underworld spirits that were believed to reside in and around these places and guarded vast treasures. People searching for such non-existent treasure have vandalized many of the ancient cairns in what is now the United State and elsewhere. Other megaliths, including some dolmens, were actually blown up in the 19th century by people who were certain that they could uncover such treasures. Some of these beliefs may have been founded in fact, if we consider Estonian folklore. Tvauri noted, "according to oral heritage, people had buried silverware near a cup-marked stone in Viljandi parish." Silverware — but not gold treasure.[143]

143. Tvauri, Andres. "Cup-Marked Stones in Estonia" in *Folklore* Vol. 11, October 1999. Tartu: Institute of the Estonian Language, 142.

CHAPTER 2. MAGICAL STONES AND CHARMS

The history of using stones for protection against illness, evil and demons is a long one. Stones have also been used to seek profit, power and happiness. Ancient texts prescribe certain stone combinations to be strung as necklaces or to be carried on the person in leather bags. Thomsen noted that certain stone necklaces were worn "against the anger of specific gods, bad omens, ghosts, fear and diseases, to undo witchcraft, or in order that the god should take pity on a man." [144]

In ancient Mesopotamia, certain consecration rituals were conducted to purify the selected stones — these rituals normally included submerging the stones in water, along with such purification items as cedar, salt, and tamarisk. Stone necklaces were worn until an illness was cured or for prescribed time depending on the purpose. For example, Thomsen writes, "after an apotropaic ritual against evil portended by a malformed newborn animal, the man affected by this omen had to wear a necklace with stones for seven days."[145] The use of "magical" gems as amulets was widespread in ancient Egypt for healing, love and requesting the death of an enemy.

Practitioners of the dark arts also valued amulets, to protect themselves from the very demons that they called forth. One ancient text calls for the use of an amulet made from "sweet-smelling lodestone" cut in the shape of a heart and

---

144. Thomsen, Marie-Louise. "Witchcraft and Magic in Ancient Mesopotamia" in *Witchcraft and Magic in Europe: Biblical and Pagan Societies*, ed. Bengt Ankarloo and Stuart Clark. Philadelphia: University of Pennsylvania Press 2001, 59-60.

145. *Ibid.*, 60.

engraved with the image of Hecate.[146] Hecate was the Greek goddess of the underworld and sorcery.

The common use of stone amulets during the early Christian period worried the Church. These obviously Pagan practices were a threat to the new religion as it sought to drive out all others and in 355 CE formal prohibitions were adopted at the Council of Laodicea. The decree stated, "priests and clerks must be neither enchanters, mathematicians, nor astrologers, and they must not make 'what are called amulets,' for these were fetters of the soul, and all who wore them should be cast out of the church."[147] It is interesting to note that the church condemned mathematicians along with users of Pagan symbols. Both were seen as indicative of "hidden" knowledge, which the church leaders found heretical.

Nonetheless, the use of certain gems and stones during the Middle Ages for healing, love spells and other occult purposes became popular at court as well as among the common populace. Sixteenth-century priest Marsilio Ficino, one of the first Western humanist scholars to bring magic, astrology and healing together into an effective practice, stated, "Christ himself...healed the sick and taught 'his priests' to do so with words, herbs, and stones. Should it be scandalous, then, if [I, a priest] did likewise?" [148]

The continued habit of crediting stones with various powers demonstrated that the Church's prohibitions fell, for the most part, on deaf ears. French writer Marcelle Bouteiller wrote that "magical objects and stones were passed from father to son. One would never part with them, but would not refuse to lend them. Occasionally, someone would consent to rent them out to oblige a sick person. Certain of these pieces had to be utilized while the possessor of a secret recited the ritual incantation, others functioned solely by their virtue of being." [149]

Magical gems were sought out and used extensively during the Middle Ages for protection or favor in such diverse situations as childbirth, illness, and combat, for the detection of poison and untruths, to render a garment fireproof,

---

146. Kunz, George Frederick. *The Curious Lore of Precious Stones.* New York: Dover Publications, Inc., 1971, 40.

147. *Ibid.*, 42-43.

148. Kieckhefer, Richard. *Magic in the Middle Ages.* Cambridge: Cambridge University Press, 1989, 148.

149. Bouteiller, Marcelle. *Medicine populaire: d'hier et d'aujourd'hui.* Paris, 1966, 57.

aid in prophecy, create a sense of peacefulness, and, according to Richard Kieckhefer, such a stone could "even render God favorable to supplication." [150]

Quartz charms were worn in Scotland to protect against malevolent spirits and other evil powers that haunted the landscape. The Church disapproved of such amulets but the practice was so ancient and so deeply imbued in the local culture that is was impossible to eradicate.[151] Moreover, in any case, even the Church viewed some stones as objects of great power and holiness.

Certain stones believed to hold great power were used in the initiation of shamans around the world. Crystals in particular were thought to have great significance and have been referred to as "solidified light," among other things. Shamans of the Australian Aranda tribe are said to have magical crystals in their bodies, which were placed there by other shamans during their initiation. In fact, these crystalline stones are supposedly produced by the shaman, at will, from his body. It is through these stones that the shaman retains and exerts his power. Mexican Indians still believe that the spirits of the dead live in quartz crystals.

In a similar fashion, Eskimo shamans are also initiated through certain stones. Mircea Eliade noted in his book, *Shamanism*, that the initiate was isolated in a lonely place near a lake or grave, where he would rub two stones together while he awaited a particularly "significant event." "The neophyte rubs his stones all through the summer," he wrote, "and even through several consecutive summers, until the time comes when he obtains his helping spirits."[152] The extension of the powers of the stone to the neophyte includes the neophyte's linkage with the spirit world and the acquisition of spirit helpers that will stay with him throughout his life.

Two pebbles inscribed with thunderbirds were discovered near Assawompsett Lake, Massachusetts, in the 1950s. Dating as far back as 4300 BCE, they are believed to have been part of a shaman's kit, serving as magical or ritual charm stones.[153] The thunderbird motif was most widely utilized in the Pacific Northwest, but it was important to Native Americans throughout North

150. Kieckhefer, *op. cit.* 103.

151. Ross, Anne. *Folklore of the Scottish Highland.* Glouchestershire: Tempus Publishing Inc. 2000, 95.

152. Eliade, Mircea. *Shamanism: Archaic Techniques of Ecstasy.* Princeton University Press/ Bollingen Foundation, 1972, 59.

153. Lenik, Edward J. "Sacred Places and Power Spots: Native American Rock Art at Middleborough, Massachusetts," in *Rock Art of the Eastern Woodlands: American Rock Art Research Associations Occasional Paper 2.* San Miguel: American Rock Art Research Association, 1996, 33.

America. It symbolizes strength, nobility, wisdom and peace. The two pebbles, one approximately four inches long and the other 1½ inches in length, must have been carried by a shaman in his medicine bag much as some modern men carry a worry stone — and for much the same reason. The stone provides a bit of beauty and comfort and relieves the stresses of living. In primitive societies, these stones were considered sacred and were thought to carry power.

Lakota Sioux shamans still regard certain stones as living entities with great powers. As animists, the Sioux believe that all things, animate or not, have a spirit within them that may become a helper spirit to the shaman. As Mark St. Pierre wrote, "small, round rocks may be charged with great power and attach themselves to a living person, returning to them even when discarded. These rocks belong to a class of spirits known as the 'rock nation.'"[154] These rock spirits assist the shaman in ritual.

These small, round stones are an important part of Sioux ritual and belief to this day. Called wašicun tunkan, they are placed in small buckskin bags that are lined with sage and are given to a person in need of assistance to address an immediate problem. "When a personal spirit is given to a layman," writes anthropologist William Powers, "the stone is named after a person who is deceased, and the deceased person's spirit is said to inhere in the stone and may be called upon in time of need." [155]

Because rocks are part of the Mother Earth — her skeleton, figuratively speaking — they have great powers. They are the oldest part of creation. These powers may be enhanced if the stone is made into an amulet to give to a person in need so that the powers may be called upon at will.

Practitioners of voodoo in the United States have imputed vast powers to certain black pebbles. Charles G. Leland, well known as the 19th century writer of *Aradia, or the Gospel of the Witches*, claimed to possess one of six such stones. "To become an ordinary Voodoo," he wrote, "the postulant must fast and watch, and undergo revolting penances, and cultivate 'power' and 'will' all his life. But the possession of an authenticated 'cunjerin,' or conjuring-stone, renders all this unnecessary, the owner by the mere act of possession becomes a grand past-master Voodoo, or multote, and requires no further initiation."[156] Leland states

---

154. St. Pierre, Mark and Tilda Long Soldier. *Walking in the Sacred Manner: Healers, Dreamers, and Pipe Carriers—Medicine Women of the Plains Indians.* New York: Touchstone Books, 1995, 108.

155. Powers, William K. *Oglala Religion.* Lincoln: The University of Nebraska Press, 1975, 146.

that, at the time of his writing, "black believers have been known to make a pilgrimage of a thousand miles to be touched with this marvelous stone — or to hold it in the hand...It must...be carried in a wrapping, or a bag, which may be closed by wrapping a string round it, which must not, however, be tied, as that would prevent the egress or ingress of the spirit which dwells in it."[157] The pebble should also be dipped once a week in whisky, he says. The wrapping of sacred and powerful stones is a common practice around the world as is the nourishing of such stones with food, drink and/or blood.

The Blarney Stone and The Stone of Destiny

Perhaps the most famous stone in the world is the Blarney Stone, which rests in the high battlements of Blarney Castle in Ireland. The stone is believed to be half of the legendary Stone of Scone that originally belonged to Scotland. Thirty-four Scottish kings were crowned over the stone, because it was believed to have special powers.

The Blarney Stone is not so richly imbued with history as the Stone of Scone but it does have its own lore. The most well known story is that a witch cast a spell upon the stone as a reward to a king who had saved her from drowning. When the king kissed the stone, he was given the gift of eloquent speech so that he could talk anyone into doing or believing anything that he desired.

In 1314, Robert the Bruce gave the stone to Cormac McCarthy as a reward for McCarthy's support in an important battle. Since the 14th century, the stone has rested in the battlements of Blarney castle and has no doubt been kissed millions of times by visitors seeking the "magic tongue."

The Stone of Scone, also known as the Stone of Destiny, has a much longer and nobler tradition, and a more confused provenance. Physically, it is a 336-pound slab of sandstone, 26 inches long, 16 inches wide, and 11 inches high. An equi-armed cross is carved on one side. It is important to note that such crosses were not Christian in origin. The Celtic cross was already an ancient symbol before Christianity came along, and its four branches are equal. The equi-armed cross represents the cardinal axes, the four points of the compass, and the four

156. Leland, Charles G. *Etruscan Roman Remains*. Blaine: Phoenix Publishing, Inc. n.d., 372.

157. *Ibid.*

elements of the world that are united in the center. Legend has it that the Stone of Scone originated in the Holy Land, where it was used by Jacob as a pillow on the night he saw the angels of Bethel. This stone, according to legend, became the coronation stone of the early kings of Israel. It was brought to Scotland in 850 CE via a circuitous route through Egypt, Sicily, and Spain. The stone was kept in Ireland from approximately 400 CE to 850 CE, where it was used for coronations of the Irish Kingdom of Dalriada. Upon its arrival in Ireland, St. Patrick blessed the stone for its use in coronation ceremonies of Irish kings. Legend has it that the stone could identify the rightful ruler by emitting a loud cry — many equate the Stone of Scone with the Lia Fáil, or the "Speaking Stone," or "Stone of Destiny." The stone was said to shriek the number of times that a king's descendants would become kings of Erin.

The Lia Fáil was also traditionally called Bod Feargius, or "Fergus's Phallus," after the Pictish king. Early writers linked the Lia Fail to the Celtic sun gods Nuada and Lugh. Old legends say that the spirit of Scota, the goddess for whom Scotland was named, inhabited the stone and prophesied from it. Still others say that "such royal monuments were haunted by a 'demon,' who exclaimed in recognition when the rightful monarch of Ireland took his seat upon it."[158]

But is the Lia Fáil the Stone of Scone? There appear to be two stones of similar character. The Lia Fáil was always an Irish treasure and is still believed to rest on the holy Hill of Tara, while the Stone of Scone, with similar ability to announce a king, was locally produced in or near Scone.[159] Lewis Spence wrote that the idea "that this stone [the Lia Fáil] still remains there [in Ireland] is indeed common knowledge among Irish antiquaries. It is a pillar, and by no means an easily portable one, and does not at all resemble the Coronation Stone at Westminster."[160]

However, popular lore states the following: Kenneth I, 36th King of Dalriada, moved the capital of his kingdom from Ireland to Scone, in what is now Perthshire, Scotland, in 850 CE. While the stone was moved several times over the years, it was always taken back to Scone for the coronation of Dalriadic kings. The Stone was last used in a Scottish coronation in 1292, the coronation of King John Balliol. Then, the English king, Edward I, invaded Scotland and con-

158. Spence, Lewis. *The Magic Arts in Celtic Britain.* Mineola: Dover Publications, Inc., 1999, 102.

159. *Ibid.*, 101.

160. *Ibid.*

fiscated the stone. It was housed in the English Coronation Throne in Westminster Abbey, specially constructed to hold and contain the stone, in 1301. Queen Elizabeth II was the last English monarch to be installed upon the Stone of Scone, in 1953. While the English had signed a treaty in 1328 to return the stone, they did not return it until November 1996. Nineteenth-century Scottish folklore still said that anyone who laid hands against the Stone would never prosper; with a bit of a stretch, willing minds may still say that England's power did wane, long after the theft of the Stone, even if not sufficiently to reduce the British to actual poverty.

Other Royal Stones

Around the world, there are several large stones reputed to have the footprints of kings and mythical leaders carved upon them, many dating from the Mesolithic age. One such place is Tintagel, the supposed birthplace of Arthur. At the summit of the high cliffs, upon which the ruined castle is perched, a rock outcrop exists which has a curious carved depression on its surface. Worn and obviously very old, the depression resembles that of a left footprint, slightly smaller than an average man's today. Researcher Paul Broadhurst says that the depression "is typical of early royal inauguration marks, where an incoming ruler confirmed, by placing his foot in the symbolic shape, his domination over the land."[161]

Another site sporting a stone footprint is near Dunadd, in Argyll, where the early kings of the Scottish Dalriadic empire were crowned. The proposed king's feet had to fit within the stone's footprint or he was not "fit" to rule. Similar sites are found throughout the world, such as the Zasliai Stone in Lithuania; they attest to the ancient sanctity of Mother Nature and the desire of those in power to assert some linkage in order to bolster their positions.

"The Romans were accustomed to carve pairs of footprints," says researcher Nigel Pennick, "on a stone with the inscription *pro itu et reditu*, 'for the journey and return,'"[71] Pennick notes — in other words, as a protective travel ritual to mark the beginning and end of a journey.

161. Broadhurst, Paul. *Tintagel and the Arthurian Mythos.* Launceston: Pendragon Press, 1992, 133.

Similar prints can be found on stones in Brittany where, MacKenzie writes, they "are depicted surrounded by meandering and serpentine lines. Perhaps these 'luck lines,' as they may be called, were inscribed with purpose to secure magical protection for individuals setting out on a journey."[162] Another theory is that the footprints carved in stone represent an individual person who has died and the lines surrounding the prints were meant to restrict the movement of the person's spirit or ghost.

Footprints in stone are not confined to Europe. The Tibetan Buddhist reformer Tsong-kha-pa, who lived 1357 to 1419 CE, was said to have had a miraculous birth and at the age of three was able to leave his foot prints in stone, as well as turning earth into food and a river to ice during the summer.

On a different note, stone prints were also used for other purposes. The Giant's Lap-Stone, located on the North York Moors (northern England), contained a large foot-shaped depression approximately two feet deep. Local belief held that it could determine a woman's virtue. If the lady could not fit her foot within the depression, she was surely a virgin! (Some of these legends appear to be more generous than others.) The Giant's Lap-Stone was also sought out for its reported powers to ensure healthy children. The ritual called for visiting the stone on a Monday and for the seeker to climb to the top, recite a verse and then throw a shoe into the nearby brook.

Stone circles were also used to enthrone kings. Up to the 14th century, stone circles in Cornwall were an important part of the coronation ritual. The king would stand in the middle, near the center stone, with his nobles arranged on the outside, standing at the other stones. The royal center of the Pict kingdom, now in a churchyard at Clackmannan and a circle near Cavan are two such examples of these "crowning places."[163]

Stones have been an integral part of kingship, law- and oath-giving for centuries, around the world. Danish historian Saxo Grammaticus wrote some nine centuries ago: "the ancients, when they were to choose a king, were wont to stand on stones planted in the ground, and to proclaim their votes, in order to foreshadow from the steadfastness of the stones that the deed would be lasting."[164]

162. MacKenzie, Donald A. *Crete & Pre-Hellenic Myths and Legends.* London: Senate, 1995, 33 (originally published 1917).

163. Pennick *op. cit.* 45.

164. Frazer, Sir James. *The Magic Art and the Evolution of Kings, Vol 1.*London: Macmillan & Co. Ltd., 1955, 160.

Another royal stone is St. Columb's, located near Londonderry, N. Ireland. A large stone, 7 ½ feet square, it has two impressions of feet and it is said that the chief of the O'Dohertys would stand in the prints "and absorb the energies which pulsed forth."[165] Historian Ronald Hutton notes that two such sites in Ulster "were used until the end of the sixteenth century." One "is a rock with the famous holy well Tobar an Duin at its foot. It was presumably in this well that the king bathed."[166] Other sites of kingship also contain both footprints in stone and bathing places. Next to a carved footprint on a fortified summit in the Kilmartin Valley of Argyll is a bowl carved in the rock with a wild boar design engraved upon it. The combined use of stone and water was a potent factor in the sacred kingship.

The King's Stone at Kingston-upon-Thames was the coronation stone of four English kings in the 10th century: Athelstan, Edmund, Edred and Edwy. The name "Kingston," by the way, is derived from "King's Stone."

The Ritual Use of Stones

Stones — magical, mysterious and imbued with supernatural powers — have been used for thousands of years for healing, cursing, luck and divination. In 1900, John Rhys wrote of the winter bonfires in Wales:

> A bonfire was always kindled...on the eve of the Winter Calends...Besides fuel, each person present used to throw into the fire a small stone, with a mark whereby he should know it again. If he succeeded in finding the stone on the morrow, the year would be a lucky one for him, but the contrary if he failed to recover it. [167]

A similar ritual was undertaken in Scotland on Halloween, when families would kindle a bonfire and place a stone circle around the fire — each stone representing a member of the family. The next morning they would return and carefully examine the stones to see if they had moved; if so, the person whom the stone represented was considered "fey" and would not be expected to live the year out. [168] In Greece, a bonfire would be lit at midsummer and boys would

165. Bord, Janet and Colin. *Mysterious Britain: Ancient Secrets of Britain and Ireland.* London: Thorsons, 1972, 31.

166. Hutton, Ronald. *The Pagan Religions of the Ancient British Isles: Their Nature and Legacy.* Oxford: Blackwell Publishers Ltd., 1993, 173.

167. Rhys, John. *Celtic Folklore: Welsh and Manx.* Vol. 1. New York: Gordon Press, 1974, 224-225.

dance around it with stones tied to their heads so that they would become as strong as a stone.

New Guinea natives wrap "magical" stones in bast[169] and bury them at sowing time; they leave them in the soil until time to harvest, in the belief that the stones promote the growth of plants. Maringer wrote, "they wrap them in bast so as to preserve that power, and guard them jealously, to prevent an enemy from stealing them and using them for his own ends."[170] This contemporary practice seems to be a parallel to a custom in ancient Neolithic Swiss lake-dwelling sites, which would indicate that similar beliefs were held by early agricultural societies around the world.

Anthropologist Robert H. Lowie noted that a Crow Indian "who found a peculiarly shaped rock suggestive of an animal would treasure it, grease it, wrap it up with beads and other offerings, and believe it capable of reproduction. Periodically the owner would pray to the rock to grant him long life and wealth."[171]

Laplanders will place offerings of bird and fish remains on certain stones in the belief that the stones will produce other birds and fish that they can hunt in the future. All hunted animals, according to Lap tradition, have their own guardian spirits that are manifested in these stones.

Using stones to curse an enemy was also a common practice in the ancient, and not so ancient, past. In Ireland, the "Fire of Stones" ritual was used to curse enemies. According to Conan Kennedy, the ritual calls for the collection of as many fist-sized stones as possible. They were placed in a pile to resemble a fire, then "the curser places his/her curse on the enemy...praying that, until the heap of stones shall burn, the curse shall stay in place." [172] After the incantation is made, the stones are scattered because, should the enemy find the stones and collect them all together again, the curse could be removed. Kennedy states that another form of stone cursing involved "turning" the stones on an altar. Kennedy

168. Radford, Edwin and Mona A. *Encyclopaedia of Superstitions.* New York: The Philosophical Library, 1949, 229.

169. "Bast" is a fibrous material made from bark, commonly used to manufacture ropes and mats.

170. Maringer, Johannes. *The Gods of Prehistoric Man: History of Religion.* London: Phoenix Press 2002, 179.

171. Lowie, Robert H. *Indians of the Plains.* Garden City: The Natural History Press, 1963, 168.

172. Kennedy, Conan. *Ancient Ireland: The User's Guide—An Exploration of Ireland's Pre-Christian Monuments, Mythology and Magic, Ritual and Folklore.* Killala: Morrigan Books, 1997, 72.

mentions "turning the stones around three times in an anti-clockwise direction" with other incantations offered.[173] The most notable success recorded for this curse was the sinking of the HMS Wasp, a British gunboat sent to evict the residents of Tory Island off County Donegal. Reportedly, the island's resident curser activated the curse stone, which resulted in the Wasp striking rocks and sinking, drowning the whole crew. According to official records, the iron-hulled HMS Wasp struck an "isolated rock" near the island and sank on September 22, 1884.

A different version of this legend also involves a sacred stone, but it is a standing stone called a gallaun — a monolith with a vaguely human shape with outstretched arms, which, according to writer Lyall Watson, "serves the islanders as a secret weapon. When threatened they gather on the cliffs and point it in the direction of marauders, tax-gatherers and other forms of piracy. And, they say, it never fails to spell disaster for an invader."[174] It is this gallaun that some believe doomed the HMS Wasp to a violent and unexpected storm.

A similar method was employed in Scotland, where "certain river stones were believed to have magical properties and these could be used both as amulets against evil, or, in the case of black magic, as charms to promote harm."[175] Ross notes that these river stones of power were "often blackened in the fire, and incantations were made over them in order to bring harm to some unfortunate person who had incurred the hostility of the charmer."[176]

Pepper and Wilcock noted that cursing stones were used on the Irish island of Inishmurray and that the antagonist "is expected to undergo a ritual while bare-headed." Assuming that potential victim had knowledge of this curse, in order to be protected from it he "was to lie in a freshly-dug grave and have three shovels full of earth thrown over him while the gravedigger recited rhymes."[177] This ritual contains elements that must be continuations of ancient Pagan traditions associated with death and incantations.

Cursing stones of a different form were used until recent times in Ireland. Individuals would place smooth stones in the cupmarks anciently carved in

---

173. *Ibid.*

174. Watson, Lyall. *The Nature of Things: The Secret Life of Inanimate Objects.* Rochester: Destiny Books, 1992, 35.

175. Ross, *op cit.*, 90.

176. *Ibid.*

177. Pepper, Elizabeth & John Wilcock. *Magical and Mystical Sites: Europe and the British Isles.* Grand Rapids: Phanes Press 2000, 285.

boulder surfaces and turn the smooth stones three times against the sun, thus ensuring that the curse would be effective. Evans wrote, "I was told of the example illustrated at Killinagh in Co. Cavan, that 'you would think twice before turning the stones, because the curse would come back on you unless the cause was just.'"[178]

Other stones seem to be naturally cursed and cause disaster without a human catalyst. Over the years, tourists have picked up bits of volcanic rock from Mauna Loa in Volcanic National Park, Hawaii. Each day, the park service receives an average of 40 packages sent back by those tourists. Each package contains the stones taken as souvenirs. Evidently, the people who had thought that they were taking simple reminders of their trips found that the stones brought very bad luck and they could not wait to return them: Mauna Loa is the legendary home of the Hawaiian goddess Pele, who jealously guards her property.

Those seeking some fortune have also used "Wishing stones." The Glenbuckie Stone kept by the Stewart clan in Perthshire, Scotland is one. Reportedly, the owner of the stone dipped it in a vessel of water and walked three times around the vessel, whereupon the person seeking his or her fortune would drink the water and make a silent wish.

Stones have also been used to secure a promise or a contract. The Ring Stone at Avebury is used to this day for "handfastings" (i.e. weddings) and other rocks such as the Stone of Angus, Odin's Stone and the Blackstone have been used for centuries to bind one's word to a deed or promise, or, like the Stone of Scone, to crown a king.

Stones with holes in them were useful not only for healing purposes but for seeing spirits. Nineteenth-century writer Charles G. Leland wrote that in Tuscany, one should take from the sea a stone with a hole in it, "then go to a burying-ground, and, standing at a little distance from it, close one eye, and, looking at the cemetery with the other, through the stone" and repeat the words:

> In the name of great Saint Peter
> And for Saint Blasius' sake,
> By this stone I fain would see,
> What form the spirits take![179]

---

178. Evans, E. Estyn. *Irish Folkways*. Mineola: Dover Publications, Inc., 1957, 300.
179. Leland, *op. cit.* 333-334.

After the invocation is said, the various spirits may be seen, either as flames (for those who died without peace) or in their previous forms while alive.

Stones with naturally occurring holes in them, as previously discussed, have often been considered to possess a wide variety of supernatural powers to heal and to protect. They also were used in attempts to control the weather. Noted folklorist Sir James Frazer noted that the shamans of New Caledonia could create a drought "by means of a disc-shaped stone with a hole in it. At the moment when the sun rises, the wizard holds the stone in his hand and passes a burning brand repeatedly into the hole, while he says: 'I kindle the sun, in order that he may eat up the clouds and dry up our land, so that it may produce nothing.'" [180]

The New Caledonians, according to Frazer, "have stones of the most diverse shapes and colours to serve the most diverse ends — stones for sunshine, rain, famine, war, madness, death, fishing, sailing, and so forth....Different families have different kinds of stones, which according to their diverse shapes and colours, are supposed to promote the cultivation of the various species of yams. Before the stones are buried in the yam field they are deposited beside the ancestral skulls, wetted with water, and wiped with the leaves of certain trees."[181] As an oceanic people, New Caledonians relied on fish as the basis for survival and the standard of their economy and social organization. Frazer notes, "every kind of fish has its sacred stone, which is enclosed in a large shell and kept in the graveyard."[182] Stones among the native New Caledonians act as direct links to the gods and the dead and as intermediaries between the sacred and the profane. It is a combination of the sacred stones and the reinforcing power of their ancestors that is seen as accomplishing the requested favors.

In Japan, at the Kasima Shrine, a first century CE Shinto temple, a sacred "Pivot-stone" is located. Referred to as one of "Kasima's Seven Wonders," the stone is described as projecting several inches above the ground, with a depression (cup mark?) on the top. According to Japanese legend, the stone holds down a "monstrous subterranean cat-fish, which is traditionally supposed to be the cause of earthquakes." [183]

---

180. Frazer, Sir James. *The Golden Bough: A Study in Magic and Religion.* Hertfordshire: Wordsworth Editions Ltd., 1993, 78.

181. Frazer, Sir James. *The Magic Art and the Evolution of Kings, Vol. 1.* London: Macmillan & Co Ltd., 1955, 162-163.

182. *Ibid.*, 163.

Certain stones were commonly used in Native American rituals, although it is obviously hard to ascertain the exact purpose for which early pre-historic sites were used. On the basis of contextual and ethnographic correlation and a lot of guesswork, it can be determined that certain stones were preferred for religious and ritualistic use. Clues lie in the physical characteristics of the stone, its design, and its location in a specific area as well as in evidence from similar cultures existing today. Amulets made from crystal and unusually shaped stone were used by the Incas as well by North American Indian groups.

"Charm stones," according to ethnologist Alfred Kroeber, "were hunting amulets...they are almost always found in or near water...the stone was known to be of value in attracting game."[184] Because these stones were most often found in the vicinity of water, they have often been misidentified as fishing sinkers. Some of these stones were found as late as the 1920s in California suspended over trails and streams, and they have been found in or near water in archaeological excavations and surveys.

The Chumash Indians living along the Channel Islands and California Coast used "plummet-shaped" charm stones, which were regarded magically, according to Kroeber, and, he says, "made much of." He notes that seeds and grain were ground into meal using these stones and the food was used as offerings during rituals.[185]

A few stone discs found in Southern California appear to represent the ritual life cycle of members of certain Indian groups as well as "the structure of the sacred enclosure and the universe."[186] According to archaeologist Charles Irwin, one of these stones "is circular, (9 ½" diameter), flat (3/8" thick), contains a hole in the center (3 ¾" diameter), bears a constriction showing two opposing sets of parallel grooves, one containing seven grooves and the other six."[187] Irwin summarizes the significance of the artifact by saying that it "may have been (a) material symbol of the social order, a dual system through which everyone passed to reach the 'Milky Way'"[188] — the Milky Way being the transition from

183. Anon. *Sinto Shrines (Zinsya): With a Brief Explanation of Sinto Ceremonies and Priesthood.* Board of Tourist Industry, Japanese Government Railways n.d., 13.

184. Kroeber, A.L. *Handbook of the Indians of California.* New York: Dover Publications Inc., 1976, 361-362.

185. *Ibid.* 567.

186. Irwin, Charles N. "A Material Representation of a Sacred Tradition," in *The Journal of California Anthropology*, Summer 1978, Vol.5, No.1, 94.

187. *Ibid.*, 91.

188. *Ibid.*, 93.

death to afterlife. Further, Irwin states that the artifacts may have represented the stage in time when an individual was initiated into the mysteries of the tribe's religious universe.

An unusual sandstone amulet found at a Tillamook (Oregon) village site called Chishucks was carved into a face; the eyes and nose were drilled through and the mouth etched across the stone. It was discovered in the middle of a firepit; no one knows if the stone was intentionally burned in a ritual or was discarded or dropped in accidentally. While smooth stone discs were rare, fishermen would use them as net weights and would sometimes carve faces on them to bring the fisherman good luck.[189]

Cog Stones

In Southern California peculiar items known as "cogged stones" have been found, in areas stretching from San Diego to Ventura. These stones were fashioned some 5,500 to 8,000 years ago, but how they were used is anyone's guess. It is assumed that they had some religious or healing purpose. They can be described as flat discs of stone with a series of depressions around the perimeter, which produces projections, or "cogs," that appear similar to gears or spokes. Some of them have been drilled through the center and appear donut shaped.

For some reason, the cogged stones have all originated in one area of California: what is now Orange County. However, two specimens have been found in Inyo County, along with the normal distribution from San Diego to Ventura, and one was found as far away as Chandler, Arizona. [190]

An unusual cog stone made from red ochre, found at Bolsa Chica in Orange County and dated between 7607 and 7529 BP, indicates that these stones were not created for utilitarian purposes but rather for religious purpose. This stone and 400 other cog stones were found at what was perhaps the last Early Holocene coastal village site in Orange County. At least 25 burials were found here, along with other artifacts carved of soapstone. The site is on a list for consideration for the National Registry of Historic Places, but its preservation is

189. Sauter, John and Bruce Johnson. *Tillamook Indians of the Oregon Coast.* Portland: Binfords & Mort, 1974, 156.

190. Koerper, Henry C. and Roger D. Mason. "A Red Ochre Cogged Stone From Orange County" in *Pacific Coast Archaeological Society Quarterly*, Vol. 34, Number 1, Winter, 1998, 59.

very much in jeopardy as the housing industry has blocked its designation and new housing units are being built that encroach upon it.[191]

Koerper and Mason noted that some archaeologists have "offered the hypothesis that they were ritual paraphernalia of a religion having its center in the lower Santa Ana River drainage." [192] The assumption that the cog stones were for intended religious use is based on several observations:

1) they do not show signs of wear that would be typical of stone utensils

2) some are made from soft lithic material that would crumble if used for utilitarian purposes

3) they were crafted with great effort and care, which would indicate that they were valued highly

4) some were found in locations that associate them with burials, and

5) they were sometimes found in a context suggesting that they were ritual items.

During an archaeological excavation, one of the stones was recovered from the chest cavity of a male skeleton and eight of the stones were found stacked one on the other in another burial.[193] In addition, a group of seven stacked cogged stones was found in 1930 in a Long Beach excavation.

A very similar group of stones simply called "stone disks" were excavated during 1936-1938 by Smithsonian Institution archaeologists. These disks were not recovered in Southern California, however, but in the Pickwick Basin in portions of Alabama, Mississippi and Tennessee. These disks were made from a variety of stone materials including sandstone, shale, slate and fine grained gneiss. They varied in size from 12.5 inches to 4.5 inches in diameter and some were elaborately engraved with mythological and mystical scenes, and all were "notched" on the edges to give them a similar, although more refined, "cogged" shape. Their uses or purposes are unknown, but the majority were found in burials. "Many are broken," archaeologists reported, "which may suggest intentional breaking in some cases." In one instance, fragments of a single disk were found in five different burials and the disk completely restored." [194] These stones

191. Robles, Rhonda. "Whispers in the Wind" in *Acjachemen Nation*, June 2002, 4-5.

192. Koerper & Mason, *op. cit.* 65.

193. *Ibid.* 66.

194. Webb, William S. and David L. DeJarnette. *An Archaeological Survey of Pickwick Basin in the Adjacent Portions of the States of Alabama, Mississippi and Tennessee*, in Smithsonian Institution Bureau of American Ethnology Bulletin 129. Washington: Government Printing Office 1942, 289-290.

are thought to have originated in the area around Moundville, Alabama, spreading throughout the area of the interior Pickwick drainage basin. The Mississippian culture was responsible for these artifacts along with other stone and copper artworks dating to the period of 700 to 1700 CE and there is some speculation that this culture was directly associated with the Mexican cultures of the time.[195] Because thousands of miles and thousands of years separated these stones from the cog stones of California, they are not believed to be related — although a similar independently arrived at purpose and style undoubtedly occurred.

Offerings of Stone

"The great offering of stones," writes Bernal, "are unique in Mesoamerica. There are five of them at La Venta. 'The characteristics of these massive offerings...seemed to be that large deep pits were dug to receive them, and the offerings themselves consist of a very great quantity of stone.'"[196] Bernal notes that these offerings were normally immediately covered with layers of clay and obviously were "true offerings" as they did not serve any practical purpose. Some of these stone offerings consisted of hundreds of polished celts (a polished but un-grooved axe or adze head) that were always arranged in a cruciform design.[197] Many of these stone offerings had been carved with the features of the jaguar or stylized human faces. Many of these celts were made from serpentine, which is a rock that resembles jade; it is believed that jade was the desired look for these votive items. Bernal notes that jade "was the most precious of all materials, superior to gold itself...Jade objects were offered in great ritual ceremonies and were placed in the tombs of priests. The association of jade with the heart of the earth or of the mountains and the heart of the people continued until the end and was to become eventually the symbol of the individual heart."[198]

It is interesting that the same reverence for the stone celt is found in Mesoamerica as in ancient Egypt, where the image of the axe actually repre-

---

195. Silverberg, Robert. *Mound Builders of Ancient America.* Greenwich: New York Graphic Society Ltd. 1968,301

196. Bernal, Ignacio, trans. by Doris Heyden and Fernando Horcasitas. *The Olmec World.* Berkeley: University of California Press, 1969, 41-42.

197. *Ibid.* 42.

198. *Ibid.* 100.

sented "god" in Egyptian hieroglyphs (see Chapter 11). The ancient Peruvians erected standing stones as representatives of their god of the coast and creator Pachacámac. "Pachacámac" means "The One Who Animates the World" and he is associated with volcanoes, earthquakes and the sun. He was believed to be the reason that the world stayed in balance and was the important oracle god to the Incas. Offerings were made to the stones to ensure good favor.

Certain types of stone were also used as grave offerings among Native Americans. Arikara burials that have been discovered in South Dakota contained obsidian, flint, quartz crystals, white pebbles and engraved, perforated stones and pendants. These offerings were normally placed near the head. Children, according to an archaeologist, were "buried with considerable care and with an unusual number of personal property items."[199]

The Power of Crystal

Rock crystal is perhaps the most frequently used stone in the occult sciences. Clear, colorless quartz, hard and glossy, it has been sought out for healing, foretelling the future, and for channeling energy. Crystal represents purity, knowledge and spiritual perfection; it has been used since ancient times and around the world for a variety of purposes. In the Greco-Roman world, it signified the moon goddess Selene, and, to Christians, the light of God. Crystal also is a symbol of the Great Spirit to Native Americans. Rock crystal charm stones were, and still are, an important aspect of North American, particularly Southwestern, Indian ritual belief. Crystals are a common find in 8,000-year-old archaeological sites in California. Contemporary tribes living in the region (including the Paipai, Kumeyaay, and Kiliwa), "without exception" refer to the stone as a "living rock," "live rock," or "alive." [200] Anthropologist Jerome Levi calls these stones "the most powerful objects in the supernatural universe. Its unique vitality, its efficacy for individual gain, and its potency in malevolent magic all make it a paranormal force that is regarded with the utmost fear.

---

199. Wedel, Waldo R. "Archaeological Materials from the Vicinity of Mobridge, South Dakota," *Anthropological Papers, No. 45*. Washington: Smithsonian Institution Bureau of American Ethnology. Bulletin 157, 1955, 90.

200. Levi, Jerome Meyer. "Wii'pay: The Living Rocks—Ethnographic Notes on Crystal Magic Among Some California Yumans," in *The Journal of California Anthropology*, Summer 1978, Vol. 5, No. 1, 43.

Clearly, it is one of the most potent and distinctive objects in the witches' paraphernalia."[201]

What is it about these stones that so appeals to the human imagination and makes them seem so powerful? Even Levi does not claim that the stone itself has power for good or evil, but he says it has the capacity to absorb power and to have that power focused by a shaman to do either good or evil. The worst scenario, in this view, is for a layperson who has no training as a shaman to possess a crystal, thus placing the power in an uncontrolled state. The only way to neutralize the crystal in this instance is to submerge it in water, insulating the power and protecting the person who would otherwise be in mortal danger.

In Australia, the shaman placed crystals in water and then drank the water to induce visions. This was supposed to enable him to see and speak with spirits of the dead who would give other magic stones to the shaman. In Borneo, shamans referred to crystal as "light stones," and believed they could reflect the individual soul and reveal what flaws may exist that could be healed by the shaman.

Similar to those stones said to contain the human spirit, "live" crystals are said to be alive because they contain beings inside their hard surfaces. Some crystals are simply crystals, being neither alive nor able to focus power. Levi states that the living crystals, in the Yuman language called *wii'ipay*, "are like people....it should be understood that they are unlike ordinary people because the stones can tap, if not generate, cosmic power. Thus, a wii'ipay is more like a powerful Yuman shaman than it is like an average lay person."[202] In addition, the wii'ipay may be male or female, may have emotions, move freely on its own, and speak; it must be fed and given attention.

A similar belief existed among the Cherokee, in the East, who thought that crystal had "great power to give aid in hunting and also in divining."[203] Kunz wrote of one Cherokee man who kept "his magic stone wrapped up in buckskin and hid it in a sacred cave; at stated intervals he would take it out of its repository and 'feed' it by rubbing over it the blood of a deer. This goes to prove that the stone...was considered to be a living entity and as such required nourishment."[204]

---

201. *Ibid.*, 44.
202. *Ibid.*, 46.
203. Kunz, *op. cit.*, 254.
204. *Ibid.* 254-255.

Noted anthropologist James Mooney, who studied the Cherokee in the late 19th century, elaborates on the magical crystal of the Cherokee which, he observed, was called the Ulûñsû'tî, "Transparent":

> It is like a large transparent crystal, nearly the shape of a cartridge bullet, with a blood-red streak running through the center from top to bottom. The owner keeps it wrapped in a whole deerskin, inside an earthen jar hidden away in a secret cave in the mountains. Every seven days he feeds it with blood of small game, rubbing the blood all over the crystal as soon as the animal has been killed. Twice a year it must have the blood of a deer or some other large animal. Should he forget to feed it at the proper time it would come out from its cave at night in a shape of fire and fly through the air to slake its thirst with the lifeblood of the conjurer or some of his people.[205]

This problem could be avoided if the owner told the crystal that it would not be needed for sometime, for then the stone would simply sleep until needed again. Mooney went on to say that "no white man must ever see it and no person but the owner will venture near it for fear of sudden death."[206] Upon the owner's death, the stone is buried with him to protect the rest of the tribe. Why take such fearsome risks for this crystal? The owner is assured of success in hunting, rainmaking, business, prophecy and love.

Indians of the Mount Lassen area in California also valued quartz crystal as charm stones, and kept them safely hidden in rattlesnake dens. The owner of such charms "would secretly rub them on himself to gain good luck in gambling or other pursuits...."[207]

Kwakiutl shamans claimed to obtain their power through rock crystal and other Indian shamans were said to be able to fly if they swallowed a crystal.[208]

Crystal was used as a rainmaking tool in both Australia and the Upper Nile. Frazer wrote that the Upper Nile shaman-chief "plunges the stones in water, and taking in his hand a peeled cane, which is split at the top, he beckons with it to the clouds to come or waves them away in the way they should go, muttering an incantation the while."[209]

The power of healing is also attributed to this stone. Crystal, ground into fine powder and ingested, was believed to have the power to cure mental illness.[210] Mayan shamans would pass a crystal over an ill person's body to "pull

205. Mooney, James. *Myths of the Cherokee.* New York: Dover Publications, Inc., 1995, 298.

206. *Ibid.*

207. Schulz, Paul E. *Indians of Lassen.* Mineral: Loomis Museum Association, 1988, 158.

208. Eliade *op. cit.*, 138.

209. Frazer, *op. cit.*, 85.

out" the cause of the disease. Crystals have been an important part of the shaman's tool kit around the world for healing and transferring evil.

By contrast, the Luiseño Indians of California claimed that clear rock crystal were the arrows of the sacred raven and caused internal pain.[211] The Luiseño used tourmaline instead of crystal in healing. Tourmaline is a group of related but different minerals that often occur in attractive natural crystal formations; they can vary in color from rose to sea green, sometimes within the same individual crystal. The Luiseño rubbed tourmaline crystals over the body of the ill person to effect a cure. Only the shaman was allowed to use them; anyone else who touched one of the stones was punished.

Quartz crystal has been credited with a wide array of uses both in healing and in causing pain and death. Convulsions, epilepsy, diarrhea, and whooping cough were treated by pouring water or milk over "thunder arrows" and having the patient ingest the liquid. Such treatments were used in the Slavic countries as well as the Unites States. Infertility was treated by having the barren woman wash her feet in running water in which a quartz stone had been placed. During the 19th century both the Australian aborigines and conjurors in the United States would place nails or sharp pieces of quartz in the footprints of an individual to cause pain and in Canada deathly illness could be caused by throwing a piece of quartz at the intended victim.

The use of crystals in contemporary society appears to be increasing in popularity as well. They are placed on the body during massage, used in meditation, and said to be helpful to cure infection, hearing loss, restore emotional health, lower cholesterol, boost the immune system, and to alleviate kidney stones, food disorders, and headaches, improve vision (both normal vision and psychic), and stabilize blood sugar. Many mystics stress that crystals should not be handled by anyone other than the user; to neutralize them of stored energy, some recommend that the crystals be soaked or buried for 24 hours before each application. There seems to be a different type of crystal for every purpose. After all, it is far more fun and far less effort to gaze at a colored crystal than to stick to a restricted diet or health regimen; and whole industries are ready and willing to

---

210. Curtin, Roland G. "The Medical Superstitions of Precious Stones, Including Notes on the Therapeutics of other Stones." *Bulletin of the American Academy of Medicine*, 8 (December 1907), 467.

211. Johnston, Bernice Eastman. *California's Gabrielino Indians*. Los Angeles: Southwest Museum, 1962, 70.

promote this approach. Perhaps, since health and pleasure are both desirable, the wisest course is to do both.

Japanese tradition states that smaller examples of rock crystal originated in the breath of the White Dragon and larger crystal was the saliva of the Violet Dragon. The importance of this analogy is that the dragon is considered the highest element of creation. Kunz notes that the name given to rock crystal by both the Japanese and Chinese people is *suisho*, which refers to water that was frozen so long that it could no longer be liquefied.[212] This same perception was common in early Christian traditions. Speaking about crystal, St. Jerome said that, "while a stone to the touch, it seems like water to the eye." [213]

The legendary ability of crystal to foretell the future and to find lost objects reaches from Europe to Asia and the Americas. Crystal balls, the tool of witches, sorcerers and those professing clairvoyant powers, were used by the ancient Greeks and Romans and were widespread in Europe during the Middle Ages. During the 5th century, the Church ruled that anyone who believed that a spirit resided in such crystal balls was to be ostracized until he renounced his belief and diligently performed his penance. The crystal ball was also regarded as a powerful amulet and many royal scepters have been surmounted with them. In the 18th century, crystal balls were still known in the Scottish Highlands as "Stones of Power." Native American shamans also used crystal to find lost objects.

John Bourke, a US Army Cavalry captain who conducted a great deal of ethnographic work in the 1890s, wrote that "to recover stolen or lost property, especially ponies, is one of the principal tasks imposed upon the medicine-men. They rely greatly upon the aid of pieces of crystal in effecting this ...I can not say how this property of the crystal is manifested. Na-a-cha, the medicine-man alluded to, could give no explanation, except that by looking into it he could see everything he wanted to see." [214]

Crystals were used by the Mayan Indians to locate herbs as well as lost objects and many crystals have been found in caves used by Mayans, indicating that they used them extensively in ritual. Devereux notes that when quartz crystals "are struck or rubbed together rapidly they glow with a surprisingly bright light"[215] that would certainly add to the mystery of rituals performed in

212. Kunz, *op. cit.*, 217.
213. *Ibid.*, 100.
214. Bourke, John G. *Apache Medicine-Men.* New York: Dover Publications, Inc., 1993, 11.

the darkness of a subterranean cave. Tourmaline, too, has piezoelectric and pleochroic properties such that may cause a crystal to vibrate in the presence of electricity, develop an electrical charge if heated, and appear to change hue when viewed from different directions.

The Mystery of Jade

Other than crystal, jade has perhaps been the stone most revered throughout the world. In the Orient, jade symbolizes the yin and yang. It represents purity, benevolence, justice and sincerity.

Jade beads were placed in the tombs and mummies of Egyptian rulers as representatives of the heart. Jade amulets and charms have been used in most every culture of the world. Contemporary Pacific Southwest people say that to give a piece of jade is to give a piece of one's soul.

A cherry-sized jade bead was placed in the mouth of the Mayan ruler Bird Jaguar at his death to act as the receptacle of his spirit.[216] This practice was apparently ancient, as some Crô-Magnon skeletons found in the Grimaldi caves in France had small green stones placed between their teeth or inside their mouths.[217] In Mesoamerica, jade was regarded as the most precious of stones and was identified with maize, water, vegetation, the sky, and life itself and the renewal and rebirth of life. Jade also was symbolic of rain and water in Mesoamerican cultures. [218] In Aztec society, only the nobility and the priestly class were allowed to wear and possess jade, as Aztec law stated, "no man of low quality might possess jade."[219] If a member of the "lower" classes was caught possessing a piece of jade, he would be executed by stoning. Jade was the most important of offerings found in the Sacred Cenoté at Chichen Itzá. "Finding

215. Devereux, Paul. *Mysterious Ancient America: An Investigation into the Enigmas of America's Pre-History*. London: Vega 2002, 134.

216. Fagan, Brian. *Into the Unknown: Solving Ancient Mysteries*. Washington, D.C.: The National Geographic Society, 1997, 160.

217. Mackenzie, Donald A. *Ancient Man in Britain*. London: Senate 1996, 33 (Originally published 1922).

218. Rands, Robert L. "Some Manifestations of Water in Mesoamerican Art," *Anthropological Papers, No. 48*. Washington: Smithsonian Institution Bureau of American Ethnology. Bulletin 157, 1955, 356.

219. Peterson, Frederick. *Ancient Mexico: An Introduction to the Pre-Hispanic Cultures*. New York: Capricorn Books, 1962, 227.

jade," wrote Frederick Peterson, "was a special talent among the Aztecs, who said that they located it by standing on a hill on a misty morning and watching the vapours rise from the stones. When a certain vapour arose from a stone its nucleus was probably of jade."[220]

The Aztecs regarded jade as a curing stone for internal ailments, in particular diseases of the spleen, liver and kidneys and referred to it as the "loin stone."[221] Both the Greeks and the Spaniards believed that jade was a healing stone, the Greeks calling it the "kidney stone" and the Spaniards the "colic stone."

In folk medicine, jade has had a significant role into the 20th century. Even into the 1960s, in rural Ohio, jade was worn to prevent illness and ground jade was taken to treat kidney problems. Pacific Southwest cultures in the 1970s still believed that wearing jade would bring good luck and a long life. In 1960 Utah, a piece of jade was often tied around a baby's neck to prevent colic. Other cures involving jade include the treatment of snakebite (India), poison (16th-century England), and epilepsy (Greece, Rome). Barama Carib shamans used jade to commune with certain spirits; Chinese workers living in New York City in the 1890s would wear jade wristlets to gain arm strength. The ancient Chinese also would boil jade in a mixture with rice and dew water as a cure-all. Taken as a drink just before death, it was also thought to prevent decomposition of the body.

FLINT

Certainly not as beautiful as crystal or jade, flint is, however, steeped in its own lore. Flint was one of the earliest stones worked by humans, as they were able to shape it into very hard and sharp tools and weapons. The pre-historic flint arrowheads found during the Middle Ages became known as "elf shot," mentioned earlier, in the belief that they were the projectile points used by the faery folk. "Elf shot" was often sewn into the lining of children's clothing in 19th century Scotland to protect them from the "evil-eye." Flint was also valued for the sparks that can be generated by striking two pieces together, to light a fire.

---

220. *Ibid.*

221. Miller, Mary and Karl Taube. *An Illustrated Dictionary of the Gods and Symbols of Ancient Mexico and the Maya.* New York: Thames and Hudson, 1997, 102.

This property gave it the nickname, "spark of love." Modern day practitioners of the occult use flint as a divination tool.

Flint has also been used in folk medicine. In the early years of the 20th century, warts were treated by rubbing them with a piece of flint and then tossing the flint over the left shoulder — an example of transference. Native Americans treated pain by scarification, or cutting the area with a piece of flint. In the Ozark Mountains, it was a practice for epileptics to "pack a flint rock" in order to stave off any seizures. Such a flint was much more powerful if it had a natural hole in it. Flint "thunderstones" were much prized as a cure for certain diseases in the Old World; they would be immersed in water, and drinking that water would bring a cure. Another, more recent technique used in Cornwall was to wash flint arrowheads and drink the water as a healing tonic. A similar method was used in North Carolina for kidney ailments. For added strength, farmers in Arkansas used to sew flint in their shirtsleeves so that they could absorb the stone's strength and hardness in their muscles.

Obsidian

Obsidian was one of the most prized stones in the world, used for arrow and spear points, scrapers, sacrificial blades, votive and grave offerings. Obsidian is one of the best materials for controlled flaking and perhaps one of the sharpest — a finely chiseled obsidian knife can rival the surgical scalpels used today. The Aztecs considered obsidian the source of life and also the bringer of death. It was obsidian blades that were used to cut the living hearts from the chests of sacrificial victims.

Obsidian was an important resource to every California Indian and it was collected reverently. The Wintu traveled to Glass Mountain to obtain obsidian. (Glass Mountain is located between Bishop and Mono Lake in eastern California, a two- to three-day journey for them.) According to Heizer, "these men fasted through the duration of their journey, since the act of obtaining obsidian was in the nature of a semi-religious quest." [222] Ceremonial obsidian flakes up to three feet long were produced by the California Indians and were important components to Native American rituals. Obsidian was also a form of payment

222. Heizer, Robert F. and Adan E. Treganza. *Mines and Quarries of the Indians of California.* Ramona: Ballena Press 1972, 303.

made to shamans for their services and were usually used in the ceremony that was contracted for.

The sacredness of obsidian undoubtedly is connected with the sacredness of the volcano, as obsidian is volcanic glass and not actually "stone." The trade in obsidian by the ancient residents of Çatal Hüyük (a goddess centered city in what is now Turkey, constructed more than 8,000 years ago) seems to have been one of the main economic resources for that city and was, perhaps, the actual reason that the city was founded where it was. The people living in the vicinity of the volcano and who obtained obsidian from it, according to archaeologists, attributed to the volcano "a magical aura, for not only was obsidian a gift from mother earth but it was also intimately associated with fire and the underworld." [223]

The mining and quarrying of obsidian evidently was instrumental in the founding of certain centers of civilization in both the Old and New Worlds. The Aztec city of Teotihuacán grew to its size not only because it lay in a fertile valley but also because it was near a major source of obsidian. Teotihuacán was, in fact, a major trade center for this material. Obsidian was "the ancient Mexican equivalent of steel."[224] In fact, obsidian blades were used long after the introduction of metals in many areas around the world. Obsidian mirrors were also an important part of Mayan religion and were believed to have oracular powers. Spanish conquistadors recorded that the Cakchiquel Maya communicated directly with the sacred obsidian mirror, called Chay Abah. Other Central Mexican deities also were linked to obsidian, including Tezcatlipoca, who was the "omnipotent god of rulers, sorcerers and warriors."[225] His name means "smoking mirror," which is certainly a good description of obsidian. Statues of this god were appropriately crafted from obsidian.

The Aegean civilization as well grew and prospered due to the production of obsidian, and its trade with Egypt. It was this obsidian, according to historian J. B. Bury, that "may explain her early prosperity."[226]

Obsidian was a treasured grave offering in many cultures, from South Dakota's Arikara Indians, who left in burials obsidian flakes that had originated

---

223. Rudgley, Richard. *The Lost Civilizations of the Stone Age.* New York: The Free Press 1999, 20.

224. Harpur, James. *The Atlas of Sacred Places: Meeting Points of Heaven and Earth.* New York: Henry Holt and Company, Inc. 1994, 98.

225. Miller, Mary and Karl Taube. *An Illustrated Dictionary of the Gods and Symbols of Ancient Mexico and the Maya.* New York: Thames and Hudson 1993, 164.

226. Bury, J.B. *A History of Greece to the Death of Alexander the Great.* New York: The Modern Library, n.d., 9.

some 500 miles away,[227] to the ancient Mycenaeans, who left obsidian blades in their tombs.

The importance of obsidian in Aztec, Mayan, and North American Indian life can be illustrated by the continued use of it in contemporary folk medicine and folklore. Midwives continued, at least into the 1940s, to insist on cutting the umbilical cord not with a metal knife but with an obsidian blade. In addition, pregnant women who observed an eclipse were cautioned to wear a small obsidian knife over their bare bosoms to protect the unborn child,[228] and folklore recorded in 1939 in Idaho indicates that elderly Indian women carried pieces of obsidian to ward off disease.

Druid's Eggs

The Roman historian Pliny wrote of "Druid's Eggs," also known as "Serpent's Eggs," or "Adder Stones," which were said to be made from the spittle of snakes and were valued by the Druids for their ability to bring victory in law courts, among other things. The eggs were also believed to enhance the rhetorical powers of the Druids and, in later years, to gain free access to kings. Several "Druid's Eggs" that appear to date to Roman times have been discovered, including five stone eggs found in Scotland made from serpentine and other "unusual and visually interesting stones." Two of these stones, according to historian Miranda Green, "come from what is arguably a ritual deposit, made in an earlier stone cairn."[229] Folklorists Edwin and Mona Radford wrote in the early 20th century that "many adder stones are still preserved as charms in those rural areas of Britain where the Celtic population still lingers. In some parts of Wales the stones go by the name of Gleini na Droedh and Glaine nan Druidhe" (the Magician's or Druid's glass). [230]

Folklorist Lewis Spence wrote that the Druids would wear these stones, which he believed were made from "an oval ball of crystal," around their necks as symbols of Druidic office.[231] According to Spence, "this magical amulet was

227. Wedel, Waldo R. "Archaeological Materials from the Vicinity of Mobridge, South Dakota" in *Anthropological Papers, No. 45*. Smithsonian Institution Bureau of American Ethnology, Bulletin 157. Washington: Government Printing Office 1955, 116.

228. Nuttall, Zelia. "Ancient Mexican Superstitions" in *Journal of American Folklore*, 10 (1897), 278.

229. Green, Miranda J. *The World of the Druids*. London: Thames and Hudson Ltd., 1997, 58.

230. Radford, *op. cit.* 12.

known to Celtic tradition as the Glainnaider or the Glain-nan-Druidhe, the Druid's glass...[and was] chiefly employed for counteracting incantations."[232]

Folklore, as well as historical accounts of the stones, says that the stones were made from the secretions of snakes as they massed together in a slimy ball once a year (thought to be on Midsummer Eve, in Cornwall, and the eve of May Day, in Wales). The snakes then shot the stones into the air by using their jaws as powerful slings.

The stones occurred in various colors, including green, blue, pink, red and brown, and some have perforations. Welsh folklore says that if you carry one of these stones in your pocket, all eye ailments will be cured and in Scotland it has been said that the stones, if hung around a child's neck, will protect him from whooping cough.

The one sure way to test the genuineness of a Druids Egg, say the Radfords, is to throw it into a moving stream. If it floats against the current, the stone you have is truly one of these magical stones. [233] That is a pretty rigorous test, which would seem to guarantee that claims of possessing such prizes will remain limited.

Gifts from Faeries

Certain stones have been associated with Faeries. Many powers have been ascribed to Faeries, of course, and at times they are said to be willing to favor a human with a gift of those powers. (However, the gift often turned out to have some disadvantages attached.) One such human was Connrach Odhar, respected in the 16th century as a seer. Odhar claimed that his power came from a magic stone given to him by the Faery. He was put to death in 1577 on Scotland's Black Isle after telling the Countess of Seaforth that he had "seen" her husband with another woman. Lord Seaforth had Odhar put in a barrel of pitch and set afire. Before he died, however, he predicted that the last of the Seaforth line would be a mute whose sons would die before him. This prediction turned out to be accurate. [234]

---

231. Spence, *op. cit.* 21.
232. *Ibid.*
233. Radford, *op. cit.* 12.
234. Alexander, Marc. *A Companion to the Folklore, Myths & Customs of Britain.* Gloucestershire: Sutton Publishing Limited 2002, 34.

Chapter 3. Standing Stones and Ancient Cultures

Standing stones are found throughout the world, from Stonehenge in England to the Nubian Desert to Polynesia and the Americas. In little hidden spots of Ireland and France, in great ritual centers like Avebury and Easter Island, stone monuments have been created, destroyed, and rebuilt for thousands of years.[235] Standing stones, like the World Tree, are seen as the *axis mundi*, the supreme support of the universe. And in the "modern" era, standing stones are once again coming into play. In California's capital city, standing stones can be found at the entranceways to Korean churches and government buildings. Why? What is the psychic tie between these inanimate solid masses and the human soul?

Menhirs, another term for standing stones, have come to be seen as symbols of the masculine creative force. The dolmen, on the other hand, is the feminine gateway to the Earth Mothers womb — the underworld. A dolmen is a megalithic (large-stone) slab placed across a number of upright stones, like a table; often, dolmens were covered by earth to create a small hill, or barrow. While the menhir represents the world's axis, the dolmen symbolizes rebirth

235. It has not only been in historic times that standing stones and other megalithic sites have been destroyed. At Berrybrae, Scotland a large stone circle and cairn were destroyed in 1750 BCE by an alien culture who savagely broke the stones apart—using them as the Puritans did later to construct walls, others had their nature changed by people altering the stone circles into passage graves or cemeteries. Even the famous blue stones of Stonehenge were torn out of the ground when the massive uprights were set up. According to Aubrey Burl this type of destruction "was almost commonplace." (*Rings of Stone*. New Haven: Ticknor & Fields, 1979, 30).

and the beyond. Together they represent the yin and yang of nature, and all complementary forces.

Even those standing stones erected for utilitarian purposes, such as boundary markers used by the Roman Empire, were accorded ritual treatment. Archaeologist Ralph Merrifield notes that these stones, named after the Roman god Terminus, "were set up with a religious ceremony...Siculus Flaccus tells us that the stones themselves were garlanded and anointed, that animal sacrifices were burnt in the holes where the stones were to be set, and that incense, grain, honeycombs and wine were thrown on the fires before the stones were set on the hot ashes." [236]

Other, more ancient, menhirs were obviously part of a society's religious structure. The unusual menhir of La Bretellière, 40 km east of Nantes, France, attests to the religious nature of the stones. This menhir is actually one of twenty standing stones on the north side of the River Moine. On one side a series of crosses has been carved as part of the effort to Christianize the site. But the other side interests researchers more. Visible only in oblique light, around sunrise, from April to October and sunset from February to November, is a tracing of a serpent. While carvings of serpents are fairly common on such megaliths in Iberia, they are rare in the territory of what is now France. Archaeologist Paul Raux, who discovered the carving in 2000, writes, "the fact that the serpents were carved as if rising from the earth ...echoes the chthonic character often attributed to serpents in documented mythologies." [237]

For the most part, standing stones and other megalithic monuments are regarded as being a part of the death cult — like large gravestones, in a sense. This is probably true, to some extent, but may be only as accurate as saying that Christianity is a death cult based on the inordinate attention focused on the image of Jesus on the cross. As Ó Riordáin noted in his book *Antiquities of the Irish Countryside*, "the erection of modern gravestones is essentially similar to the erection of an ancient standing stone, and indeed serves the same purpose as did some of those."[238] Dolmen are almost always associated with burials; while

---

236. Merrifield, Ralph. *The Archaeology of Ritual and Magic.* New York: New Amsterdam Books, 1987, 38.

237. Scarre, Chris & Paul Raux. "A new decorated menhir" in *Antiquity*, Vol. 74, Number 286, December 2000, pgs 757-8.

238. Ó Riordáin, Seán P. *Antiquities of the Irish Countryside.* London: Methuen & Company Ltd., 1979, 143.

many other sites also have burials associated with them, the dolmen constructs are generally much more than that.

Some standing stone monuments in certain cultures appear to represent ancestor worship. An ancient complex of over 2500 standing stones located in Turkish Thrace is still being looted, as the locals still cherish the stones. Rabia Erdogu writes that "complexes are important for present people in a spiritual way: standing stones are removed by local people and are brought to modern cemeteries. This may be explained by the connection to the ancestors through standing stones."[239]

However, there are also indications that such sites were important religious and even scientific locations to an ancient people. Many, such as Stonehenge, mark celestial events that were closely tied to agriculture and fertility, and are certainly not focused on death. The rising sun was as important to these people and was associated with the belief that spirits must be appeased. Other sites, such as those at Carnac, appear to represent ritual processional avenues. Still other stones, such as the sacred rock at Kenko, Peru, are regarded as living representations of gods that stand in witness of public festivals. Around 1,000 BCE, during the formative stage of Incan culture, a large ceremonial center along the Marañon River tributary was built. Within one of the oldest structures was "found a standing stone of white granite," writes archaeologist G.H.S. Bushnell, "nearly fifteen feet high shaped more or less like a prism tapering downwards, carved in low relief to represent a human figure with feline fangs. This in its setting is still an awesome thing and must have been an object of worship." [240]

Other standing stones were erected to mark boundaries, roadways, important religious or historical events, and the inaugurations of kings or ritual centers. Standing stone complexes, and even individual dolmen, were probably for mixed use. Like many cathedrals today that serve as the final resting places for prominent leaders and artists but also as places of worship and cultural centers, so too did these stones represent places of internment for the important people of the time and also places of worship and community.

In 1911, folklorist-theologian W.Y. Evans-Wentz noted that contemporary Dravidians in India continued to use dolmens for worship. The Dravidians are a short, dark-skinned people believed to have originated in the Middle East and to

---

239. Erdogu, Rabia. "A major new megalithic complex in Europe," in *Antiquity*, Vol. 77, Number 297, September 2003.

240. Bushnell, G.H.S. *Ancient Peoples and Places: Peru.* Lima: Libreria ABC Bookstore, SA, 1963, 47.

have been the forerunners of the Brahman class. Some trace the Brahmans to the same people who became known as Druids when the Celts migrated westward across the globe and arrived in Britain around 600 BCE. The continuation of traditions is easily explained by the cross fertilization of ideas brought by the migrating Celts. The Dravidians are believed to be an ancient goddess-worshipping people responsible for many of the great achievements in the Indus Valley. The Dravidians have also been regarded as the builders of the Indian dolmens. Evans-Wentz wrote that one Dravidian "medicine-man" was seen one night "sitting on the capstone of a dolmen with heels and hams drawn together and chin on knee, evidently thus to await the advent of the Sun-god." [241]

The practice of erecting sacred standing stones did not immediately die out when Christianity became the dominant religion. In Corsica, the practice continued at least into the 12th century CE, even though 600 years earlier Pope Gregory had admonished the Corsicans for their stone worship. Dorothy Carrington, in her book *The Dream-Hunters of Corsica*, remarks, "sinister legends attached to the megalithic monuments echo the long hard struggle of the Christian Church against the earlier faith."[242] The dolmen scattered around Corsica are known as Satan's forges or the homes of ogres.

The folklore of Corsica's megaliths is imbued with a sense of dread rather than the sense of wonder and awe that is usually inspired in the monuments of other lands. Carrington writes, "rock has given the Corsicans security; yet the legends connected with it are charged with violence and grief. In Corsican tradition rock has a punitive function; the theme of petrification is prominent."[243] It is possible that the creators of these stone monuments waged a war of terror on the inhabitants of the island that is still felt in the deepest parts of the Corsican soul. It is also possible that the Corsicans attempted to maintain and protect these megaliths against the threatened destruction by the Church and the terrible violence they experienced has created a lasting sense of gloom around these sites. History is silent. Megaliths seem to have the continuing power to generate the energy and life force of their creators and to convey a sense of their original purpose to future generations.

Many of the standing stones have an enigmatic history. The nearly 70-foot fairies' stone located in Brittany near the town of Locmariaquer, made of quartz-

---

241. Evans-Wentz, W.Y. *The Fairy-Faith in Celtic Countries.* Mineola: Dover Publications 2002, 408.

242. Carrington, Dorothy. *The Dream-Hunters of Corsica.* London: Phoenix, 1995, 171.

243. *Ibid.*, 170.

grained granite, was placed on a bit of high ground overlooking the sea. The stone, which weighed 340 tons, was quarried some 50 miles away. Why did the people place such a huge stone looking over the sea? The answer may be simple. It acted as lighthouses do today — it was probably a beacon used to mark the moon's passage during certain times of its phases. The stone was near a dolmen made of the same imported material. Lit by fires, the stone would have been "a distant foresight, visible from megalithic observatories throughout the Carnac area as marking the extremes of the moon's orbit." [244] We know that early people also sailed and fished the oceans so that lighthouses of this type certainly may have played an important part in their lives.

Other stones have lost some of their allure and wound up in less honorable locations, such as those that were incorporated into the walls of the pub known as the Oxenham Arms Free House and apparently built in the 13th century, in South Zeal, Cornwall.

There may be other, just as mysterious, factors behind the construction of these stone monuments. It is known that certain types of stone can hold and generate energy. Crystal is used today in the form of microchips that power computers and machinery. There has been some speculation that the feelings that people receive at megalithic sites are a result of such energy. In experiments involving some of the larger stone circles, animals such as sheep and cattle appear to be drawn to the center of the stone circles. Scientists have discovered that abnormal energy sources appear to exist in stone circles and in other holy places around the world. A special investigation into this phenomenon, called the Dragon Project, "confirmed that certain types of sacred sites the world over occur in close proximity to fault lines...which tend to be the scene of tectonic stress, magnetic and gravitic anomalies, and enhanced mineralisation"[245] which can cause variable electromagnetic fields.

Paul Devereux, who participated in the study, says "we have discovered naturally-magnetic stones at stone circles (usually just one at a site and in a key position) and at natural holy spots — such as a rock outcrop, an Indian power place, on Mount Tamalpais, near San Francisco, and a mountain peak called Carn Ingli...of south-west Wales, where a Celtic saint had visions and where modern people have reported physiological and mental effects."[246] Such electro-

244. Michell, John. *Megalithomania*. Ithaca: Cornell University Press, 1982, 85.

245. Deveruex, Paul. *Symbolic Landscapes*. Glastonbury: Goth Image Publications, 1992, 50.

246. *Ibid.*, 49.

Standing Stones in wall of the
Oxenham Arms Free House

magnetic anomalies can affect certain parts of the brain and alter dreams, memory and cause visions or hallucinations, especially in individuals who are or who have trained themselves to be highly sensitive.

Standing stones were also believed to hold the souls of the dead that waited until called to inhabit the stone. These souls were able to "animate" the stones and impregnate women who sought them out for that reason. The custom of touching and rubbing against standing stones to ensure pregnancy lasted into the 20th century and was commonly used by women in such diverse areas as France, England, Africa, the United States and Asia. It was also a common ritual among Native Americans and other indigenous people around the world.

STONES OF ENERGY, STONES OF POWER

Researchers have discovered, according to architectural historian Alastair Service and researcher Jean Bradbery, that electromagnetic charges in standing stones are spread out in seven layers; if the stone is over five feet in height, five of those layers are above ground. The layer immediately above the ground level is reportedly the strongest.[247] Tests done at the Rollright Stones "found that only twelve of the seventy stones kept the same charge throughout — the rest changed frequently, sometimes from hour to hour."[248] It is believed that the presence of quartz in the stones is responsible for the fluctuations in the charge.

Devereux's statement that only certain stones appear to have a powerful electromagnetic charge and that these stones were positioned in key locations indicates, if it is true, that the ancient shamans were extremely aware of their surroundings and the forces of nature, and how these forces can be focused to produce desired outcomes. Michell called for further tests to verify that "stone circles were erected at sites where, under certain astronomical conditions, a source of natural energy would be generated, for which the ancient priests found a practical use to the benefit of themselves or the people."[249]

It is possible that this power source, whatever the cause, has produced the various legends that are abundant concerning standing stones and stone circles — including the inability to count the stones, etc.

Watson thought that energy could be transferred between living and inanimate objects via an "organic bridge." Such a bridge would be something that is or was living, such as wood, leather, or feathers, and a process, more than likely an unconscious one, that acts as a trigger. According to Watson, such a trigger "is often better left to operate at unconscious levels through superstition, ritual, incantation or scientific protocol." [250]

It is possible that traditions such as a belief in healing stones can be proven to be more than superstition. Devereux notes that the circular stone of Men an Tol, which children and adults were and are passed through for "treatment"

---

247. Service, Alastair & Jean Bradbery. *Megaliths and Their Mysteries: A Guide to the Standing Stones of Europe.* New York: Macmillan Publishing Company, 1979, 36.

248. *Ibid.*

249. Michell, *op. cit.* 104.

250. Watson, Lyall. *The Nature of Things: The Secret Life of Inanimate Objects.* Rochester: Destiny Books, 1992, 54.

actually has a radioactive reading on the inside of the circular hole that is double that of the surrounding area.[251]

That certain stones can and do hold power in reserve is a scientific fact. As we have discussed, crystals are valued for their ability to transmit energy. Because of this characteristic, they are used extensively in computer and electronic operations today. It is possible that ancient humans sensed something about these properties of certain stones and that the stones were carefully placed and erected with that understanding in mind. Three standing stones located in Monmouthshire, called Harold's Stones, reportedly discharged enough energy to fling back two dowsers who had placed their hands on the stones.

A different form of energy has been observed from stones with cup marks. Ley-line researcher David Cowan found that "the waves associated with the cup-marked stone...are quite different from the straight leys which most people associate with Earth energy or telluric energy."[252]

Ley-lines continue to be objects of scorn in the scientific community and are often associated with "New Age" thought. Aubrey Burl, perhaps the world's foremost expert on stone circles and other megaliths wrote, "the most lunatic of ideas about prehistoric monuments is that of ley-lines. These are fabrications of the twentieth century..."[253] However, many strange things can be found along these lines. It seems that researchers have discovered that the majority of sacred sites around the world are situated upon these lines. However, one should be cautious in making any assertions as to what this may actually mean. So many sacred sites exist throughout Britain, Europe and the Mediterranean region that any line drawn at random would stand a good chance of intersecting with several of them. Cowan notes, however, that the energy lines from cup-marked stones, while generally traveling in straight lines across open ground, would also suddenly veer in right angles, switch back, expand, and contract. Cowan believes that such energy forces are "cavity seeking" due to their resonant nature.

---

251. Devereux, Paul. *Places of Power.* London: Blandford, 1990, 188.

252. Cowan, David & Chris Arnold. *Ley Lines and Earth Energies.* Kempton: Adventures Unlimited Press 2003, 32.

253. Burl, Aubrey. *Rings of Stone: The Prehistoric stone circles of Britain and Ireland.* New Haven: Ticknor & Fields, 1979, 80.

The Folklore of Standing Stones

Standing stones create their own traditions of odd and mysterious happenings and tales. Many times, holy wells are part of those tales. A legend about Our Lady's Well located at Lower Swell in the Cotswolds recalls that at midnight the "Wittlestone" (one of the standing stones nearby) walks to the well to drink.[254] This is not an isolated tale. The Long Stone in Gloucestershire is said to run around its field when the nearby town clock strikes midnight. As noted previously, folklore provides abundant examples of stones that move. There have been 39 tales of standing stones moving, dancing or bowing to nearby wells in England and Wales in the 20th century alone. Twenty of those 39 tell of stones going to the nearest well to drink or bathe and 27 of them are said to go into action at midnight.

As noted elsewhere it is a universal belief, still existing today among indigenous cultures, that stones are alive — and most other inanimate objects, as well. The huge stone complex at Avebury was believed to be alive — "an organism drawing its life from the vital spirit of the landscape," as Michael Dames remarks.[255] As the Church struggled to eliminate nature worship and Pagan ways, they chose an innovative approach to the problem at Avebury — a way that validated the Pagan belief that the whole site actually lived. They summoned a surgeon with a metal probe to figuratively operate on the living organism and kill its spirit.

While some standing stones may mark burial sites, others were used to help the dead proceed on their journeys. An ancient custom at the "Godstone" in Merseyside, England, stipulated that the bodies of the recently dead were to be carried around it to persuade the spirits to move on and not to haunt their former home.

Avebury

Avebury is one of the great, ancient sacred sites of the world. At one time, hundreds of megalithic stones created a huge serpent across the landscape. This was perhaps the most important religious-ceremonial site in Europe. While the

254. Hope, Robert Charles. *The Legendary Lore of the Holy Wells of England*. London : Elliot Stock 1893, 17-18 (A facsimile reprint by Llanerch Publishers, Felinfach Wales 2000).

255. Dames, Michael. *The Avebury Cycle*. New York: Thames and Hudson Inc., 1977, 125.

28-acre site in which a whole town is situated still appears massive today, it is but a small remnant of what once was. The central 21-foot tall obelisk was destroyed around 1725 — and its rubble used to build the town church that stands nearby. "Much of the destruction at Avebury," says Leon Fitts, "was deliberate, even systematic, and occurred as recently as the medieval period....the Church held a dim view of what it considered a pagan temple, and in its efforts to suppress persistent pre-Christian traditions, it destroyed some of the stones by heating them with fire, and then dousing them with cold water so that they cracked. Other stones were simply toppled and buried on site."[256] During 2003, archaeologists using geophysics surveying techniques rediscovered 15 of the megalithic stones that had been buried in the 13th and 14th centuries. They had been buried next to their original positions, but the British National Trust does not plan to raise them; still, three-dimensional computer replicas may be produces for future displays. [257]

Construction of Avebury began around 2800 BCE, within a hundred years of the beginnings of Stonehenge. Silbury Hill and West Kennet Long Barrow, two other sacred sites, are situated nearby.

The original construction of Avebury, says J.D. Wakefield, was to serve as "a spectacular 'winged temple.'"[258] The temple was the cultural and trade center of the region and the force of its attraction at that time can only be guessed at. Relics including 77 Egyptian faience beads dating from 1600 BCE have been found in the area, as well as axes from Wales and pottery from Cornwall.

Avebury has had a long and difficult history. A huge ceremonial gathering place, it was vilified in the 14th century when the Church and local populace attempted to dismantle and destroy the stones. It is possible that only the ravages of the plague prevented its total destruction. At times, it seems that the stones themselves fought back. In 1938, when a 13-ton stone was being raised back up to its standing position, the skeletal remains of a man's body were found underneath. Evidently, the man was a traveling surgeon who joined in the activities of toppling the stones; one of them fell on him and crushed him. Coins in his purse were dated from 1320-1325. Another unfortunate fellow was killed in the 1700s by a lightning strike that shattered the stone at whose feet he was seeking

---

256. Fitts, Leon. "Stone Circles" in *British Heritage*, March 1997, 35.

257. Brown, Amanda. "Discovery of buried megaliths completes Avebury circle" in *The Independent News*, December 3, 2003.

258. Wakefield, J.D. *Legendary Landscapes: Secrets of Ancient Wiltshire Revealed.* Marlborough: Nod Press, 1999, 81.

Avebury

shelter. Attempts to plot the original layout of the stones in the 1800s met with disaster when sudden and violent storms drove the researchers away.[259]

Folklore that is more recent says that the Avebury stones are gravestones for King Arthur's men who fell in the Battle of Mount Badon.

STONEHENGE

No discussion of standing stones is complete without including the 4,000-year-old Stonehenge. One visit is not enough. Visiting it in person after seeing all the images on posters, TV, and optimized photographs, at first some people are disappointed — it seems smaller, in real life. However, one cannot help but be amazed at the massiveness of the place and the effort and focus of the people who built it so long ago. An early tale has it that the structure originated in

259. Burl, Aubrey. *Prehistoric Avebury*. New Haven: Yale University Press, 1979, 60.

Africa and was brought to Salisbury intact by Merlin, through his magical arts. The long-held theory that the Druids built it has been discredited for some time, as the monument was already standing thousands of years before the Druids and Celts came to the shores of Albion — it is quite possible that the Druids used it in some of their rituals, but there is little evidence to support that view.

Stonehenge

An extremely well organized society, possibly governed by a warrior elite, must have planned and constructed the megalithic structure. The size of Stonehenge is such also that only a few people could have utilized the inner portion at any one time. Currently, it is believed that the leaders of the local people might have used the structure to enhance sound in the inner area but muffle it before it reached the people outside. Various monographs have been published extolling the use of Stonehenge as an astronomical observatory or calendar, and this is not the place to elaborate on the merits and weaknesses of those theories. It is probable that Stonehenge had a variety of uses and it is known that Stonehenge was part of the Avebury temple complex.

Recent discoveries have fueled much new speculation. The burials of two men who were contemporaneous with the erection of Stonehenge were recently discovered just two miles away. The men were obviously wealthy, and possibly royal, judging from their dress, jewelry and weaponry. The older man was buried with 100 valuable items including arrowheads, gold earrings, copper knives and pottery. The gold objects are some of the earliest gold items found in Britain. Even more amazing is the fact that one of the bodies has been genetically linked to a Swiss Alps origin. One theory is that these two men were the designers of the monument and the leaders of the people living within the region that used Stonehenge. [260]

Stonehenge has its own set of myths attached to it. Like the Rollright Stones, it has been said that no one could accurately count the stones at Stonehenge or, if he did, death would quickly follow. History tells us that Charles II, Samuel Pepys, John Evelyn, Celia Fiennes, and Daniel DeFoe all were unable to count the stones or, rather, they came to different totals. [261]

The inability to count stones or cup marks in stone is a fairly widespread notion. The Kawaiisu Indians of the Great Basin in Southern California tell of a stone with many mortar holes in it at Walker Basin. The Indians say that to count the holes is dangerous, as it belongs to the Rattlesnake. One woman reportedly dismissed the story, counted the holes, and was immediately bitten by a snake and died — no one else saw the serpent. [262]

Beth-el: Did the Hebrews Worship a God of Stone?

Today, Beth-el is far removed from its past status. It was a thriving commercial trading center from the 3rd millennium BCE until its gradual decline and subsequent destruction, in 587 BCE, during the Babylonian invasion. Present day Beth-el is known as the little Muslim village of Baytīn, or Beitin, situated approximately 17km north of Jerusalem.[263] What makes this little spot on the map important is its biblical past. It was here that Jacob dreamed of the ladder stretching from the earth to the heavens and God's voice promising him that the

260. http://www.bbc.co.uk/history/archaeology/king_stonehenge_01.shtml.

261. Westwood, Jennifer. *Albion: A Guide to Legendary Britain.* London: Paladin/Grafton Books, 1985, 81.

262. Zigmond, Maurice L. "The Supernatural World of the Kawaiisu," in *Flowers of the Wind: Papers on Ritual, Myth, and Symbolism in California and the Southwest.* ed. by Thomas C, Blackburn. Socorro: Ballena Press, 1977, 59-95.

263. Avi-Yonah, Michael. *Archaeology of the Holy Land.* Jerusalem: Keter Publishing House Jerusalem Ltd, 1974, 46.

land he rested on would be his and his descendants'. In thanks, Jacob erected a "mazzevah," or a "sacred pillar," over which he poured oil as an offering. What is the connection between the pillar and the God to whom an offering should be made? The clue may be in the word "beth-el," which means "home of god." According to the biblical passage, Jacob said, "and this stone which I have set up as a mazzevah will be the house of God. And of all which you give me, I will give a tenth to you." Did the Hebrews believe the spirit of their god resided in the stone pillar, as the Egyptians believed that the spirit of the sun god resided in the Ben Stone? Clifford notes a parallel story in Ugaritic mythology:

> The meaning of the mazzevah is not clear. Jacob expressly says it will be the house of God. The stele, as the Septuagint translates mazzevah, was a feature of Canaanite religion as we know from many Old Testament passages and Philo Byblios. In Eusebius' *Praeparatio Evangelica*, 1.10.10, Ousoon consecrates two pillars to fire and wind. He worships them and pours libations of blood upon them from the wild beasts he had killed in the hunt.
>
> Krt makes a vow at the shrine of Asherah of Tyre and Elath of Sidon to make payment of gold and silver..., just as Jacob vows a tithe." [264]

Hebrew mythology includes a "big stone" in the creation. After The All-Father and Creator created the invisible universe, he decided to create the visible. To do so, he called upon Advel:

> And there came forth a very big stone called Advel, and He, the Creator, saw it and lo, Advel had in its body a big light. And He said: "Burst asunder, Advel, thou fiery stone, and let the visible issue forth from thee." And Advel, the fiery stone, burst asunder and out of it broke forth an immense light and forth came an immense aeon which revealed the whole creation as it had been conceived and designed by the Creator, the All-Father. And out of it He made His own throne, and sat upon it.[265]

This story is reminiscent of other stories about stones with a "light" or "spirit" within them. The association of stone, creation and life appears across all cultures, to some degree. This creator-rock concept is also found in Deuteronomy 32:18:

> Of the Rock that begat thee thou art unmindful, and hast forgotten God that formed thee.

> These early traditions of the Hebrews have continued into Christianity as well, with the "Father rock," "Peter the rock," and other symbols of the strength and per-

---

264. Clifford, Richard J. *The Cosmic Mountain in Canaan and the Old Testament.* Harvard Semitic Monographs Volume 4. Cambridge: Harvard University Press, 1972, 107.

265. Rappoport, Angelo S. *Myth and Legend of Ancient Israel: Vol. 1.* New York: Ktav Publishing House Inc., 1966, 17.

> manency of the deity — but also as thinly veiled references to older, Pagan symbolism. The words Pater and Peter are related to the roots of the designation "petra," used to indicate the pillars that were representative of the fertile god's phallus. A large petra located on Vatican Hill was worshipped as the father-rock since the Etruscans occupied the area.[266]

Similar concepts apply to other Middle Eastern religions as well. Mithras, the savior god of the Persians and a rival to early Christianity, was referred to as "rock born" and "God out of the rock" by his followers.[267]

THE SACRED STONES OF BELARUS

Since the waning of the cold war, the West has had access to more information about Eastern European nations, their history, pre-history and mythology. Like many other areas of the world, Belarus has its own standing stones and associated folklore. Many of the sacred stones of Belarus were deposited by glacial action, which transported massive boulders from what is now Finland and Sweden to the Belarus countryside. Because they are obviously out of place in the associated landscape, myths sprang up to account for their presence. Along with myths, religious traditions also sprouted around these stone giants.

One of the pagan beliefs, dating back to the Paleolithic era, is tied to the cult of Volas. Volas was the pagan god of prosperity and of cattle. He was reportedly worshipped into the 20th century and may still be revered in the isolated rural areas of the country. Volas Stones are a direct link to this ancient religion. They are large recumbent stones, usually found in small clearings in forests. Cattle skulls would be placed in trees around the stone, where a priest would seek to see into the future and to cure diseases. Travelers would visit these stones in pilgrimage to offer sacrifices before and after certain ventures.

Other stones were dedicated to the god of agriculture, Dazhdzhbog who, like other gods of agriculture, was also the god of the sun and rain. Dazhdzhbog Stones were recumbent stones that served as altars. They are characterized with cup depressions that were used to mill sacral grain for the sacrificial bread which was made as an offering for the continuation of the crops. Many of the forest

---

266. Walker, Barbara G. *The Women's Dictionary of Symbols and Sacred Objects.* Edison: Castle Books, 1988, 27.

267. Gaskell, G.A. *Dictionary of All Scriptures and Myths.* New York: Avenel Books, 1981, 636.

clearings used in these rituals were strewn with rock alignments, cairns and standing stones.

Like other sacred areas of Europe, stones in Belarus were also believed to be inhabited by an evil form of Little People, regarded as "devils." Their stones are called Devil Stones, and they are located in swamps and other sinister places. These devils were known to try to confuse travelers so that they would lose their way.[268]

Belarussian folklore also contains stories of men and beasts who were turned to stone for angering local pagan gods.

268. "Belarusian Sacred and Historical Stones." http://www,belarusguide.com/historyl/stones.html. January 9, 2004.

Chapter 4. Standing Stones In America

Most Americans are aware of the standing stone alignments and monuments in Great Britain and some of those in France, Sardinia, Easter Island and elsewhere around the world; but few are aware of the many similar standing stones in America. For some reason, the New England area of the United States appears to have most of its standing stones, but there is evidence of monuments that were very similar to those of England, Ireland, Wales, Scotland, Brittany and other European locations. These monuments are not only standing stones but also dolmen, stone circles and cairns.

Tom Paul, a researcher with the New England Antiquities Research Association, has found cairns, formed cairns, dolmen, walls, "prayer seats," and possible stone chambers in a relatively small area of Connecticut, along the Killingworth and Hammonasset Reservoirs. Paul determined that a nine-mile long line stretches across the landscape with possibly more than 1000 stone structures situated along the line — and that these megalithic structures marked a "summer solstice line." [269] Paul also found that the winter solstice sunrises could be observed along the same line as the summer solstice sunsets.

Native Americans watched the stars, the sun and the moon very carefully. Their positions in the sky marked important dates for hunting, planting, weather changes and the movement of time. It is not difficult to imagine these people marking paths and other places that were useful for such astronomical

---

269. Paul, Tom. "Hammonasset Line," a talk given at the Spring 2001 NEARA meeting. Text available at www.neara.org/PAUL/Hammonasset02.htm.

observations in much the same way as other peoples around the world have done for countless centuries. But more intriguing still, there are other locations where stone structures and other artifacts appear to be the work of people who were not native to North America.

Chambered stone structures have been found in New England whose purpose remains unknown, but structurally they resemble the Celtic chambers of Britain and Europe. Imbrogno and Horrigan note that the "Balanced Rock" dolmen located in North Salem, New York, is the world's largest dolmen, the capstone weighing over 40 tons. "The Balanced Rock," they write, "is located at the focus of all the chambers that lie north of it. This means if you draw a straight line on a map with all the chambers that are north of the Balanced Rock they will all line up with the huge North Salem dolmen."[270] Imbrogno and Horrigan, among others, believe that the ancient Celts, Druids in particular, are responsible for these structures. However, other scholars have noted that stone was commonly used as a building material around the world and, regardless of when they were put together and by whom, there are only a few ways to build a structure using the raw materials of the earth in the form of uncut stone slabs and blocks. The mixed data that is available does little to settle the dispute over who built these structures and when. More of the artifacts found at these sites are related to what we generally call Native Americans than to any other people, although the majority of the 50 chambers evaluated appear to have been built during the late 18th and early 19th centuries.[271] Why they were built, however, remains a mystery as does the actual builders — Native Americans or American settlers?

However, there are many more enigmatic structures and artifacts that, if legitimate, indicate that people from other cultures and areas of the world visited North America long before Columbus and long before the Spaniards and English wrested control away from the indigenous people. Unfortunately, the vast majority of inscribed tablets and other artifacts that were purported to indicate trans-global visits to the Americas have been proven to be fakes, so many in fact that most archaeologists refuse to evaluate new finds.

One of the few artifacts that may indicate Viking visitations to America's shores is the Kensington Rune Stone. Discovered in 1898 on a farm near Kens-

270. Imbrogno, Philip & Marianne Horrigan. *Celtic Mysteries in New England.* St. Paul: Llewellyn Publications 2000, 116.

271. Devereux, Paul. *Mysterious Ancient America.* London: Vega 2002, 101.

ington, Minnesota, the 200-pound slab appears to be covered in 14th century runic (ancient Scandinavian) characters. Put on display in the Smithsonian Institution, some researchers have called it a hoax perpetrated by the neighbor, one Olaf Ohman, with the assistance of a book of runic alphabets. Research continues on the stone, however, and the last chapter has not been written on its authenticity. Other runic stones of unknown authenticity have been found in other places in the United States. Researcher Ole Landsverk wrote that three similar stones with dates of 1012, 1017, and 1022 CE have been found in Oklahoma. One of the stones was reportedly well known by the Choctaw Indians in the area in the 1830s; the other two were found in 1943 and 1967. [272] An additional stone with apparent runic inscriptions known as the Dighton Stone is located on the Taunton River in Massachusetts.[273] The Dighton Stone has been noted by antiquarians since 1680.

It is likely that trade networks did exist across the world, from times stretching far back into humankind's dim past. New evidence continues to be found that suggests it was common for people of many races and cultures to travel great distances, far more so than we used to think; and that these cultural diffusions continued until the domination of Christianity, the break-up of the Roman Empire, and the concomitant loss of knowledge during the Dark Ages. The recent dating of the Vinland Map to 50 years before Columbus' voyage proves that the northeast coast of America was visited and mapped by Vikings and it may be that those voyagers constructed some of the ruins now extant in this area. The scientist and historian communities today are disinclined to accept evidence that would shatter their carefully worked-out explanations of history, and that will make it much more difficult to prove any new theory. Regardless of the origins or the creators of these monuments, America does have a significant number of unusual megalithic sites.

When we speak of American megaliths we do not mean only those mysterious remnants that defy explanation. Many stone structures are known that were sacred to Native Americans. Philip Staniford, in his study of the Kumeyaay sacred mountain of Cuchama (also known as Tecate Peak) in Southern California, "found a monolith over 10 feet tall which, when viewed from one direction, represented the female force with her genital cleft...viewed from

272. Landsverk, O.G. *Ancient Norse Messages on American Stones.* Glendale: Norseman Press, 1969, 52-57.

273. Anderson, Robert E. *The Story of Extinct Civilizations of the West.* New York: S.S. McClure Co., 1909, 28.

another perspective, the cleft receded and the column became...undeniably, a giant lingam. It is a formidable monument symbolizing creative male generative power within which is contained female fertility."[274]

With some sites, little information remains to tell us of their history or their meaning to native people; sometimes, only a name survives that implies a special purpose. One of these is Ceremonial Rock at Patrick's Point near Trinidad, California. Patrick's Point is a gorgeous area now protected in a state park. Located along the Pacific coast in Humboldt County, the park includes a reconstruction of Sunmeg Village. Sunmeg Village is used today by the Yurok Tribe for seasonal ceremonies and teaching. In Yurok lore, the village and Patrick's Point was the refuge of the Immortals, a supernatural race who often appeared as porpoises. As human beings began to populate the world, the Immortals gathered in the refuge of Sunmeg for protection. Approximately one half mile from Sunmeg is a rock jutting out of the ocean waters called Cone Rock. Here, archaeologists have discovered over 1,000 sea lion skulls that appear to have been placed in offering to the Immortals to ensure a successful sea lion hunt. Each of the skulls had a two-inch hole bored into the bone similar to traditional practices of Arctic tribes that drilled holes in the skulls of bear and walrus, for the same reason.

A short walk along a fern- and tree-lined trail near Sunmeg leads to a spectacular forest glen, heavily treed with giant redwoods, pines, spruce, hemlock, pine, fir and red alder with house-sized boulders in every direction. A deep feeling of awe and respect overcomes the visitor as well as a feeling of a mysterious power. This is one of those sites that simply feel different from the mundane world of our daily experiences. While there was no outward sign of use, it is hard to believe that this place was not one of ritual importance. Ceremonial Rock has a trail to the top that affords a terrific view of the ocean and coastline; today, couples come here to be married in a continuation of timeless ritual.

In response to inquiries about Ceremonial Rock, District Park Superintendent John Kolb wrote:

> According to our archeological files and our District Resource Ecologist, there is no recorded archeological significance for Ceremonial Rock. There are several stories about the rock that were never recorded or verified and a pre-field literature

---

274. McGowan, Charlotte. *Ceremonial Fertility Sites In Southern California: San Diego Museum of Man Papers No. 14.* San Diego: San Diego Museum of Man, 1982, 16-17.

search did not include references as to the importance of the Ceremonial Rock area in Yurok tribal recordings.

According to Patrick's Point State Park Interpretive Specialist, Brent Montgomery, several factors would tend to question some of the stories:

- One legend involves a tribal chief, and the Yurok people did not have chiefs
- The meadow next to the rock is a man-made meadow and would have been covered by trees and vegetation prior to the coming of settlers, thereby obscuring the rock from sight.
- There are no known Yurok trails in the vicinity of the rock. [275]

While these points certainly tend to discourage belief that Ceremonial Rock was sacred in the Yurok cosmology, they do not disprove the notion that the Yurok people regarded this area as holy. Oft-repeated folklore is ripe for alteration and the fact that there are no "known" trails in the vicinity might simply mean that they were not found — they may have fallen out of use or they may not have been clearly marked or frequently used — perhaps intended only for a few, initiated people, probably shamans, at certain times of year. Mr. Kolb's response also points to the difficulty in working with incomplete ethnographic records.

Patrick's Point is an example of a sacred site that will not be found in contemporary literature or recorded in field notes, although, like so many others, it exudes a profound sense of the sacred and is daunting in its magnitude. The close proximity of Sunmeg Village, the last abode of the Immortals as well as the massive offering on Cone Rock, speaks of the sacredness in which the Yuroks held Patrick's Point.

275. Kolb, John. District Superintendent, California State Parks, Trinidad Sector. Personal communication. January 12, 2004.

CHAPTER 5. STONE CIRCLES AND ALIGNED STONES

Stone circles are closely linked to the Faery. Irish lore in particular cautions against stepping into a ring of stones lest you become invisible, a slave to the Little People. [276]

Circles of standing stones were also used in a positive way to intervene in legal events. The Refugee Stone in Scotland was so named as any criminal or debtor was given safe haven, should he reach the circle. [277]

That stone circles were long ago associated with the Earth Goddess is certain. MacKenzie, citing the Greek Pausanias who wrote of a town called Hermione in the Peloponnese, stated, "the Cretan Great Mother was also associated with stone circles. Pausanias says that near it [Hermione] 'there is a circle of huge unhewn stones, and inside this circle they perform the sacred rites of Demeter.'"[278] Stone circles were also burial places of honored individuals and offerings were commonly made to honor and appease the spirits of the dead, who were intimately linked to the Goddess. Over time, the folklore and mythology associated with these sites changed to reflect the Christian view of Pagan sites of power. MacKenzie reported the statement of a Scottish ploughman who was asked about the circles: "It is said that if you walk round it three times against the sun at midnight, you will raise the devil."[279]

---

276. UCLA Folklore Archives Record # 2-5775.

277. Livingstone, Sheila. *Scottish Customs.* New York: Barnes & Noble Books, 1996, 78.

278. MacKenzie, Donald A. *Crete & Pre-Hellenic Myths and Legends.* London: Senate1995, xlv.

279. *Ibid.*, xlvi.

Stone circles are a worldwide phenomenon. However, it is not clear that they had the same meanings and purposes everywhere. Today, there are more than 900 stone circles across the British landscape, although this is a small fraction of the original number. There are many stone circles in America as well — many of them apparently mislabeled as "sleeping circles" or round house foundations.

Some were certainly used as astronomical aids, as they are in alignment with the summer or winter solstices. It is possible that hominids have been constructing stone circles since they became bi-pedal. Mary Leaky discovered a stone circle more than fifteen feet in diameter made of lava cobbles and blocks at a site in the Olduvai Gorge, in northern Tanzania; it is approximately 1.8 million years old. The significance and implications of this site are still very much debated among archaeologists. [280]

Throughout the world one can find carefully arranged cairns of large (sometimes massive) stones and small boulders. These arrangements are particularly prevalent in the northern countries and into the artic circle. Among the Laplanders, this is known as the "cult of the seidas," or sacred stones. Some of the huge boulders have been raised to rest atop much smaller stones. The Laplanders believe that spirits reside in or near these stones and will provide help in times of need, if they are sacrificed to. Such sacrifices consisted of reindeers or the blood of reindeer. Located along gentle, rocky slopes, there are two types of seidas. Some appear to resemble animals; they were used by hunters. Others were considered as shrines to ancestors. Finnish researcher Matias Alexander Kastren, one of the first to study these monuments, believed that they were used in witchcraft.[281] Women were prohibited from approaching the stones and the use of the stones in ritual continued into the 20th century.

Stone alignments were, and still are, an important part of Australian Aborigine religious tradition and theology. Like other animistic peoples, they believe that all of existence has a life force, including topographic features, plants, animals and stone. Objects which Western man considers inert and inanimate are totemic ancestors to the Aborigine — very much alive and interactive with Aborigine society. Mulvaney wrote about the difficulty facing researchers who seek to determine the sacredness of natural features: "a pre-historian

280. Schick, Kathy D. and Nicholas Toth. *Making Silent Stones Speak: Human Evolution and the Dawn of Technology*. New York: Simon & Schuster, 1993, 214.

281. "Saami Sacred Stones in Karelia," http://heninen.net/seid/english.htm.

realizes that rocks did not require human 'arrangement' before they played an intimate role in ceremonial life; yet unless human agency was involved in erecting them, he cannot identify them archaeologically."[282] Stone alignments were representative of totemic beings that interact in "creation dramas" as well as markers of unusual or sacred events.

Australia has its share of standing-stones and cairns, as well. Mulvaney notes "possibly the most striking 'megalithic' structures are stark, up-ended sandstone slabs situated in the Great Victoria Desert. One alignment of twenty upright arrangements about three feet tall continues regularly for more than thirty yards; the entire complex covers hundreds of square yards and the dominant impression is of systematic planning." [283]

The use of aligned stones in Dartmoor, England, was important during the 3rd millennium BCE. Seventy alignments have been discovered so far and most are found in association with burial cairns or barrows. The Merrivale Stone Rows are perhaps the finest example of these monuments that were used for ceremony and ritual during the Neolithic. The Merrival Row is a double row of upright stones that stretches 596 feet to the north and 865 feet to the south. Interestingly, the ends are blocked off with an upright, which seems to fit one theory that similar stone rows were meant as pathways for the dead. The blocked end may have marked the end of the path for the spirit, or might have directed the spirits to turn in another direction.

Other rows in Dartmoor seem to lead to stone circles and are singular in nature. A most impressive double row set is found at Avebury. Constructed some 4500 years ago, the stone avenue had over 100 pairs of standing stones; one side being tall pillar shapes referred to as male stones, the other being wider, leaf shaped stones referred to as female. Archaeological evidence indicates that people walked on the outside of the avenue and not down the middle. [284]

Early researchers have suggested that the avenue "might have been not only a processional way but also a representation in stone...symbolizing male and female sexual organs" and dedicated to fertility.[285] Similar, although smaller in nature, stone-lined avenues also occur in the United States. In Yuma County, Arizona, is a 600-foot long double rowed alignment of boulders that was con-

---

282. Mulvaney, D. J. *The Prehistory of Australia.* New York: Frederick A. Praeger Publishers, 1969, 169.

283. *Ibid.*

284. Francis, Evelyn. *Avebury.* Powys: Wooden Books Ltd. 2000, 35.

285. Burl, Aubrey. *Prehistoric Avebury.* New Haven: Yale University Press, 1979, 70.

The "Female Stones" at Avebury

structed for unknown reasons. The boulders are approximately 200 pounds each, which reflects only the materials at hand. It has been noted in archaeological analysis that most ceremonial structures were boulder outlined and did not have lined pathways.

North American "medicine wheel" constructions may have served more than one purpose. Investigations of medicine wheel alignments in Saskatchewan, Canada, found that while several of the alignments appear to match astronomical measurements of stars for the solstices, some were probably used as markers of burials of important people. The astronomical alignments were sighted with stars of mythic importance as well as stars useful for telling the time of night and indicating the direction.[286] There is some evidence, both ethnographic and archaeological, that the construction of the Canadian medicine wheels were directly related to the Hopewell culture of the Mid-West dating from around 1 CE and, according to the Kehoes, "to the astronomically sophisticated Mesoamericans."[287]

---

286. Kehoe, Alice B. & Thomas F. *Solstice-Aligned Boulder Configurations in Saskatchewan.* Canadian Ethnology Service Paper No. 48. Ottawa: National Museums of Canada, 1979, 35.

287. *Ibid.*, 36.

Some of the Medicine Wheels ("Medicine" in this case refers to supernatural powers) probably pre-date the arrival of what we would consider the contemporary American Indian stock by several thousand years, even though contemporary tribes have continued to use them. The Crow believe "the little people" (again, the common theme of the Faery living in and being responsible for stone circles), constructed the Wheels. These Little People are said to create havoc and confusion to those who venture to these circles without the proper respect.[288] It is possible that later people used the designs of these Wheels as the basis for the designs of tepees used as medicine lodges or in the Sun Dance rituals — many of the Wheels are perfectly matched to the spokes used in these constructions. Archaeologists have determined, however, that none of the Wheels was used as tepee foundations; many of them are aligned with the solstices or are connected with other religious sites.

Other stone circles are also found in Native American sites. Begole wrote that two small circles found near a cairn in the California desert were possibly "clearings...for placement of offerings or perhaps for small hearths used in connection with a religious ceremony." [289]

Many of the stone circles in Ireland, similar to the Medicine Wheels, have burials associated with them either in the center of the circles or nearby and outside of the circle. Some of these are known as "boulder-burials" and consist of a group of low boulders with a stone cover, the burial being beneath the cover stone.[290] Archaeologist Seán Ó Nualláin notes that those stone circles with burials mostly occur in northern and western Britain and Ireland, while the stone circles in southern Britain were probably used as gathering places for religious or secular purposes. [291]

Like the ancient circles, the alignments are also problematic in their interpretation. Noted San Diego archaeologist Malcolm Rogers spent forty years in the Southern California deserts exploring the remains of the ancient San Dieguito culture. Dating back some 10,000 years, the San Dieguito were Paleo-Indian big game hunters who settled in the American West. One of the San Die-

288. Brockmann, Norbert C. *Encyclopedia of Sacred Places.* New York: Oxford University Press, 1997, 169.

289. Begole, Robert S. "Archaeological Phenomena in the California Deserts" in *Pacific Coast Archaeological Society Quarterly*, Vol. 10, No. 2, April 1974, 56.

290. Ó Riordáin, Seán P. *Antiquities of the Irish Countryside.* London: Methuen & Company Ltd., 1979, 153.

291. Ó Nualláin, Seán. *Stone Circles in Ireland.* Dublin: Country House, 1995, 45.

guito sites is a "ceremonial" site comprised of several snake-like alignments, the largest being a 400-foot long double row of stones.[292] Other stone alignments in the American Southwest may also be ceremonial in nature or may have been used as a "blocking" technique by later people to keep the spirits of the ancient ones at bay. Many of the existing shrines and alignments have been damaged by treasure seekers who assumed that the stone works had been created by the Spanish to hide buried treasure. [293]

Similar arranged alignments can be found in the Whiteshell Provincial Park in Manitoba, Canada. Called "petroforms," these aligned stones have been fashioned into representations of snakes, sweat lodges, turtles and mythological figures. These sites are still used by the Midewewin, or Grand Medicine Society, and members of the Ojibwa tribe for ritual, healing and learning purposes. Ojibwa lore says that these petroforms are doorways to other worlds and their location in Whiteshell is known as Manito Ahbee, or "the place where God sits." One petroform represents a human figure in stone. Ojibwa legends indicate that one of the people asked the god Waynaboozhoo, who is both human and spirit, good and bad, for immortality. It was granted when Waynaboozhoo turned the man to stone. The Ojibwa continue to leave offerings at these stone figures.

---

292. Rogers, Malcolm J. *Ancient Hunters of the Far West.* San Diego: Union-Tribune Publishing Company, 1966, 51.

293. *Ibid.* 77.

CHAPTER 6. STORIES FROM THE STONES

The folklore of stones is fascinating for the timeless tales of mystery and fantasy — and implausible possibilities. There is a vast amount of folklore concerned with stones. At one time, it was considered bad luck to be the first person to pull a stone from a church, even if a new one was replacing it. The poor workman would often meet with a violent end. Bits of folk medicine from near and far called for an ill person to be passed through a hole in a stone. Surely, illness was caused by the devil and by squeezing through such a hole the evil one would be scraped off.

In this chapter, various sacred sites will be presented with each site's lore and history explored. Perhaps one of the most famous of these sites is that of the Rollright Stones in Oxfordshire, England. It is with the Rollrights that we start our tour.

THE ROLLRIGHT STONES

The Rollright Stones form a perfect stone circle located on a prehistoric track way on an Oxfordshire ridge. This stone circle, 104 feet in diameter, was created and utilized from the Late Neolithic to the Early Bronze Age.[294] Originally consisting of 80 shoulder-to-shoulder standing stones, the Rollright stone circle was probably built as an "unequivocal astronomical sightline," according

294. Burl, Aubrey. *A Guide to the Stone Circles of Britain, Ireland and Brittany*. New Haven: Yale University Press, 1995, 74.

to researcher Aubrey Burl.[295] Located in an area of many other ancient stone groupings, the Rollrights have many legends attached to them, including one that says that witches or faeries cast a spell over the site so that no one may get an accurate count of the stones. Mark Turner tells us, "indeed it is said: The man will never live who shall count the stones three times and find the number the same each time." In fact, authoritative books list the number of stones at 60, 72 or 80.[296] There are other legends involving witches, as well. One name given to the Rollrights is "The Whispering Knights." It is said that a king, his troops, and traitors who were following the royal band were turned to stone by a witch. The traitor stones have been given the name of the "Whispering Knights." Other stones in the circle are called the King Stone and the King's Men. In the legend, the witch turns herself into an elder tree. It is true that witches have used the stone circle for rituals at least from Tudor times and probably into the 21st century. In fact, on May Day, 1955 a split-end hazel wand was found at the Rollrights, left behind from a ritual held the night before. The wand is now in the Museum of Witchcraft at Boscastle, Cornwall.[297]

Researcher Cheryl Straffon believes that this story is indicative of the ancient practice of kingship arising from the land and the goddess of that land. The witch was in reality the Goddess of nature and she refused to grant the power to rule to the king — turning him instead to stone. When the witch turned herself into the elder tree, she once again became the Goddess of nature. The elder was sacred to the Celts. The elder that was present at the Rollrights was ritually "bled" on Midsummer Eve until the 1700s and, according to Straffon, "at the climax of this bleeding ritual, the King Stone was supposed to move its head."[298]

Another legend tells of a miller who took one of the stones to dam a stream for his waterwheel. Much to his dismay, the water drained away every evening from the dam. While the miller had to use three horses to acquire the stone, he only needed one to return it. The story says that witches had placed a spell on the stones.[299]

---

295. *Ibid.*, 73.

296. Turner, Mark. *Folklore & Mysteries of the Cotswolds.* London: Robert Hale Limited, 1993, 100.

297. Grinsell, L. V. "Witchcraft at some Prehistoric Sites" in *The Witch in History*, ed. by Venetia Newall. New York: Barnes & Noble Books, 1996, 78.

298. Straffon, Cheryl. *The Earth Goddess: Celtic and Pagan Legacy of the Landscape.* London: Blandford, 1997, 117.

Stories of dancing Faeries that frequent or live under the stone circle are also told, if hard to document; but one thing is still certain: people continue to leave offerings of coins and flowers at the stones and others have chipped pieces from the King Stone in the belief that they may be used as powerful amulets. Other legends speak of young women and infertile women who were rumored to touch the King stone with their breasts at midnight during the full moon to ensure fertility. This bit of sympathetic magic was used to get the attention of the spirits of the dead, who "must have been expected to assist the purposes of the rites, or even to incarnate themselves in the children born as a result of barren women resorting to these stones."[300]

The link between the ancestors and megaliths is a strong and eternal one. The Whispering Knights were also visited by girls and young women in the belief that they could hear the stones whisper the names of their future husbands to them. The stones are also said to dance at certain times and the King Stone, along with the Whispering Knights, have been said to walk down to the nearby stream at night to drink. [301]

That there is some unusual power source at the Rollrights has been documented over the years by the Dragon Project that found that the Rollrights like all other stone circle arrangements in England and Wales are located within a mile of geological fault lines.[302] Magnetic anomalies and photographic oddities have also been recorded at this site. An unusual "cloud" effect has been seen in infrared photographs taken at the Rollrights. This "cloud" was not visible to the photographers and has not been explained. [303]

One explanation for the construction of the Rollright stone circle is that it was used for the observance of the Divine Marriage — that is, the celestial movements that occur during certain times of the year (the solstices) wherein the standing stones of certain stone circles cast a long, phallic shadow into the entryway of the circle representing the vulva, thus the copulation of the Gods.[304]

---

299. Burl, *op. cit.* 74.

300. MacCulloch, J.A. *The Religion of the Celts.* Mineola: Dover Publications, Inc. 2003, 330.

301. Bord, Janet and Colin. *Mysterious Britain: Ancient Secrets of Britain and Ireland.* London: Thorsons, 1972, 41.

302. Devereux, Paul. *Earth Memory: Sacred Sites—Doorways into Earth's Mysteries.* St. Paul: Llewellyn Publications, 1992, 282.

303. *Ibid.*

304. Meaden, Terence. *Stonehenge: The Secret of the Solstice.* London: Souvenir Press Ltd., 1997, 149.

An article in *Notes and Queries* for May 14, 1859, stated that the stones are "daily diminishing in size 'because people from Wales kept chipping off bits to keep the devil off.'"[305] The name given to this circle, so claims the article, was probably derived from Bel Rex, or "the King of Fire."

THE MERRY MAIDENS

The Merry Maidens stone circle is located in a field near the B3315 roadway four miles southwest of Penzance, in Cornwall, England. It was restored in 1860 and is one of the most perfectly circular stone circles surviving into the present age. The circle is 78 feet in diameter and composed of nineteen stones spaced twelve feet apart. Two additional standing stones, called the Pipers, are located one-quarter of a mile away. These two stones are 13 and 15 feet in height as compared to the Merry Maiden stones, which are about four feet in height.

The Merry Maidens

According to legend, nineteen girls were caught dancing one Sabbath day and were turned to stone; the two pipers who accompanied their dancing were turned to stone as well. This story probably did not originate until Puritans spread it in the 1600s as an edifying example of the consequences of not obeying

305. *Notes and Queries*, Vol. 7 2nd S. (176), May 14, 1859, 393.

the Sabbath. However, such stories are common in folklore, with similar tales occurring in Native American mythology (i.e. the story of Standing Rock). [306]

A more mundane legend says that the Saxon King Athelstan erected the Pipers in the 10th century CE to commemorate the conquest of Cornwall. The two standing stones marked the signing of the treaty between Athelstan and Howel, the Cornish ruler.[307] This legend is probably somewhat closer to the truth. However, the stone circle is thousands of years older than that.

Boscawen-un

Located four miles west of Penzance lies the stone circle of Boscawen-un. Like the Merry Maidens, Boscawen-un is also comprised of 19 stones. Unlike the Merry Maidens, it has a standing stone in the center. The standing stone appears to be intentionally inclined to provide a sundial effect as the sun moves across the sky. One stone in the southwest is pure quartz and current lore is that anyone suffering from any ailment may find relief by touching the stone or laying the afflicted part on its surface. There is evidence — mostly in the form of ashes located at the base of the center stone — that the circle is still used for contemporary Pagan rituals. Michell noted that this circle is still used by Britain's bards and augurs as one of their three main assembly points. [308]

There are several circles in the Land's End area of Cornwall, with the same number of stones, and the question begs to be asked: did the same group of people, under the same religious or civil leader, construct them? In Welsh, according to Burl,[309] "'Beisgowan' was one of the three great gorsaddau of Britain, and may have been the moot or judicial assembly-place of West Wales down to AD 926." Eighteenth-century scholar William Stuckeley stated that this circle was the first to be built in Britain and he attributes it to the proto-Christian Tyrian Hercules. There has never been any proof of this, however.

---

306. While humans are normally the creatures turned to stone, in Iceland it is the Night Troll who suffers that fate. Legend has it that these Trolls are unable to tolerate daylight; it turns them to stone. Numerous rock features in Iceland are considered to be Night Trolls who were caught at dawn, unable to get to the safety of their homes. Numerous tales of these beings can be found in Jacqueline Simpson's book, *Icelandic Folktales and Legends*, published by the University of California Press, Berkeley.

307. Michell, John. *Sacred England.* Glastonbury: Gothic Image Publications, 1996, 190.

308. *Ibid.*

309. Burl, *op. cit.*, 31.

A nearby outcrop of stones reportedly has a huge imprint of a foot left by one of the old Cornish giants. The atmosphere here is one of sadness, rather than of the light and mischievous air of the Merry Maidens. It is a beautiful spot with an old, probably ancient, path leading to the stones through the sometimes-heavy gorse ground cover. It may be the deep sense of isolation that comes when one stands in the ancient circle that creates the feeling of sadness; or perhaps it comes from the knowledge that the people who built this sacred site and their old ways are no longer.

The London Stone

Today, the London Stone is a rather insignificant piece of blackened limestone about 18 inches square, secured behind an iron grate in the wall of a London bank at 111 Cannon Street: an ignominious fate for a stone with a very mystical history.

The London Stone is the omphalos of London — the sacred center of the city. The original stone was certainly grander than this 18-inch square of rock. It may have been a standing stone, a Celtic cross, or a Roman boundary stone (Cannon Street at one time was a Roman road). Some have suggested that the stone is a piece of the altar from the Temple of Diana that was located at the present site of St. Paul's Cathedral. The stone may have been fashioned more than 3,000 years ago, and while its origin is in doubt, it has taken on an importance to London that cannot be denied. For some reason, that importance became more focused in the Middle Ages. The first recorded reference of the stone came in the 10th century, when it was mentioned on a list of lands and rents belonging to Ethelstone, King of the West Saxons. Some of the property was listed as being "near unto London stone."[310] During the 12th century, it was placed on maps as "Londenstane." Eventually, the stone became the central place of government, where laws were passed, oaths taken and proclamations made. Fragments of legends indicate that the fate of the stone reflects the fate of London. In 1450, the leader of a failed peasant rebellion against Henry VI entered London with his 40,000 men and promptly rode up to the stone and struck it with his sword, proclaiming his place as the Lord of London.

310. "The London Stone," http://www.bbc.co.uk/dna/h2g2/classic/A791101 January 14, 2004.

The future of the London Stone is somewhat in doubt. On July 23, 2002, the City of London Corp. approved a plan by the owner of the building where it currently resides, the Overseas Chinese Banking Corporation Ltd., to demolish the building and put up an eight story office-retail building. Supposedly, the stone will be relocated to the "retail frontage" of the new building.

EXTERNSTEINE

The sacred site of Externsteine is located in the heartland of Germany. It is here that Arminus defeated the Romans and it is here that the birthplace of German mythology is acknowledged. The Externsteine site is located in the geographic center of this important region. The Externsteine rocks are 70-million-year-old sandstone spires with the remains of a temple still extant on the top. While it is unknown when the rocks were modified by humans into the complex of sanctuaries, tunnels, and dead-end stairs that characterize the site, it was a Saxon center of Pagan culture until 782 CE when Charlemagne outlawed its use for rituals in an effort to crush Saxon Paganism. The temple has definite astronomical purposes as its rounded windows align with the moon and the sun during the summer solstice. Some researchers believe that the Persian god Mithras was worshipped here but others believe that the Germanic gods and goddesses were the intended objects of devotion.

There appear to be signs that Pagan rituals are still practiced here. During the Nazi era, "Pagan hymns" were sung here by the Nazi youth during the solstice and on Hitler's birthday. A decidedly Neo-Nazi element is still active. A series of hand-hewn caves are located in the base of the spires and, while their original purpose is unknown, Christian monks occupied them in the 12th century. More than likely, the caves and other holes dug into the rock were regarded as entryways to the otherworld. Beautiful carvings adorn the base of the rock, which were executed in the 12th century as commemorations of the Christian defeat of the old religion. [311]

311. Brockman, Norbert C. *Encyclopedia of Sacred Places.* New York: Oxford University Press, 1997, 79, 297.

The Externsteine (photo courtesy Aloha Montgomery)

THE KA'BAH AND OTHER BLACK STONES

The "Ka'bah" is actually the enclosure of the sacred stone of Islam. Believed to be a black meteorite, the stone is said to have been brought to Abraham by

God so that Abraham could finish building a temple called the House of God. God had originally given the black stone to Adam and today is the holiest item at the most sacred site of Islam. Another legend says that the stone was originally white, but has turned to black as it absorbed the sins of humankind.

As part of the annual Hajj pilgrimage, Muslim worshippers make a circuitous path around the stone, first stopping at the stone to kiss it and then to pray at the Station of Abraham. In a golden cage rests a stone with the footprints of Abraham imprinted upon it. On the last day of the 15-day ritual, the pilgrims gather either 49 or 70 small stones, which they use to stone three pillars that represent the devils that tempted Abraham.[312] Prior to Mohammed's day, the Ka'bah was home to over 300 gods representing the deity of each clan. The first act that Mohammed did when he captured Mecca was to smash each of the idols in the Ka'bah.

Many of the goddesses worshipped around the world are associated with particular stones that hold incredible power. The Amazons in particular were said to have worshipped at a black stone (presumably obsidian, which is prized for its hardness and its shiny surfaces) on an island in what is now known as the Black Sea. The Amazons' stone figures in the tale of Jason and the Argonauts.

It should be noted that black is considered the color of wisdom and other sacred black stones, such as the stone at Petra, were dedicated to and symbolic of the goddess.

The black stone or meteorite at Mecca was originally a sacred stone of the Earth Goddess. At one time, the stone was called "the Old Woman," and it is still tended by men called Beni Shaybah — which means "Sons of the Old Woman." Lynn Webster Wilde writes,

> maybe those who guarded the [stone] idols were armed priestesses, Amazons, 'moon women' to whom this 'stone from the moon' was sacred.
>
> To me, the black stone was a connection to something very old and not human, something abstract, terrifying and yet absolutely essential to our lives. We try to pretend this level of reality is not there, but it is, and in the Bronze Age the moon-women knew it and valued it above everything else. [313]

Egyptologist Wallis Budge noted that this holy stone is relatively small, considering its importance among the Arab people. Measuring only 6 by 8 inches, the original reason for which it was regarded as sacred is forgotten. It

---

312. *Ibid.* 103.

313. Wilde, Lynn Webster. *On the Trail of the Women Warriors: The Amazons in Myth and History*. New York: St. Martin's Press, 1999, uncorrected advance copy, 102.

may be that it was seen streaking in from space, in which case it might have been considered a direct message or messenger from the gods. [314]

The Romans' goddess Rhea Cybele is said to have fallen from the sky in 205 BCE in the form of an irregular shaped black stone. During the war between Rome and Hannibal's armies, imperial envoys were sent to the king of Pergamum requesting that the sacred black stone of the goddess Cybele be moved from its resting place to Rome. The Romans wanted to make sure that the goddess residing in the black stone was in their territory. And so, the stone was transported from her temple in Emesa, the Pergamum territory, to Rome by ship in 204 BCE.[315] The Belgian historian Franz Cumont, in his 1911 publication *Oriental Religions in Roman Paganism*, noted that "we all know the audacious *pronunciamento* of the year 218 that placed upon the throne the fourteen-year-old emperor Heliogabalus, a worshipper of the Baal of Emesa....The ancient authors narrate with indignation how this crowned priest attempted to elevate his black stone, the coarse idol brought from Emesa, to the rank of supreme divinity of the empire..."[316] Aphrodite as well appeared and was worshipped in the form of a black stone at Paphos, this time a stone that was conical in shape, and as a black meteor that was covered with "depressions" similar to cup-marked stones. The Greek and Roman goddess Artemis/Diana fell from heaven in the form of a black stone and a stream of fire in the lake at Ephesus.

In Kabbalism, the black-robed goddess Shekhinah, regarded as the source of the created world, was called "Queen, Daughter and Bride of Yahweh" as well as the "Stone of Exile" and the "Precious Stone." [317]

The Juaneño Indians, in the south of California, attributed the creation of the world and all of its life forms to Tukuma ("Night"). Tukuma "fastened the earth by means of the smooth, black, hard rock called tosaut."[318] The Chumash Indians on the California coast also had stones called tosaut that were the charm stones used by shamans.

---

314. Budge, E.A. Wallis. *Cleopatra's Needles and Other Egyptian Obelisks*. London: Religious Tract Society, 1926, 2.

315. Baring, Anne and Jules Cashford. *The Myth of the Goddess: Evolution of an Image*. London: Arkana/Penguin Books, 1993, 400.

316. Cumont, Franz. *Oriental Religions in Roman Paganism*. New York: Dover Publications, 1956, 114.

317. Baring & Cashford, *op. cit.*, 640-641.

318. Kroeber, A.L. *Handbook of the Indians of California*. New York: Dover Publications Inc., 1976, 638.

But not all black stones are seen as purely good. The Black Stone of Arddu on the Llanberis side of Snowden, in Wales, said to be haunted. It would either cause one to be "inspired" or "mad," after spending a night under it. [319]

The Lore of the Dolmen

Dolmens are those strange standing stone structures that normally have three upright stones supporting a large stone slab roof, or capstone. When originally made, most of these were covered over with sod, but today the majority of those we know eerily rise out of the landscape like monstrous bones. The majority appear to be associated with burials but may also represent much deeper purposes. Legends in Brittany say that a race of dwarfs still resides in the dolmen and they can be seen dancing and singing near them on Sabbath nights. Remnants another vanished legendary race, the Nains, are also said to populate these monuments. Having the legs and feet of goats, the Nain is said to have a harsh voice and an evil countenance with eyes that blaze like the fires of hell — a depiction of the Christian devil or demon, indicating the early Church's attempt to dissuade people from their reverence for stones.

A variety of offerings have been found in these dolmen from weapons, jewelry, pottery and even horses and oxen, but one of the more interesting items is the thunder stone — a small, smoothly polished axe head used over the years as protectors against lightning and as powerful healing stones. Pepper and Wilcock state that these thunderstones were "made in special sanctuaries by a religious caste of priests or magicians."[320] The image of the axe head is often found carved in various stone assemblages including Stonehenge, indicating that the axe represented an important and powerful religious item.

Dolmens are a widespread phenomenon in Europe, Britain, Asia, Africa and the Mediterranean area but they are also found in the United States on the east coast and in the mid-western states, as well as in South America. The structures are almost identical and it seems safe to assume that the purposes were as well. In Europe, they served as tombs of important leaders, fighters or religious people. They were also used as places of worship.

---

319. Squire, Charles. *Celtic Myths & Legends*. New York: Portland House, 1997, 305.

320. Pepper, Elizabeth & John Wilcock. *Magical and Mystical Sites: Europe and the British Isles*. Grand Rapids: Phanes Press 2000, 191.

One dolmen is located in North Salem, New York. The top of this structure weighs 90 tons and it rests on five smaller standing stones. Supposedly, in the early morning hours strange-cloaked figures have been reported at this dolmen who disappear when approached. Also, according to authors Phillip Imbrogno and Marianne Horrigan, globes of light have been seen floating around the stone and visitors become disoriented and have even collapsed.[321] Devereux's findings of electromagnetic anomalies at British stone circles are apparently common the world over.

Why such identical stone structures are found on both sides of the Atlantic is anyone's guess. There is no way to accurately date those structures in the United States, so it is uncertain whether they were constructed around the same time periods or not. There is some indication, however, that the dolmen in the United States and those in Western Europe are roughly from the same time period, as both examples have identical measurements of "megalithic yards." The dolmen and stone circles in Europe were constructed using the megalithic yard or multiples thereof. A megalithic yard measures 2.72 feet. The length of the North Salem dolmen is exactly two times a megalithic yard. Until a few years ago, the creation of these chambered tombs was believed to have resulted from a Mediterranean influence during the 3rd and 4th millennia BCE spread by seafaring peoples along the Atlantic coast of Europe into northern Europe and Scandinavia[322] and possibly across the Atlantic into the eastern coast of North America. Contemporary research, though, has shown that the Western European dolmen are much older than those in the Mediterranean area, dating in France and Spain from 4500 BCE, England from 4300 BCE, Ireland 4200 BCE, Scotland 4100 BCE and Denmark and Portugal from around 3900 BCE. The latest are those in the Netherlands, dating back to 3400 BCE. There are a few anomalies in specific site dates, though, that makes the gradual spread of these tomb structures difficult to pin down. One site in Brittany yields dates of 4700 BCE and one in Ireland, 4600. [323]

It should be noted however, that dolmen found in North America have not been found with cultural artifacts that would indicate who created them or even

321. Imbrogno, Philip & Marianne Horrigan. *Celtic Mysteries in New England.* St. Paul: Llewellyn Publications 2000, 116.

322. Ó Riordáin, Seán P. *Antiquities of the Irish Countryside.* London: Methuen & Co. Ltd. 1979, 100.

323. Hutton, Ronald. *The Pagan Religions of the Ancient British Isles: Their Nature and Legacy.* Oxford: Blackwell Publishers Ltd., 1993, 20.

if they were human-made. Dolmen in Europe were obviously built and used by the local inhabitants, mostly for burials. Due to the biases of contemporary archaeology, many of the reported megalithic structures in North America have not been excavated or even surveyed by archaeologists, who prefer not to think about crosscultural contacts in prehistoric times. It is also possible that many supposedly ancient dolmen may have been naturally created by glacial or erosional actions, when large stones are moved across the surface of the ground by sheets of ice or running water, depositing stones atop one another in unusual ways.

John Rhys, in his 1900 study of Celtic folklore, notes that other traditions apparently coincided with the construction of dolmen: "The geographical distribution of rag-offerings coincides with the existence of monoliths and dolmens."[324] Rag-offerings are still found today at many of the holy wells of Europe and the Mediterranean area and act as vehicles of transference of disease from an individual to an inanimate object. While the coincidence of rags and monoliths may be entirely that, it is also possible that these traditions are carried over from the pre-existing culture of the dolmen builders.

Writers jumping on the alien visitation theme have advanced fanciful theories over the years. Roger Joussaume, in his excellent book *Dolmens for the Dead*, repeats one of the more ludicrous theories:

...it was spacemen, who visited earth in order to mine our uranium supplies. Standing stones and mounds served as beacons on the road: they were just crude signposts, visible from afar...the Earth, then, was an inter-galactic service-station, marked out by mounds and standing stones.[325]

Stones with Eyes

Many ancient megaliths have symbolic eyes carved into them. Strangely enough, this eye motif not only is found in Britain among the standing stone monuments but also in the American Southwest. Why they were carved, we may only guess; the stones' general context and locations in relationship to other

---

324. Rhys, John. *Celtic Folklore Welsh and Manx, Vol. 1.* New York: Gordon Press, 1974, 358.

325. Joussaume, Roger. *Dolmens for the Dead: Megalith-Building throughout the World.* Ithaca: Cornell University Press, 1988, 21.

important features is pretty much all we have to go by, plus perhaps some scanty information about the people who created them in various regions.

One remarkable site featuring a series of deeply bored eyes is located in Arizona. Just a few miles north of Winslow is an ancient Pueblo settlement called Homol'ovi. The Homol'ovi people are believed to have been the precursors of the Hopi. The Hopi to this day continue to visit shrines and to obtain plant and animal resources from this ancient settlement, continuing a tradition thousands of years after the settlement was abandoned.[326] Near the site designated by modern archaeologists as Homol'ovi II is a ritual area with stunning rock outcrops and dozens of examples of rock art. Many are so ancient that the patina on the surface of the stone almost makes it impossible to see the pecked and carved images left for us to decipher. Hundreds of rock tools, including scrapers, blades, grinding implements and hammers litter the surface near the rock outcrops. Some of the images are of "stick figures," some are of spirals, and others depict images similar to large eyes peering out of the stone. The Homol'ovi settlement was abandoned around 1400 CE.

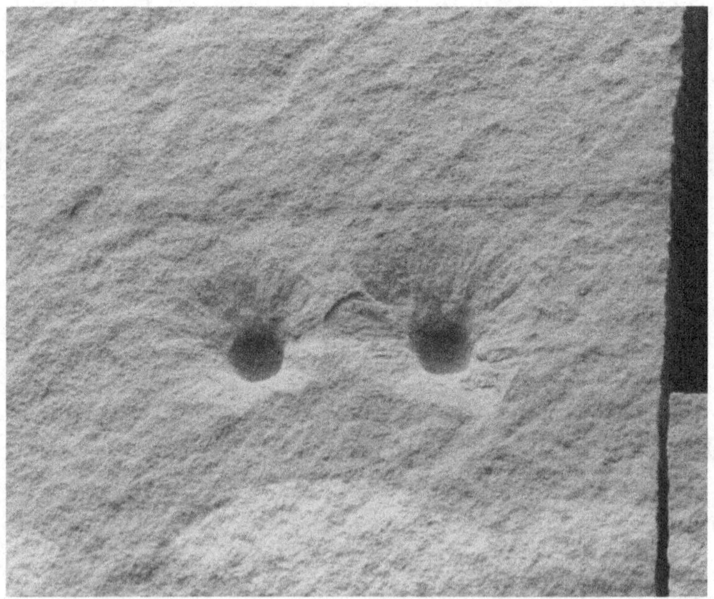

Stone "Eyes"

326. Adams, E. Charles. "Homol'ovi: An Ancestral Hopi Place" in *Archaeology Southwest*, Vol. 14, Number 4, Fall 2000, 1-3.

One of the interesting aspects of these eye carvings is that they were made on the flat sides of huge rocks looking out over large valley areas as well as the ritual site itself.

Stone eyes are also found at Avebury and West Kennet Avenue, near the monument. Eyes are also engraved on many of the Bronze Age "pygmy cups" found in many burials. Researcher Michael Dames refers to these markings as "goddess's eyes."[327]

Use of eye symbolism on megaliths should not be surprising. The eye is perhaps the oldest and most widespread representation of the sun and the moon. It represents the all-seeing and the all-knowing divinity. As Tamra Andrews noted, it was "the most powerful attribute of the most venerated gods."[328]

"Rocking" and Balanced Stones

"Rocking stones" are large boulders that rest perfectly balanced upon smaller stones and that can often be gently rocked back and forth with the touch of a hand or even a gentle breeze. Most of these were probably left in place by retreating glacial action, while others, it is presumed, were placed in their positions by human interaction.

One of these remarkable stones is located in the Sierra Nevada town of Truckee. Today the stone has been cemented in place, but Indian lore says that the 17-ton rocking stone was used to keep birds away from fish and dried meat that was laid out at the site. [329]

Another "balanced rock" in the United States is situated in North Salem, New York. The rock weighs 40 tons and while there is no evidence that it was intentionally created it does appear to be located at the end of a series of many other aligned and standing stones in the area. Local legends speak of strange lights, odd currents and Druid ghosts associated with the balanced rock. [330]

Recently, I journeyed to Mount Lassen in Northern California, while researching sacred water sites and found, much to my surprise, a balanced stone

327. Dames, Michael. *The Avebury Cycle.* London: Thames and Hudson Inc., 1977, 160.

328. Andrews, Tamra. *A Dictionary of Nature Myths.* Oxford: Oxford University Press, 1998, 67.

329. Truckee-Donner Historical Society http://truckeehistory.tripod.com/panorama9.htm.

330. Imbrogno & Horrigan, *op. cit.*

overlooking the southeastern slopes of the mountain and the nearby Yana and Maidu Indian territories. No folklore appears to be associated with this stone, so we cannot determine whether it was viewed as a sacred formation, or not. It is even possible that it was created naturally, as a result of the last volcanic eruption here in the early 20th century. However, the use of rocks in magic by the nearby tribes has been documented. Paul E. Schulz quotes ethnographer Thomas Garth:

> There once was an earthquake that shook this country up and down and made those boulders out on the flat shake. It shook so much that it made people sick. There was a very old woman...she picked up a rock and pounded it on another rock while she sang. She was praying for the world to stop shaking. Soon she got an answer, and the shaking ceased. Many people were killed...[331]

The local Indians reportedly used a rocking stone at Fall River, Massachusetts, weighing 140 tons, as a means of punishment. Evidently, the limbs of the victim were placed so that they would be crushed when the stone was rocked back and forth over them.[332] This stone, like so many others, was locked into position in the 1860s, so that it no longer has free movement.

Most of the well-known rocking stones are located in Britain (England, Ireland, Wales and Scotland) and Europe. Geologists say that all of these stone occur naturally. That said, these stones have become known more for their attached legends than from their peculiar existence. Like other stone monuments, rocking stones also faced a violent time during the English Civil War when the Puritans, in their religious zeal, toppled many of them. In the ancient past, these stones were often used as oracles. One of these is the Roulter Rocks in Derbyshire. Evidently, the winter winds caused these rocking stones to be in perpetual motion, which produced some eerie noises thought to be the spirits or gods communicating with those who would listen. Rocking stones were mentioned by Pliny the Elder, who died in 79 CE, in his *Natural History* and by Apollonius of Rhodes, who lived in the 3rd century BCE. In his *Argonautics* (ll. 1296-1314), Apollonius wrote:

> Hapless ones, assuredly a bitter vengeance came upon them thereafter at the hands of Heracles, because they stayed the search for him. For when they were returning from the games over Pelias dead he slew them in sea-girt Tenos and heaped the earth round them, and placed two columns above, one of which, a great marvel for men to see, moves at the breath of the blustering north wind.[333]

---

331. Schulz, Paul E. *Indians of Lassen.* Mineral: Loomis Museum Association, 1954, 145.
332. Moore, Jim. "Some Balanced Rocks Across Massachusetts," field report for the New England Antiquities Research Association 2002, 3.

Balanced rock on Mt. Lassen

The "columns," of course, are rocking stones.

Perhaps one of the most venerated rocking stones was that of the Logan Stone near Treen, in Cornwall. Until 1824, children were rocked on the stone to obtain cures for illnesses. Such visits usually coincided with a visit to the St. Levan holy well located nearby. In 1824, a Royal Navy crew toppled the stone — on a bet. The officer in charge, Lt. Goldsmith, was forced to restore the stone to its original location due to public outcry; however, the stone has never rocked as well as it did before.

Rocking stones were, at one time, regarded as divinely operated or as the tools of evil. One stone was said to move only at midnight, when witches were abroad; of another, it was said that if it were touched nine times at midnight, the person who touched it would turn into a witch. Other rocking stones were used as "judgment stones." These rocking stones were said to remain steadfast if a

333. The electronic text can be seen at: http://sunsite.berkeley.edu/OMACL/Argonautica/book1.html.

man with a guilty conscience attempted to move it. If the stone swayed, that proved his innocence. Such judgments were final, as a divine hand had obviously proven the individual's guilt or innocence.

Chapter 7. Simulacra — Nature's Artwork

The New World Dictionary defines "simulacrum" as "1. an image; likeness 2. a vague representation; semblance 3. a mere pretense; sham." In nature, we use the term "simulacra" to designate objects, usually of stone, which look like something else — usually animal or human forms. According to Rickard and Michell,

> these spontaneous images are often prominent in local folklore, and in times of pagan religion they were symbols of the gods and other characters of mythology. They give hints about the spiritual qualities...of the country around them. Certain spots on earth are seen...as "generation centres"...because they are spots where nature seems to manifest the prototypes of Creation. [334]

Such images occur both in England and in the United States. Sometimes they seem to jump out of photographs taken at sacred sites — such as the one below, from West Kennet Long Barrow. A decidedly human face can be seen on one of the upright slabs at the left of the entrance of the tomb, another more monstrous face appears from the top of a large slab to the right of the entrance, and two more appear at the right edge and lower left of the same slab. Did the builders already know of these images? Did they create the images? Were the stones selected for the particular sites? Are they entirely natural? While we cannot say for sure how they got there, we do know that these images in stone were important to earlier cultures and still are, in many parts of the world. They suggest a physical tie between the human and the spiritual and the supernatural workings of the universe.

---

334. Rickard, Bob and John Michell. *Unexplained Phenomena: Mysteries and Curiosities of Science, Folklore and Superstition*. London: Rough Guides, Ltd. 2000, 234.

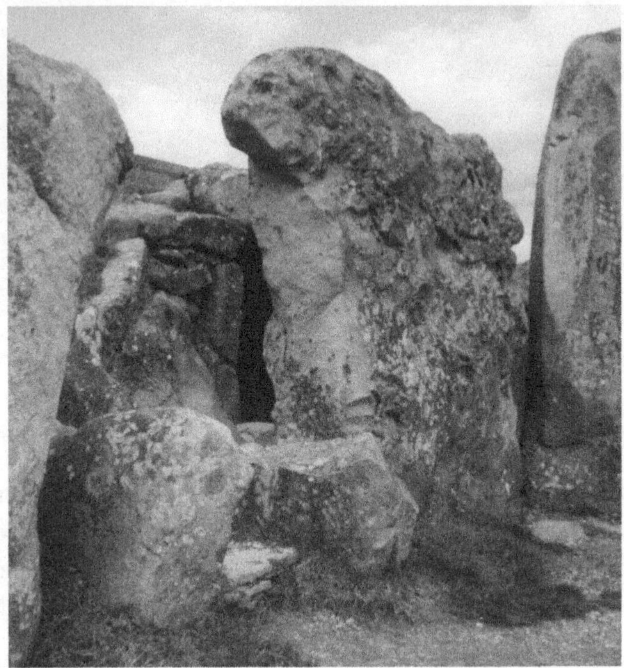

Faces Hidden in the Stone at West Kennet —
Can You Spot all Four?

The great cave art as seen in some three hundred deep caves from the Paleolithic period are examples of nature and human work in a symbiotic relationship. "The 'Great Bison' in the Bernifal Cave in the Dordogne," notes Jean-Pierre Mohen, "possesses an entirely readymade outline: only an ear and the patches on the chest have been added, as signs of human awareness of the natural forms giving birth to the animal...the animals conjured up spring physically from the rock face..." [335]

Another magnificent simulacrum is located not in the deep caves of the underworld but on the craggy, wind swept cliffs of Tintagel, in southwestern Cornwall, the traditional birth place of King Arthur. Atop the stone island lie the ruins of Tintagel castle and village, built in the 12th and 13th century. This date makes it too recent to be directly related to King Arthur (who, if his legendary figure was based on any living king at all, must have been born around 480 CE),

335. Mohen, Jean-Pierre. *Prehistoric Art: The Mythical Birth of Humanity.* Paris: Pierre Terrail 2002, 122.

but it is still a place of mystery and holiness. Local lore says that the castle disappears twice a year, but one suspects that may be due to the fog! Although the construction of the existing castle was started in 1141 by Reginald, the Earl of Cornwall, a distinctive form of Mediterranean pottery, called Tintagel Ware, has been found there that dates back to the 5th and 6th centuries. Tintagel was apparently a wealthy trading post during that time and may, in fact, have been a stronghold of Arthur or some model personality of that type. Arthurian scholar Geoffrey Ash believes that the castle was constructed at Tintagel by Reginald to take advantage of the Arthurian lore that surrounded the site.[336]

The Face of Cernunnos in Tintagel

In 1998, the organization English Heritage revealed that during that season's excavations at Tintagel, a broken piece of Cornish slate was uncovered with an inscription reading, "Pater Coliavificit Artognou," which, translated, means "Artognou, father of a descendent of Coll, had this built." "Artognou" is pronounced "Arthnou." The inscription has been dated to the 6th century and the reference to "Coll" is interesting in that King Coel Hen (the Old) was the 4th-century founder of the royal line of Dummonia. Dummonia is the kingdom that King Arthur is reported to have ruled.

336. Ashe, Geoffrey. *Arthurian Britain.* Glastonbury: Gothic Image Publications, 1997, 210.

A sacred well can be found at the top of the island crest, along with an underground passage which ends at a pool of water. Archaeologists have determined that this passage was used as a "cold storage" pit, but that may not be so. The site is located several hundred feet from the castle proper, and is confronted with the full fury of the winds that constantly sweep over the island. Most fortresses had storage rooms built within them, or closer to them, for easy access. The passage is far more likely to have served as a ritual site that mimics the Earth Goddesses' womb.

The close connection between Tintagel and the Goddess is also evident in the two labyrinths carved in stone a few miles from Tintagel. These carvings have been dated to around 1400-1250 BCE. The mazes are remarkably similar to those found at Crete and at ancient Native American sites. Below the castle ruins is a large cave with openings to the ocean, and to a cove. Known as "Merlin's Cave," it is typical of those caves believed to be representative of the Earth Goddess and the mysteries of fertility. It is lined in quartz crystal and exudes a sense of high energy within its walls.

Just outside the cave entrance and running up the left side of the cliff is a natural rock sculpture of a face. Researcher Paul Broadhurst notes in his book, *Tintagel and the Arthurian Mythos*,[337] that the face is that of Arthur. Upon closer examination, curved rams horns are seen sprouting from the rock forehead. The castle builders added onto this image by building stone walls connecting to the natural horn structure. Does that sound like a representation of Arthur? No. It is rather a classic example of an ancient, primordial, visage of the Horned God, Cernunnos. Literature on this rock face is almost non-existent. The scant mention of the image in Broadhurst's book ignores the fact of the horns. Even the accompanying photograph is devoid of horns. Perhaps it is more advantageous to maintain local tradition and boost the Arthurian legend than to discuss the alternative, better founded — and, one would think, equally intriguing — significance of the image.

The sense of wonder that comes over the viewer of such a marvel is profound. The face at Tintagel has been there for eons and is a reminder that the ancient Horned God of nature is still with us, watching over the wildlands.

The people of ancient Britain acknowledged a sacred power at Tintagel and the areas around it, by carving the labyrinths at Rocky Valley and digging or

---

337. Broadhurst, Paul. *Tintagel and the Arthurian Mythos.* Launceston: Pendragon Press, 1992, 158.

extending and enhancing a natural cave to make a ritual site at the top of Tintagel. What better place to situate Arthur's castle? Arthur was a Pagan and worshipped the old gods. His teacher, Merlin, was a Druid. The face of Cernunnos, clearly sculpted on the side of the island by the forces of nature, would give authority to the king who acted on behalf of the Horned One. Even today, those who wish to do so can infuse a chosen piece of landscape with a sense of sacred power, and draw a sense of awe, or tranquility, from the stones or the waters of the Earth — if we but look and open our hearts and minds.

Natural Image of a Human Head,
Alpine County, California

The United States has many of these natural features as well. Driving along a small country road in Alpine County, California, one may round a bend to find, directly ahead, a natural outcropping that clearly resembles the head and face of a Native American. Other such images occur in Utah National Park and along the Nevada-California border, as well as in the Appalachians and Adirondacks of the east. Near the Rock Baby petroglyphs in the Owens Valley is a large outcropping of volcanic rock that resembles a dragon flying out of the rock in a striking pose. However, we do not know whether the Native Americans in the region viewed this stone as representative of a mythic beast.

Flying Dragon

The state symbol of New Hampshire was a natural rock formation called The Old Man of the Mountain. This natural sculpture was, until its collapse on May 3, 2003, 40 feet high and 25 feet wide. It was left by geological shifts that took place some 200 million years ago — needless to say, long before humankind emerged on the earth. Native American legends recorded in the 1600s said that if one followed the Merrimack River north, a mountain with a human face would be seen.

The Anishinabe Ojibwa Indians on Manitoba, Canada, continue to make offerings at a rock that is remarkable for its resemblance to a resting buffalo, at Whiteshell Provincial Park.[338] Over the years additional "faces" have been photographed in the monoliths at Stonehenge; they are visible only in certain light conditions. It is unknown whether these images were intentionally created to be seen only during certain time of the year, or if they are naturally occurring anomalies.

Of course, the imagination and willingness to see strange shapes and creatures in the shadows can play a role, too. The concept of stone-related trolls in

338. Paul Devereux wrote of this site in his book *Mysterious Ancient America*; however, I have not been able to substantiate the information.

folklore may have originated from people seeing these strange faces and forms in stone. Barbara Walker noted, "the idea evidently grew out of the natural human propensity to see faces and humanlike figures in jumbled rocks, in dark caves, on cliff faces and outcroppings. Like trees, the rocks lent themselves to anthropomorphism." [339]

339. Walker, Barbara G. *The Women's Dictionary of Symbols and Sacred Objects.* Edison: Castle Books, 1988, 279.

Chapter 8. Caves, Rocks and Mountains: Portals to the Otherworld

Caves and rock fissures have long figured in folklore as entryways to other worlds, worlds of spirit beings, of different lands and different times. They are portals to other existences. It was in a cave on Mount Mashu that Gilgamesh became the "opener of the way" and crossed the Sea of Death to find Paradise.

Caves

As noted earlier, the Kawaiisu myth (*A Visit to the Underworld*) contains an interesting illustration of these portals between worlds. The story tells of a man who entered an opening in a rock, to find himself in another world where the spirits of deer killed in the hunt go after death. The story, as reported by Zigmond, says, "the man saw water that was like a window. He could see the mountains through it. But it wasn't water. He passed through it and did not get wet. When he was outside, he looked back and saw the 'water' again."[340] This man found himself several miles further up a canyon, just by stepping through the portal. This is a tale of a shaman's travels, a physical representation of the mental or spiritual transformations that can lead us to a different sense of reality. Archaeologist David Whitley, an expert on Southwestern rock art, states that "caves often served as vision quest locales because shamans believed the super-

340. Zigmond, Maurice L. *Kawaiisu Mythology: An Oral Tradition of South-Central California*. Ballena Press Anthropological Papers No. 18. Menlo Park: Ballena Press, 1980, 177.

natural world lay inside or beyond them; the shaman entered the supernatural when the rocks opened up for him. Caves served as portals to the sacred realm."[341] Whitley goes on to say that because the Indians believed that spirit helpers lived within rocks, caves and mountains, "it seems natural that within this region shamans received their power from rocks and mountains."[342]

Apache shamans also revered the sacred mountain and caves that lead to other worlds. Morris Opler relates one tale told by an Apache:

> My father is a shaman...A spirit came to him and told him to go into that mountain [the holy mountain known as Guadalupe Mountain]....When he thought he heard a voice telling him to go into the cliff, he turned around and started to enter the mountain. The cliff opened like a door.[343]

The shaman entered the cliff and came to another "door," which was a "great rock turning around and around. They call it by a name that means 'rock that swings around together.'"[344] As the man went through three more rock doors, he finally emerged on the outside of the mountain, where an ancient man sat. He proceeded to instruct the shaman in healing knowledge and religious ceremonies.

Not only caves but also cracks and fissures in boulders were thought by the Southwestern tribes to be entryways to the supernatural. The snakes and lizards that are seen coming out of these cracks were regarded as messengers between the worlds. When the shaman traversed into the otherworld through the rock surface, or cave, he was able to experience the ancient creation of the universe. He could also visit with the Creator.

In many cultures, stories of small, dwarfish or Faery-like creatures that live in and around rocks are common. In the Great Basin, these creatures are called "Rock Babies" and they have the ability to pass through rock. Described as looking just like a baby, with short black hair, the Rock Baby is seldom seen and is more commonly heard. To see one is to court disaster. Like the Faery, the Rock Baby is capable of stealing human babies and exchanging them for non-human look-alikes.

---

341. Whitley, David S. *A Guide to Rock Art Sites: Southern California and Southern Nevada.* Missoula: Mountain Press Publishing Company, 1996, 67.

342. Whitley, David S. *The Art of the Shaman: Rock Art of California.* Salt Lake City: The University of Utah Press 2000, 88.

343. Opler, Morris Edward. *An Apache Life-Way.* Chicago: University of Chicago Press, 1941, 269.

344. *Ibid.*

The Kawaiisu, living in the area around the southern Sierra Nevadas in California and Nevada, call the Rock Baby "uwani azi," which is derive from "uwa uwa" — which is understood to reflect the sound of a baby crying. Ethnologist Maurice Zigmond reported that the Rock Babies are believed to be responsible for many of the pictographs in the Kawaiisu territory and they are never finished working on them— as indicated by the changing patterns of the rock art. Pictographs of the Rock Baby are characterized by the use of at least five colors rather than the one or two colors used by humans. "Both the Rock Baby and his pictographs are 'out of bounds' for people," says Zigmond, "the paintings may be looked at without danger, but touching them will lead to quick disaster. One who puts his fingers on them and then rubs his eyes will not sleep again but will die in three days." [345]

Throughout the United States and Mexico, rock art drawings or carvings of Rock Baby tracks have been found. As an interesting aside, a set of footprint petroglyphs found in the 1930s in Kentucky were so convincing that Wilbur Greeley Burroughs, an area geologist, gave them a scientific name of Phenanthropus mirabilis ("looks human remarkable"), thinking that they were the fossilized tracks of an unknown species of human being. [346]

Caves have been regarded as entryways to the Underworld and as linkages to the sacred for thousands of years, at least. It is by no accident that the world's most beautiful rock art is located in deep caves or that tombs mimic the reality of the cave. Caves are traditionally the homes of the famous Little People — the Menehune of Hawaii, the Faery of Britain and Europe, the Rock Babies of America, all having similar descriptions, characteristics, powers and attitudes. One small cave in Yorkshire, known as the Hob Hole, is said to have been the home of a brownie (or "Hob") that could cure whooping cough. Local residents used to take their children to the cave seeking the Hob's help, with the following plea:

> Hob-Hole Hob,
> My bairn's gotten t'kink cough,
> Tak't off! Tak't off!"

345. Zigmond, *op. cit.* 55.

346. Coy, Fred E. Jr. "Petroglyphs and Pictographs in Kentucky" in *Rock Art of the Eastern Woodlands: Proceedings from the Eastern States Rock Art Conference*, edited by Charles H. Faulkner. San Miguel: American Rock Art Research Association, 1996, 93.

In many stories, those who successfully enter caves and return are awarded with new talents and skills by the cave Faery — musical skills were the common award, but some gained everlasting life, if they remained in the land of the Faery. These stories are commonly told in folklore and myth. Caves represent the unconscious mind that is open for instruction from the mysteries of the Underworld. Caves are also places of transformation. In addition, there were those who visited caves not for treasures or newly granted skills but for visions of the future given by oracles. "Sacred caves," writes Nigel Pennick, "were places of mediums...in the side of the Teck, an ancient Celtic holy mountain in southern Germany, is the Sybillenloch. This cavern was the seat of a benevolent being who gave counsel to local people and made fields and flocks fertile..."[347]

Such benevolent beings have been associated with caves up through the 20th century with visions of the Virgin Mary at Lourdes, France, and the Virgin of Guadalupe in Mexico among others. The fact that people still revere these sites, and make pilgrimages to them, speaks of the continuity of Pagan traditions into modern times — even if cloaked, now, in Christian theology. These sacred caves are usually also associated with water, which also has long been seen as a conduit to the underworld and divinity. Healing, such as that sought at Lourdes and the Dripping Cave at Craigiehowie, is believed to come via a direct link to the sacred through the medium of water. Water is also directly associated with female divinity and the Goddess.

Caves are invariably construed as female. They are symbolic of the womb of the Mother Goddess and therefore signify rebirth and renewal. The natural creation of stalactites and stalagmites in caves is an examples of, as Terence Meaden says, "the Goddess's life-waters...creating life pillars of rock from rock — phallic-like forms which became natural pillar shrines to the concentrated, regenerative life process."[348] When we enter a cave, we symbolically enter the Goddess. In some instances, sacred caves are located near other sacred sites that are more obvious. One example is the temple of Athena Polias at the Acropolis in Greece, built on the site of far earlier temples to the Goddess. Devereux notes that "a sacred cave lies beneath the northern horn [of the eminence of the area which is set out in a horned saddle], and an ancient cairn and a natural rock pillar all add to the sacred symbolism of the place." [349]

---

347. Pennick, Nigel. *Celtic Sacred Landscapes.* London: Thames & Hudson, 1996, 96.

348. Meaden, Terrance. *Stonehenge: The Secret of the Solstice.* London: Souvenir Press, 1997, 25-26.

A Seaside Cave in Oregon — Entry to the Earth Mother's Womb

349. Devereux, Paul. *Symbolic Landscapes.* Glastonbury: Gothic Image Publications, 1992, 21.

The connection that humans feel with the secret and special world of caves is present in many religions. Mircea Eliade noted that "caves are secret retreats, dwellings of the Taoist Immortals and places of initiation. They represent a paradisal world and hence are difficult to enter."[350]

Caves and other openings into the earth are symbolically associated with the emergence of humankind. Such beliefs are common among American Indian tribes, such as the Navajo and the Hopi, who believe that The People emerged from a great sipapu — a hole in the roof of the underworld. A large cave discovered under the Pyramid of the Sun at Teotihuacán probably also represented an emergence site for the ancient Aztecs. This cave may have been the legendary Chicomoztoc, the sacred cave of emergence of the Aztecs.

Caves were, and still are, used in religious ritual. Among the followers of Mithras,[351] the cave was used for worship and initiation purposes. The cave symbolized the "cosmos contained by the vault of heaven"[352] to the members of this mystery religion. While natural caves were available, the members would also create or extend caves, where the worshippers would gather in groups of around twenty. At times, wealthy benefactors would have them constructed especially for this purpose. Caves were also, according to Burkert, used for the activities of the Dionysian cult and "were seen and experienced as a kind of netherworld."[353]

Religious hermits of many religions, both Eastern and Western, have chosen to reside in caves where they meditate and receive inspiration and visions. This practice has held up over thousands of years; for whatever reasons, the use of caves seems to contribute to the attainment of enlightenment.

Folklore from around the world and throughout history also speaks of caves as time-altering places. The folklore of Faeries tells of individuals who are

---

350. Eliade, Mircea. *The Sacred & The Profane: The Nature of Religion.* San Diego: Harcourt Brace & Company, 1959, 153.

351. The Mithras "cult," which is the term preferred by present day scholars, was a popular religion during the Roman Empire. Roman troops brought the religion to Rome from Persia. During the early Christian era, Mithraism was more popular than Christianity and would have eclipsed the Christian religion except for the official approval given by Emperor Constantine. There are many similar traits between both religions including baptism, communion, twelve apostles, a savior who rises from the dead, and eternal life. The Mithras religion was only open to males, however. There is some evidence that the Three Magi in the Biblical story of Jesus' birth were Mithraic priests.

352. Burkert, Walter. *Ancient Mystery Cults.* Cambridge: Harvard University Press, 1987, 86.

353. *Ibid.* 101.

either invited as guests or somehow stumble into the underground Faery land and emerge years later — even though a far shorter time seemed to pass in their company. Legends that say King Arthur and his Knights of the Round Table are sleeping in a hidden cave, to be awoken when Britain is in their need, have been told for hundreds of years. Of course, Rip Van Winkle is the best known American version of these stories.

Christian mythology also has its tales of time-altering caves. *The Seven Sleepers of Ephesus* was written by the Greek, Symeon Metaphrastes (meaning "the Compiler"), in the 10th century. According to Symeon, Decius, a Pagan emperor who ruled around 250 CE, found seven noble young Christian men and sentenced them to death. The seven men gave their possessions, except for a few coins, to the poor and went into a cave on Mount Anchilos to pray and to prepare for their death. When Decius came back for the men, he found them asleep in the cave. To keep matters simple, he ordered that the cave be sealed up with the men inside. Over the years, the empire turned Christian and one day, approximately 150 years later, a farmer who wanted to use it as a cattle stall unsealed the cave. Once the seal was broken, the men awoke. They thought that they had only slept through one day, and sent one of their men to the town to buy food. The story tells of his surprise at finding crosses on buildings, since the empire was non-Christian when they went to sleep. The people in the town were amazed, as well, to see such old coins being offered for food. Eventually, the Christian emperor Theodosius (who had banned paganism) arrived at the cave to talk to the seven men whom the people had already called miraculous. After the emperor was satisfied that they were what they seemed to be, the men died, praising God. The emperor had the cave adorned with precious stones and had a church built over it and every year the Feast of the Seven Sleepers is held. The feast is held according to the Byzantine Calendar on August 4 and October 22. The story has been incorporated not only into Christian tradition but into Muslim tradition as well. Versions of the story appear in German, British, Slavic, Indian, Jewish and Chinese traditions, too. Of course, the seven noble men have been made Catholic saints as well. [354]

In Brittany, at Plouaret, is a chapel into the structure of which the builders incorporated the remains of an ancient dolmen. In fact, the roof of the chapel is the roof slab of the dolmen. Built in 1702, the chapel is dedicated to the Seven

354. See the Catholic Encyclopedia on-line version at http://www.newadvent.org/cathen/05496a.htm for more details.

Sleepers and at least through the 19th and early 20th centuries, seven dolls of varying sizes were kept near the altar to represent the seven saints. Spence noted that the dolmen, according to local lore, "dates from the creation of the world...built by the hand of the Almighty at the time when the world was in process of formation." [355]

Caves also house strange creatures, like the Rock Babies and Faeries, that at times prey upon unsuspecting humans. In Sweden there is a shallow cave, called the Snuvestuan cave. Here lives a creature, which, from the front, appears to be a beautiful girl, but from the back she is hollow, with a fox's tail. She could bring the hunter good luck or bad, depending on the day, and would enchant young men so that they could never love a human girl. To break the spell, one had to either speak the name of Jesus, wear his jacket inside out, or wear his hat backwards.

Australian lore speaks of a mysterious cave situated in a protected valley, near a stream of pure and refreshing water. On the cave's walls were paintings of strange creatures and also rocks that were shaped like humans and animals. "This spot," reports folklorist William Smith, "was regarded with much superstition and a great deal of fear. The elders of the tribes around had given strict instructions that no one was to be allowed to camp there, or even to visit the place."[356] But caves also were the source of life. In the Aborigine creation myth, the Great Father Spirit instructs the Mother Goddess to go forth and create life. She does so by awakening the unconscious life forms that had existed deep in the earth's caves and caverns even before the creation of the world. The Mother Goddess's presence and her warmth (for she is the Sun Goddess as well) in the caves created all forms of life as well as the rivers of the earth. In each cave she visited, new forms of life appeared.

Many ancient tombs were artificial caves, regarded as entryways to the Goddess and to the otherworld. One of these is West Kennet Long Barrow, approximately a mile and a half from Avebury. This 4500-year-old burial mound is 330 feet long and 8 to 10 feet high, with a 40-foot long burial chamber in one end. Used for over a thousand years, it was finally sealed with huge standing stones around 3600 years ago. Meaden notes that "the forecourt entrance to the chambered barrow or passage grave is modeled on the womb-opening which

355. Spence, Lewis. *Legends and Romances of Brittany*. Mineola: Dover Publications, Inc., 1997, 41.

356. Smith, William Ramsay. *Aborigine Myths and Legends*. London: Senate, 1996, 278.

leads to a vault or chamber, the place of rebirth or regeneration for the souls of the dead."[357] Forty-six individuals were interred here, including twelve children. During the 19th century, a well-known doctor would steal bones from the tomb, grind them up, and use them for potions. West Kennet is also said to be haunted by the spirit of a Druid priest (which would be particularly odd, since Druids did not exist when the barrow was in use) or by the Lord of the Underworld — black dogs with red eyes are said to accompany the wandering spirit.

Entryway to the 40-foot burial chamber at West Kennet Long Barrow

357. Meaden, *op. cit.*, 131.

Mountains

Mountains, like caves, are regarded as portals to the otherworld, the abode of the gods and the sites of sacred revelations. It was on a mountain that Moses received the Ten Commandments; it was on a mountain that the last remnants of life were saved from the universal flood; and it is the mountain that connects the Earth with the heavens. Mountains have also been called the abode of strange beings of super- or supra-natural origin. Many, like California's Mount Shasta, have been called the homes of the lost races of Atlantis, Mu and Lemuria as well as being pegged as landing ports for alien spacecraft. Time and space can sometimes seem different in the mountains, especially at high altitudes, which contributes to the mind-altering states that shamans experience and the disorientation that can come upon travelers. All of this feeds the legends of demons and faeries of the mountains that lead the unwary to their deaths.

The Cosmic Mountain is the legendary center of the universe, which the ancient omphaloses imitate. In addition, mountains themselves have been worshipped, not just as the sacred home of the deities but also as the gods themselves.

Icelandic folklore is full of accounts of Christian priests who take on the characteristics of earlier mythic heroes that are able to open up these portals. In one story, a man goes in search of his missing wife, who has disappeared from the isle of Málmey. This island was cursed so that no one could live on it for more than 20 years. The man goes in search of his wife with the local priest. When they come to an area of steep cliffs, the priest dismounts from his horse, then "goes up to the rock and plucks a small green plant from the ground beside him; with this he strikes the mountain, and after a little the mountain opens" and the missing woman walks out. However, the woman has turned into a mountain troll![358]

Rocks

Rocks themselves are often perceived to be entryways to the otherworld. The Rock Babies and other spirit helpers of Native American shamans live in the

358. Simpson, Jacqueline, trans. *Legends of Icelandic Magicians.* Cambridge: D.S. Brewer Ltd for The Folklore Society, 1975, 40.

stone and freely pass between both worlds. The Yupa Indians of Venezuela have a tale of the Pareracha, a red stone:

> One day a woman found a great, reddish slab of stone on the bank of the river. It shone most wonderfully. How happy she would be if she could rub the very same color on her own body.
>
> So she searched and found a rough stone which she used to scrub the stone slab...until there was a little pile of red powder. She mixed some water with the powder. Then she colored her body with the shining red. Standing there, so beautifully painted, she began to sing for very joy. And as she sang, the stone slab on which she stood opened and swallowed her up.
>
> Even today, on passing this stone, one can still hear the song of the enchanted woman.[359]

The word enchantment is telling. She was swallowed up, but not harmed: she was taken through the portal into the world of spirit and Faery.

Icelandic folklore, once again, also has accounts of rocks as portals between dimensions. In the story "Eiríkur Rescues a Woman from the Otherworld," returns to the theme of the missing wife. In this tale, the newly married woman disappears from her farmstead and the worried husband goes in search, again with the aid of a priest. As the two reach the boulders marking the boundary between two districts, the priest stops and lays a large book upon the biggest stone. A great storm gathers but no rain falls upon the book and not a page is ruffled by the wind. According to the story, the priest then "goes widdershins round the rock, and mutters something between his teeth, and then he says to the farmer: 'Look carefully whether you see your wife coming.'

"Now a crowd of people comes out of the rock..."[360] As in the previous Icelandic tale, the woman had been captured by mountain trolls but was recovered by the priest's actions. It should be noted that the practice of walking "widdershins" around an object three times is an ancient one, known across the world. It normally is meant to allow an individual to enter the Faery land or some other spirit world. In this tale, it opened a doorway between two dimensions to allow spirits and trolls and their captives to enter the physical world. This story is obviously a mixture of Pagan rituals and lore disguised in scant Christian clothing.

Openings to the otherworld through rocks are also part of Polynesian lore, deep in the Pacific. In Samoa legend, Talaga wished to visit the underworld to

359. Wilbert, Johannes. *Yupa Folktales.* Los Angeles: Latin American Center, University of California Los Angeles, 1974, 97.

360. Simpson *op. cit.*, 64.

obtain fire, which was not yet known on the surface. He stood upon a rock and said, "Rock, rock, I am Talaga; open to me. I wish to go below."[361] Talaga must wrestle the fire-god Mafui'e and twist off his arm to win a firebrand. Thus, humankind comes to know fire and is able to cook food.

361. Andersen, Johannes C. *Myths and Legends of the Polynesians.* Rutland: Charles E. Tuttle Company, 1969, 216.

CHAPTER 9. CAIRNS

The use of cairns as religious objects is a very old practice, as evidenced by the Bible. In Genesis 31: 45-54, Jacob and Laban construct a cairn to act as divine witness to their peaceful intentions towards one another: "And Jacob said unto his brethren, Gather stones; and they took stones, and made an heap...and Laban said, This heap is a witness between me and thee this day...."

Rock cairns are significant in at least two ways. They delineate space, especially sacred space, and also constitute a form of offering. Each pilgrim leaves a pebble or cobble on a pile of previously laid stone, creating a landmark. This practice continues to this day, as can be witnessed at Panther Meadows on the slopes of Mt. Shasta. The Panther Meadows cairn consists of a large boulder with several cobbles and stones placed on top of it. This form of shrine cairn was common during much of prehistory. Archaeologist Malcolm Rogers noted, "a common variety has a large boulder as a nucleus, around and over which the cobbles were deposited."[362] Several of these are found in the desert between San Diego and Arizona.

However, not all cairns were used for sacred offerings. Many times, American Indians and other hunter-gatherer people would use rock cairns to designate good hunting areas, trailheads, taboo areas, initiation sites and even burials; but they also placed rocks at waterfalls or waterholes used during vision quests. There is growing evidence that Native Americans also used cairns for

362. Rogers, Malcolm J. *Ancient Hunters of the Far West.* San Diego: Union-Tribune Publishing Company, 1966, 49.

astronomical observations and in California, "shrines of stones mounded to support sacred poles have been reported in numerous locations in Chumash territory." [363]

The Apache utilized cairns as wayside shrines, as noted by ethnologist Morris Opler:

> It is a pile of rock and stones about four feet high and eight feet wide. There are four holes in the center. The foundation is east and west, and the holes are running toward the east. You pick up a stone or leaves and hold this to the four corners while you pray. Then you drop what you have in the hole. It's asking a blessing. They take this to be a holy place...I have heard ceremonial songs, a long time ago, mention these shrines. The name means that rocks churn about in this place.[364]

Similar shrines built on mountaintops were visited by individuals prior to making a lengthy journey. By placing a stone or a sprig of juniper on top of the cairn, a safe journey was assured. One cairn located in Arizona along an ancient trail has over 50,000 stones. Thought to be a trail shrine, the original measurements of the cairn were approximately 16 feet in diameter and 30 inches in height. Archaeologists have noted that "early men must have passed this shrine 50,000 times and each time placed a stone, presumably in the expectation that the ceremony would help assure a safe journey.[365] Malcolm Rogers, in writing about a large trail shrine in San Bernardino County, California, observed that "here three identical cairns grew so large that they eventually coalesced to become one. The total weight of the stones in this shrine must approximate three tons."[366]

This is another of those universal practices that appear to have a common origin. In Siberia, it was commonly believed that spirits resided in the mountains, spirits that would protect the members of the clan as long as they were well treated. Every three years, sacrifices would be held on the tops of the mountains and stones, along with rags, horsehair, and other items would be left as offerings.

---

363. Trupe, Beverly S., John M. Rafter, and Wilson G. Turner. "Ring of Pictured Stones: Astronomical Connotations of a Rock Art Site in the Eastern Mojave Desert" in *Visions of the Sky: Archaeological and Ethnological Studies of California Indian Astronomy. Coyote Press Archives of California Prehistory Number 16, 1988.* Salinas: Coyote Press, 162.

364. Opler, Morris Edward. *An Apache Life-Way.* Chicago: University of Chicago Press, 1941, 312.

365. Rogers, *op. cit.* 75.

366. *Ibid.* 51.

Similar practices continued into the 20th century in Bolivia, where shrines made of stone and mud bricks, four to five feet tall, are constructed. Each January 2, the Aymara would make a pilgrimage to the shrines, which they would circle three times, walking on their knees. After breaking a fast, they would then smash their bowls on the shrine in offering. Some modern pilgrims associated the shrines with Christian saints, but others to the spirits of the mountain that controlled weather, specifically rain, hail and frost. [367]

Native Americans continue to leave offerings on this cairn on Mt. Shasta

Cairns have been a part of sacred water sites for untold years. At St. Fillan's Pool, Scotland, which was visited for its purported cure of insanity and other medical conditions, three cairns used to grace the site; they were destroyed in relatively recent times. Under the stone cairns, left by those seeking a cure, caches of coins were found. Fillan's Pool is actually part of the river itself; it is

367. Hadingham, Evan. *Lines to the Mountain Gods: Nazca and the Mysteries of Peru.* New York: Random House, 1987, 243.

near a ruined chapel and accompanying graveyard. According to folklorist Sheila Livingstone,[368] persons going to the pool for medical reasons were to take up nine stones from the pool and walk to the top of the hill where the cairns were located. Here, they would walk around each of the three cairns three times sun wise, and deposit one stone each time the cairn was circled.

The minister of the Scottish parish where St. Fillan's Pool is located wrote, in the late 1700s:

> It is still visited...especially on the 1st of May and 1st of August....The invalids, whether men, women, or children, walk or are carried round the well three times in a direction deishal, that is, from east to west, according to the direction of the sun. They all drink the water, and bathe in it. These operations are accounted a certain remedy for various diseases.[369]

"Heaps" of small stones like these are commonly found at many sacred wells around the world. Patrick Logan made the following observation in his book, *The Holy Wells of Ireland*:

> Many writers mention the heaps of small stones seen near holy wells. Such a cairn was described at St. Patrick 's Well in Kilcorkey parish...and another at Tullaghan Well, Co. Sligo ....O'Donnovan wrote that each pilgrim added a further stone to the heap as part of the ritual of the pilgrimage. [370]

Logan believes that those who leave the stones are leaving a substitute offering to a saint, in lieu of leaving something of economic value. This would not appear to be the case, however, since the practice appears to be universal among many different cultures with many different perspectives on wealth. The 18th-century account by a parish minister at St. Fillan's Well suggested, rather, that "all the invalids throw a white stone on the saint's cairn, and leave behind, as tokens of their confidence and gratitude, some rags or linen or woolen cloth."[371] It would seem that the origin of such practices has been lost in the distant past but the contribution of individual stones and rags must have held a more complex meaning than simply to betoken confidence.

Another Scottish cairn, located at Unst, Shetland, and said to be the burial place of King Harold of Norway, has had stones added to it over the years by

368. Livingstone, Sheila. *Scottish Customs.* New York: Barnes & Noble Books, 1996, 122-123.

369. Anon. "Our Hagiology," in *Blackwood's Edinburgh Magazine*, Vol. 82, October 1857, 454.

370. Logan, Patrick. *The Holy Wells of Ireland*. Buckinghamshire: Colin Smythe, 1980, 99.

371. Anon. *op. cit.*

A cairn of cobbles and stone blocks in Eastern San Diego County, California

folks who think by doing so they will ensure that the "evil creatures" that inhabit it will be entombed.

A more unusual practice is that of stacking stones in the form of miniature dolmen. At Poulnabrone Dolmen, County Clare, contemporary visitors still stack stones in the dolmen's shape as an offering or in satisfaction of a psychic need.

Rock cairns are found on most high passes in Peru, ancient Persia, Tibet and China as well as in North America. "Mountain passes and difficult points on roads," writes Cambridge archaeologist G.H.S. Bushnell, referring to Peru, "were and still are venerated by praying and adding a stone or a quid of coca to a pile of stones by the roadside...."[372] California's deserts are also marked with these propitiary structures. Archaeologist Robert S. Begole wrote that cairns were "formed by travelers who, in lieu of leaving small bits of food, would place a pebble or small cobble at a significant spot as a token of appreciation to the spirits for past favors, for safe traveling, or for fulfillment of a future wish or request."[373] Begole also found that dozens of lines of up to 750 cairns exist in the

372. Bushnell, G.H.S. *Ancient Peoples and Places: Peru.* Lima: Libreria ABC Bookstore, SA, 1963, 140.

California desert, some dating back 10,000 years and others far more recent. Similar roadside shrines were created in Hawaii. "Travelers passing through," says Sir Peter Buck, "laid some leaves, a stone, or any material object on the shrine as a placatory offering to the guardian spirit to ward off any mishap that might otherwise befall them." [374] This custom continues today, with tourists adding to the number of stones placed on various shrines.

A similar tradition has been observed in the Nazca Valley where the farmers leave small piles of river cobbles and cotton plants during periods of draught as offerings to secure rain. These offerings have been found at the 7,000-foot elevation of sacred peaks.[375] This practice undoubtedly has continued from ancient times.

In Tahiti, cairns were built to protect the individual from witchcraft. Frazer wrote:

> The Tahitians buried the cuttings of their hair at the temples. In the streets of Soku a modern traveller observed cairns of large stones piled against walls with tufts of human hair inserted in the crevices. On asking the meaning of this, he was told that when any native of the place polled his hair he carefully gathered up the clippings and deposited them in one of these cairns, all of which were sacred to the fetish and therefore inviolable. These cairns of sacred stones, he further learned, were simply a precaution against witchcraft, for if a man were not thus careful in disposing of his hair, some of it might fall into the hands of his enemies, who would, by means of it, be able to cast spells over him and so compass his destruction. [376]

Beliefs involving cairns are much more complex than we may surmise. Cairns are simply made, and yet they evoke something concrete and powerful in their spiritual tie to the human soul. Some of the most remarkable cairns are those in the Arctic Circle, known as inuksuit. Constructed by ancient and contemporary Inuit people, these stone figures vary from small rock piles to large Stonehenge-like structures. Norman Hallendy, who has studied these structures and the Inuit who have built them, breaks their purpose down into five categories.

---

373. Begole, Robert S. "Archaeological Phenomena in the California Desert," in *Pacific Coast Archaeological Society Quarterly, Vol. 10, No. 2, April 1974*, 59.

374. Buck, Sir Peter H. *Arts and Crafts of Hawaii: XI Religion*. Bernice P. Bishop Museum Special Publication 45. Honolulu: Bishop Museum Press, 1964, 529.

375. Hadingham, *op. cit.* 244.

376. Frazer, James George, Sir. *The Golden Bough*. New York: Macmillan, 1922, 235.

1. To express beauty and joy
2. To guide hunters or otherwise relate to hunting
3. To aid in travel and navigation
4. To indicate meeting places, or serve utilitarian purposes (such as drying fish and meat, or to trap animals), and
5. For ritualistic or religious use.

The last category includes sites where shamans were or are initiated, or they are considered to contain spirits or spiritual power, to offer healing or protection. They may mark sacred sites or act as doorways between the physical and spirit worlds.[377] The Inuit also build some of these cairn works simply to pass the time and leave their mark in the wilderness! The above listed purposes may well cover the majority of reasons why many of the world's cairns and other mystical rock sites have been built throughout time.

Rock cairns in the West and Northwest of the United States were also used simply as clan and household boundaries, and also as recipients of prayer. They might be built by boys and girls as part of puberty ceremonies. Archaeologist Robert Begole reported that he had found seven cairns in the Mojave Desert on a mesa above the Amargosa River, which had one and two circles cleared in the desert pavement nearby. Begole wrote, "it is postulated that such clearings were for placement of offerings or perhaps for small hearths used in connection with a religious ceremony." [378] Begole also discovered 482 circle mounds — cairns that had large circles cleared around them. Most of these have trails leading from one to another and appear to have been in continuous use, for some reason. While the reason for their creation is unknown, two of the circle mounds had three rock-outlined figures associated with them. One was of a human shape, another was a fish and the third was that of a mountain sheep. Begole postulates that these circle mounds were used by a small band of people — perhaps by a fraternal order or by shamans — as a religious site.[379] Stone phallic symbols were also found nearby, one measuring 29 inches and the other 20 inches in length. Similar stone "pictures" have been found in Australia as well. The Australian figures are of small sailboats, house structures and "boiling hearths." [380]

---

377. Hallendy, Norman. *Inuksuit: Silent Messengers of the Arctic.* London: British Museum Press 2000, 116-118.

378. Begole, *op. cit.*, 56.

379. *Ibid.* 66-67.

It is important for us to recognize that there is not one good answer to any of the questions that we may have about stone structures and sacred sites. In fact, knowing what we do about the inuksuits, we may be totally incorrect in assuming that some of these sites were considered sacred — they may just as easily have been strictly utilitarian areas. The importance of looking at the total context of a site is paramount in arriving at any possible understanding. It is very alluring to follow one's intuitive feel, but that may tell us more about ourselves than about the people we wish to study.

In all probability, most cairns were constructed for a mixture of utilitarian and religious reasons. One example of this mixed purpose comes from Scotland. Researcher Sheila Livingstone, writing about funeral processions, notes, "if the journey was long, cairns were built along the way to rest the coffin on while a small refreshment was partaken. If the road was one regularly used by funerals then a stone was added to each cairn on passing." [381] This would appear to be more a holdover of pagan tradition than a matter of convenience, as it would surely take more effort to construct a cairn at each stop than to simply rest the coffin on the ground.

While cairns in Britain appear to almost always mark a burial or a tomb, one known as the Stone of the Lulling, located in Argyll, Scotland, has been used to cure toothaches. The patient would drive a nail into the cairn at midnight to obtain a cure and several nails are still present today — indicating the continued usage of the site for healing. [382] Cairns in other far reaches of the world are used to mark trails and in some cases act as offerings to the gods and spirits to ensure a safe journey or to request important items of need, such as rain.

Cairns were also constructed a part of the "spirit quest" ritual of young Tillamook Indians on the Oregon coast. A teenage boy would be sent to the deep forests alone for ten days with only a blanket and a knife. He was to chant and pray for the ten days until his spirit helper came to him. Specific spirits represented his course in life, from canoe builder to fisherman to shaman. One of the arduous tasks undertaken was to construct a large cairn in the forest of large, heavy stones. Two such cairn areas are still present in Tillamook County, Oregon. One "is on the ocean side of Netarts. It is in a grove of old-growth fir

380. Mulvaney, D.J. *The Prehistory of Australia.* New York: Frederick Praeger Publishers, 1969, 170.

381. Livingstone, *op. cit.*, 69.

382. Lamont-Brown, Raymond. *Scottish Folklore.* Edinburgh: Birlinn Limited, 1996, 65.

where the sunlight rarely penetrates, and it consists of a number of mounds of these large, heavy stones." [383] After the cairn was constructed, the boy would often see his spirit guide and would announce the vision at the winter festival.

383. Sauter, John and Bruce Johnson. *Tillamook Indians of the Oregon Coast.* Portland: Binfords & Mort, Publishers, 1974, 35.

Chapter 10. Carved and Painted Stones: Mystic Symbolism

Stones are perhaps the most perfect canvas in the world. Since humankind began to express itself and to depict its ideas of the heavens and the earth and the creatures that reside in both, rock has been utilized as the permanent record of those ideas. This chapter will discuss the various symbols found around the world that humans have been painting, carving and pecking onto stone surfaces for thousands of years.

Vulvas and Phalluses Galore

Perhaps the most universal representation depicted in rock art around the world is that of the reproductive organs. Fertility was extremely important among ancient people, for crops and animals as well as for humans. The continuation of the species, and food production, dictated much of the religious foundation for these societies as well as how the societies grew and cooperated with one another.

Paintings and carvings of the vulva are direct associations with fertility and Goddess worship. Natural clefts in stones were often recognized as nature's link between the Goddess and humankind, and to the Earth Mother's womb. The importance California Indian groups placed on this motif is illustrated by the Chalfant Bluffs in Owens Valley, California. Over 100 vulva forms were carved on stones at this one site.

The photo below was taken near Rancho Bernardo, in Southern California, of a natural cleft that was outlined by Native Americans hundreds or thousands of years ago to resemble the human vulva. This site is an important rock art site with eight panels of pictographs and the vulva form. While the pigment has been worn away by age and weather, the vulva image is still clearly seen. This rock art is part of a large ritual site, which may have been used for female puberty ceremonies, judging from many of the other paintings that are associated with fertility. Similar stones also existed in other locations in the San Diego County area. Whitley notes that the last Native American female puberty ritual in Southwestern California was performed in the 1890s in northern San Diego County.[384] It is possible that the site is the same one where this photo was taken in 1976.

As part of the ceremony, the girls would be subjected to sleep and sensory deprivation, isolation, fasting and ingesting tobacco, which would allow the girls to enter an altered state and would produce hallucinations. "At the culmination of the ceremony," says Whitley, "the girls ran a ritual race to a special rock — known as the 'Paha's House' — near their village. Paha is the term for shaman...the high point of the initiation, underscoring the great symbolic importance, was...to paint the spirit helpers they saw during their visions. In the majority of cases, the girls' spirit helper was a rattlesnake...rattlesnakes guard the vaginas of mythic women just as they guard entrances to the supernatural rock art sites.[385]...Zigzags and diamond-chain motifs, symbolizing rattlesnakes throughout the Far West, heavily dominate the girls' art." [386] At the San Diego site, diamond-chain motifs and mazes were drawn, presumably by the initiated girls themselves, to accompany the vulva image. Nearby, mortars were found that had been used to mix the pigments chosen for the ritual paintings.

The Kumeyaay, another San Diego area tribe, had similar puberty ceremonies but the stone that the girls ran to was considered sacred and was meant

---

384. Whitley, David S. *A Guide to Rock Art Sites: Southern California and Southern Nevada.* Missoula: Mountain Press Publishing Company, 1996, 25.

385. Years ago, when I was employed as an archaeological surveyor-excavator in Southern California, my crew chief and I stumbled upon a rock art site deep in an isolated canyon. As we approached the rock outcrop with the paintings, I stepped down on a hidden snake, which proceeded to rattle its warning until I jumped off. Although we saw the grass part as the snake slithered away, we never did see the serpent. We looked at each other, and then left the site. I can imagine that is one way that new myths are created: the snake had behaved as if it were the guardian spirit of the site, warning us to leave—it never did attempt to strike at me.

386. Whitley, *op. cit.* 25-26.

Natural cleft vulva outlined in pigment,
Southern California

to protect them. The stone was approximately 15 by 15 inches in size, said to be shaped like a yoke, and weighed 35 pounds. This sacred stone was hidden on a hillside until it was uncovered before each ceremony. Contemporary accounts of the ritual said that the "friends of the girls hung their garlands on rocks and bushes about, and the sacred stone was buried again. Grain was scattered over all and the ceremony was complete." [387]

Diamond-chain rock art depicting the rattlesnake

Similar carvings of vulvas have been found in the Aurignacian cave shelters of France dating back at least 30,000 years. One of the monoliths at Avebury obviously depicts a vulva; it was aligned with the now destroyed Obelisk, so that

387. McGowan, Charlotte. *Ceremonial Fertility Sites in Southern California: San Diego Museum Papers No. 14*. San Diego: San Diego Museum of Man, 1982, 16.

the sunrise during early May created a shadow that fell from the Obelisk to the Womb Stone, signifying the Sacred Marriage.

It is clear to most observers that the standing stones so common across the European landscape are symbolic of the phallus. The number of women who have rubbed against them and slid down their sides (such as the grand *menhir brisé* mentioned earlier) to ensure fertility attests to the strong Pagan traditions associated with agriculture and the fertility of crops, herd animals and family. The shadows cast by some of these standing stones, viewed by the ancients as the rising of the male sex organ, and their joining with the vulva in a sacred marriage, were intentionally created to instill a feeling of awe among the people and to ensure the continuation of the world.

The standing stone at Réguiny, Brittany, was referred to as the "Indecent Stone" due to its phallic shape and, as noted by Michell, "it was eventually 'cut down and made harmless'" around 1825. [388]

Those Mysterious Cup Marks

Cup marks are shallow cup-like indentations made or enhanced by human effort; they are found on boulders and megaliths that have been used in rituals the world over, from North America throughout Europe, Asia, Africa and the Pacific Islands. Their true purposes are unknown; however, they are probably tied to shamanic rituals, fertility practices and burial rites. They may have a common purpose and timeline in the development of cultures. In some cultures cup marked stones were created and used thousands of years ago while in others, such in North America, they may be only a few hundred years old. It would appear that their appearance in certain societies is dependent upon the stage of "development," such as hunter-gatherers or agriculturally based lifestyles the users had reached. In the Scandinavian country of Uppland, over 30,000 cup marks have been counted.

Many of these cup marks had been used by more recent people who would put holy water or milk in them as offerings to God — or to Faeries. Lewis Spence noted in his book, *Legends and Romances of Brittany*, that many of the tombstones in Brittany have these cup-marks, as do the roof-slabs on ancient dolmens, and that they may have served as food receptacles for the dead. [389] This may be true for

388. Michell, John. *Megalithomania*. London: Thames and Hudson Ltd., 1982, 89.

some of the monuments, but many are located on areas that are not associated with the dead — or, at least, the dead have not been located as yet. This theory falls short when you consider that cup marks are also commonly found on the underside of dolmens, rock overhangs, and cave roofs and on the sides of standing stones. Many researchers believe that these cup marks are representative of fire and the sun or were part of the thunder cult. In support of this theory, they suggest that many of the boulders that contain cup marks also have hand, foot and wheel carvings or paintings and that these are, as Maringer states, "symbols of the sky, or solar, cult."[390] Scandinavian sites where cup-marked stones are located also frequently have an association with foot and handprints. Lithuanian archaeologist Inga Marmaite, of the Department of Archaeology, Vilnius University, notes that "it would seem that foot-marked stones are related to the cult of the dead, the fact, which could be proved by the not very clear but still distinguished connection with the burial monuments, as well as appropriate mythological parallels and folklore data."[391] There are as many possible explanations for these objects as there are cup marks, and no one explanation fits all of these locations. It seems probable, however, that foot and hand representations are not only associated with a sky god but may represent the person and the person's presence in time and space — be he dead or alive. In this light, others have suggested that the hand and foot impressions found in Native American sites represent a shaman's posting of a place as one of power and importance.

Archaeologist and rock art expert David Whitley wrote, "it is likely that the grinding of these depressions was related to larger beliefs about the rock and site itself; specifically, that the rock was the entrance to the supernatural world and grinding cupules into it allowed access to the supernatural power contained therein." [392] Some Southern California archaeologists theorize that these cup-marked boulders "are related to fertility rites, and they represent the female genitalia." [393] Ethnographic evidence points to other uses as well. A cup-marked stone at Hospital Rock, in Kings Canyon National Park in California, has a number of depressions approximately one inch deep and two inches in diameter

389. Spence, Lewis. *Legends and Romances of Brittany.* Mineola: Dover Publications, Inc., 1997, 383.

390. Maringer, Johannes. *The Gods of Prehistoric Man.* London: Phoenix Press, 1956, 182.

391. http://viking.hgo.se/bsaan/papers01/marmaite.html.

392. Whitley, *op. cit.* 95.

393. McGowan, *op. cit.* 13.

that may have been used by shamans to induce rain or, "in some cases, by barren women who desired to conceive children." [394]

A cup-marked stone located in Roseville, California, at an ancient Maidu village site is said to have been an entryway for shamans to access the other world. After they had reached a state of trance, they would fly through the cup mark to the nearby stream, where they would then journey to the spirit world to learn new healing techniques. When they returned, they would have learned those new ways and could apply them to the people.

San Diego County archaeologist Gary Fink notes that the numerous cup-marked rocks in his region are often associated with villages and campsites and all date to within the last 500 years. Fink notes that "ethnographic explanations for cupule petroglyph sites include such things as 'baby rocks' made by women desirous of offspring. Rain rocks...were made in the hope of bringing rain to an area." [395]

During extensive excavations in Ventura and Santa Barbara counties in California in the early 1900s, two clusters of charm stones in distinctive cigar shapes were found. Measuring from two inches to over thirteen inches in length, they were carved from non-native stone and were laid out in a radiating circular pattern. Some of them had been placed "in a small cup-shaped boulder like a golf-ball in a tee." [396] An aged Indian called "Old George" was shown one of the cigar-shaped stones and he became terrified, saying that it "may not be dead." According to Old George, "such stones are alive and burrow in the ground like moles. To look at one would cause serious illness, perhaps paralysis. Only a medicine man could capture one and only he knew how to kill it." [397] The association of these stones with cup-marked boulders is uncertain — perhaps the cups were a way to control the "living stones" so that harm would not be visited upon the residents of the area.

In both Europe and North America, many cup-marked boulders include lines carved out between the cups and beyond. Some researchers theorize that the cup marks represent the womb and the straight lines pathways to guide the

---

394. Elsasser, A.B. *Indians of Sequoia and Kings Canyon.* Three Rivers: Sequoia Natural History Association, 1962, 11.

395. Fink, Gary. "Some Rock Art Sites in San Diego County" in *Pacific Coast Archaeological Society Quarterly*, Vol. 15, No. 2, April 1979, 67.

396. Johnston, Bernice Eastman. *California's Gabrielino Indians.* Los Angeles: Southwest Museum, 1962, 71.

397. *Ibid.*

spirit to the womb of pregnant (or barren) women to ensure a safe birth. Others think that these straight lines represent the penis, or even semen, entering the vulva. This form of rock art is more common in the Great Basin and is believed to represent the oldest style in the Basin, dating back to more than 7,000 years.

Maidu cup-marked stone. Entryway to the spirit world.

Obviously, the American and European cup marked boulders are from different eras and may have had different purposes. While the European and British archaeologists believe that they represent death, the American archaeologists believe that they represent fertility and life. Both explanations may be valid. This patterning is also found in Estonia. One such cup-marked stone in the village of Valasti has 30 individual cup marks, which "are linked together by long well-preserved channels." [398]

Estonia is one of those few remaining gems that can inform us about the evolution of civilization in Europe. Christianized relatively recently, Estonia has preserved ancient folkways that are still practiced as they have been for untold

398. Tvauri, Andres. "Cup-Marked Stones in Estonia" in *Folklore*, vol. 11, October 1999. Tartu: Institute of the Estonian Language, 132.

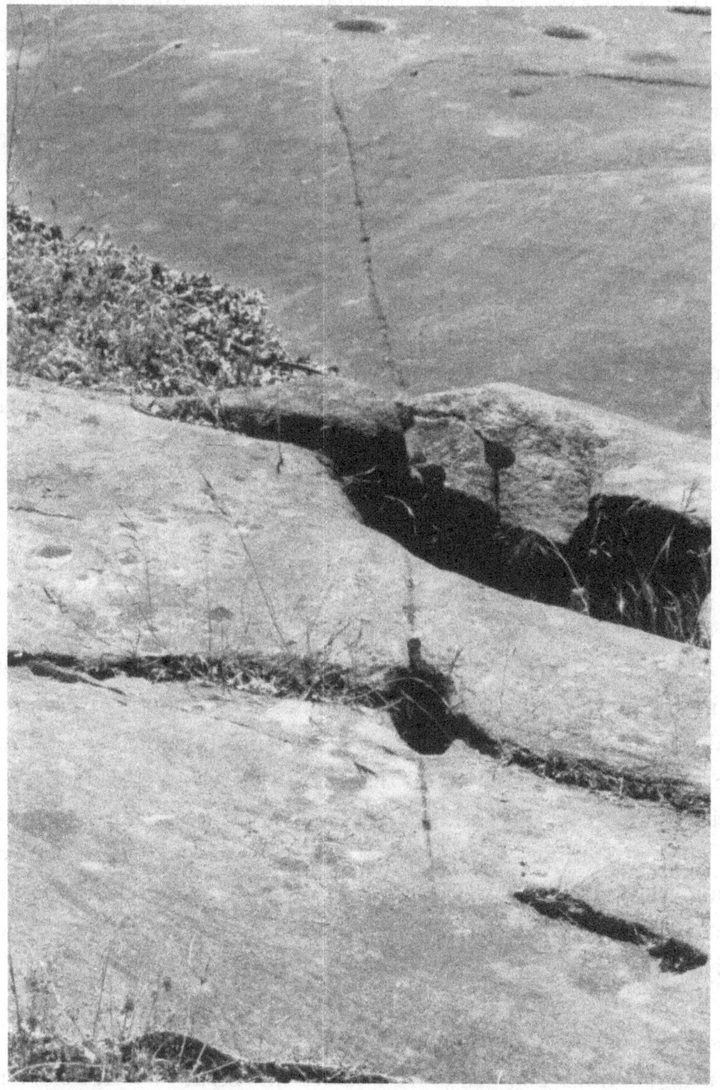

Miwok Cupule Site, Grinding Rock State Park, Plymouth, California.
Note the line from one cup to another.

generations. By looking at Estonian folklore, we may be able to glimpse the uses applied to these stones over time. As in other European and British sites where cup-marked stones are found, many of those in Estonia are located near Bronze

Age burials. However, as in these other areas, the cup-marked stones were probably of a mixed usage —both recognizing places of death and of fertility.

Folklore collected in 1939 about cup-marked stones in the Estonian village of Kaaruka indicated that the cup-marks were "passages through which dead souls entered the other world, as in the past the relatives of the deceased used to carve a small hole in the stone." [399]

Andres Tvauri, in his excellent article, "Cup-Marked Stones in Estonia," notes that a large amount of the folklore concerning these stones indicates that they have been used as "offering stones." "Sacrifices to stones," writes Tvauri, "was very common in Estonia as late as in the 19th century," with offerings still being made in the 1930s. [400] Offerings were made for the Faery, and to obtain healing. Offerings included fire, blood, milk, fresh meat and burnt grain. Many of the cup-marked stones are associated with sacred groves and the stones were probably used as altars.

These stones were also utilized in much the same manner as holy wells have been. For some reason, diseases of the eye were often treated at these sites. Using the ancient transference techniques, individuals would touch their afflicted eye(s) with a coin, or salt, and then leave the coin or salt in one of the cup-marks — thereby transferring the disease to the stone. Rainwater that collected in the cup marks was also collected and used to treat diseased eyes.

While the true original purpose of Estonian cup-marked stones remains elusive, the most probable answer is that they were part of the agricultural-fertility rituals practiced the world over. Evidence indicates that each year, at the time of sowing, one cup mark was carved into a chosen stone as part of a fertility tradition. The majority of cup-marked stones in Estonia occur in the coastal areas of the country, where agriculture was the most intense. After the stone was carved and the grain was sown, the stone's purpose had been served and it no longer had a sacred relevance. Tvauri notes that some Scandinavian rock art depicts female figures with cup-marks between their legs, and as recently as the 19th century, in India, cup-marks were carved into stones situated along roads used for bridal processions.

Cup-marked stones found in Finland date back to the Iron Age and are believed to have been "sacrificial stones." The early agricultural people of Finland, like the Estonians, used these stones to grind sacrificial grain and to

399. *Ibid.*, 143.
400. *Ibid.*, 138.

offer milk to the gods to ensure bountiful crops and successful hunts. Finnish folklore says that these stones were used as "serving vessels" to provide food and drink to the dead and to eliminate illnesses and pain. Obviously, the uses of these stones have changed over time. Ethnographic evidence indicates that these stones were used into the early 1900s in Finland.

In many sites around the world, concentric rings are carved around these cup depressions. These occur commonly during the North American Late Archaic and Woodland eras as well as in Neolithic Europe and the Middle East. Some fine examples are also found along the Russian River in Mendocino County, California. On one recumbent boulder alone near Rothiemay, Scotland, is an array of over 100 cup marks and cup and ring carvings. What do these symbols represent? Service and Bradbery wrote that the ring marks are similar to the representations of the spiral, which is found worldwide. "Where the spiral may represent the path of the life-bringer," they say, "concentric circles may stand for stopping-places on that way. Where the spiral refers to the Great Goddess, so too does this concentric sign, symbolizing the belly or womb from which all life comes...it is also seen as representing the navel of the earth — the omphalos." [401]

At certain rock art sites in Hawaii boulders with cup markings surrounded with one or two rings have been found. These stones were used, according to ethnographic evidence, as depositories for the umbilical cords of newborn children.

Other theories proposed over the years suggested that these cup and ring designs were plans for stone enclosures such as Iron Age hill-forts, aligned with star groups — making an ancient star chart, or simply pre-historic doodles! Cup marked stones have many traditions associated with them as other megaliths. The Roch d'la Sguia, or sliding rock near Bessa, Italy, is a large, egg-shaped rock with a number of cup marks on one side. It is called the "sliding rock" because women over the years have worn it smooth by sliding down its contours to ensure pregnancy. Bessa is a unique area with numerous megaliths — many with cup marks. Researchers have noted that cup-marked stones are situated so that they are exposed to sunlight and many of them are slanted towards the sun. The positioning of these stones, or rather the selection of them, would give credence to the sun or solar disc association. The vast majority of these stones are also

---

401. Service, Alastair & Jean Bradbery. *Megaliths and their Mysteries: A Guide to the Standing Stones of Europe.* New York: Macmillan Publishing Company, 1979, 40.

located near bodies of water (indeed, most megaliths fall in to this category as well).

There is some indication that solar associations were also seen in Native American cup-marked stones. At the Miwok ceremonial site, Chaw'se, located near Jackson, California, a huge slab of marble has been used to produce almost twelve hundred mortars and cupulas along with over 350 petroglyphs. This is the largest collection of bedrock mortars in North America. One of the mortars has solar rays emanating from it. Archaeologists have determined that the cupules are up to 6,000 years in age while the rock art, which has been added to the stones, is approximately 2,000 years old— showing a continuation of usage by different peoples over different times. Chaw'se is the only known location where mortars have been intentionally decorated with rock art.

A prehistoric solar designed cupola

Another very real possibility is that the cup-marked stones were created as musical instruments. This certainly would be an important ritual tool and there are other locations around the world where "singing" stones have been found. A few years ago an American rock art enthusiast, on safari in Tanzania, was taken by her guides to a large rock outcrop. On top of the rock were a number of cup marks and, as she relates the story, "before I knew what was happening, one of our drivers picked up a stone and started rapping on the cup marks!

"It was a musical instrument. The rock was tuned! Every cup mark had a different tone, and eventually the driver actually played a scale of notes. It was quite pleasing to the ear." Her driver "explained that the cup marks were carved about 200 years ago by the Masaii. After a good rain, people would come to the rock outcrop. Leaders or shamans would climb the outcrop, and 'play' the rock with the cup marks, leading the rest of the tribe below in songs of thanks." [402]

Ethnographic information indicates that the Luiseño Indians in San Diego County, California used cup marked boulders in girls' puberty rituals — also to make musical sounds. However, ethnographic information also indicates that there was no one purpose for these markings but were used in different ways by different groups and tribes. Not all cup marked stones are musical so this is only one possible reason for their creation.

It is also probable that many of the mortars (stones where food was ground and pounded into a paste) identified in archaeological surveys have been misidentified and are, in reality, cup-marked stones. Some of the areas that have been identified as mortars were located in places that are difficult to reach and a distance away from any water source, which would have been necessary for food processing.

It is hard to believe that these cup marks and cup and rings are only coincidentally identical the world over; it may be that they once did have a common origin and common symbolism. Researchers are a long way from determining what those are, though. What has been determined, so far, is that some of the cup marks, or cupules, have been dated to 100,000 years ago and were used by Neanderthal groups. At the other extreme, Whitley notes that these sometimes complex "pit and groove" work located in the American Southwest was "widely made during the historic period" and "that much (but not necessarily all) of it is relatively recent." [403] Such markings, therefore, may be the one symbol that humans have been creating for the longest continuous period in their history.[404]

Anthropologists and others are striving to analyze why such an unusual symbolism might be found in identical representations across such wide geographic and cultural areas and extreme time periods, and how these symbols came into use universally.

What was the driving force that created the need in humankind to produce the same identical symbols in the same ways? The evidence seems to indicate that early man to some extent shared a common religion. How it hap-

402. http://stones.non-prophet.org/archive/Ancient/000000/1023499901004317.html.

403. Whitley David S. *The Art of the Shaman: Rock Art of California.* Salt Lake City: The University of Utah Press 2000, 49.

404. Knaak, Manfred. *The Forgotten Artists: Indians of Anza-Borrego and Their Rock Art.* Borrego Springs: Anza-Borrego Desert Natural History Association, 1988, 60.

pened that similar beliefs cropped up or were spread, and why, are whole studies in themselves. Was there a worldwide priest-class or ruler-class that propagated the same artistic and ritual traditions in Wisconsin and California, Spain and Germany? Was a Goddess religion universally recognized around the world? Are these similarities purely a result of the type of life lived at that time, the technologies available and the aspirations of individuals and tribes, and the threats and fears they faced produced a commonly understood symbolic response? Have these traditions been carried by the human mind from place to place since our earliest ancestors began to explore the world and spread across its sphere? These are all questions that have not been asked and thusly not answered. I do not believe that we will know the answer as long as these sites are only analyzed on a regional basis without comparisons of the similarities around the world being made. The majority of sites appear to date to the Late Stone Age and the Bronze Age, which only poses another question — what was it that ignited the creative spark in humans to produce these universal symbols? British archaeologist Colin Burgess summarizes these symbols appearing on British stone monuments:

> The use of cup and ring marks on stone circles and ring monuments suggest that, like passage grave art, they were part of the total religious fabric of the Third Millennium.[405]

THE SPIRAL AND THE LABYRINTH

The spiral and labyrinth are two additional symbols found in rock art around the world. Two theories are current as to the meaning behind the spiral motif. One is that it represents the Goddess and the endless cycle of birth and rebirth, the other is that it is symbolic of a people's migrations from one world to the next, or the travels of the spirit from the inner life to the expanded and outer world. The Hopi Indians believe that they have progressed through four different worlds and the spiral is symbolic of those travels. An intricate spiral design in Eastern California, in traditional Paiute territory, is identical, although much smaller, to a design found on the Nazca Plain in Peru. Clockwise spirals have also been associated with water, either bodies of water or rainy seasons, as well as the migrations of tribes. In most areas where the spiral is found in ancient symbolism, it seems to be associated with the primary life source — the creator and the creator's path. "Wherever there appears an arrangement of stones in a

405. Burgess, Colin. *The Age of Stonehenge.* Edison: Castle Books 2003, 348.

circular, spiral or serpentine form," write Baring and Cashford, "there is the tradition of the Mother Goddess..." [406]

The labyrinth, like the spiral, appears in diverse locations including Crete, Cornwall and Arizona — and in the identical form. In Celtic folk tradition small stones, called Troy Stones, were carved with labyrinth designs. These stones were handed down by wise women (otherwise known as witches) from one to another and were used, they say, to communicate with the underworld. Pennick wrote, "the wise woman would trace her finger through the labyrinth, back and forth, whilst humming a particular tune, until she reached an altered state." [407] When the wise woman reached that altered state, she, like shamans eons before her, would be able to communicate with the otherworld. The last known Troy Stone was destroyed in 1958, at the time of its owner's death. She had stipulated that it was to be smashed to bits, when she was gone.

In the 20th century, we have seen a marked increase in interest in labyrinths. Christian churches have begun to reconstruct the large 12th-century cathedral labyrinths that earlier parishioners used to walk through; some have even created portable labyrinths, so that they may be set up on a temporary basis. The Christian concept of the labyrinth is "a fusion of the ancient and the (post) modern, of prayer, contemplation, encounter and self-discovery. It is a symbolic journey towards an encounter with God."[408] While humans were creating labyrinths as far back as 5,000 years ago, contemporary usage is based on the Roman design used as a decorative floor pattern. The essential religious significance of this symbol has not been altered over those 5,000 years and, like the Troy Stone, it continues to offer a method to communicate with the otherworld and the divine, however those might be understood in a given era.

There are several labyrinths, in Arizona near the Hopi towns of Shipaulovi and Oraibi, and in Southern Arizona at Casa Grande, that are identical to Minoan and Etruscan designs, and to the labyrinth at Tintagel. Rock art expert Campbell Grant noted that "this symbol is so intricate and so unusual that the idea that it could be independently devised twice is not credible."[409] Grant, as well as others, believes that the Spanish, who were familiar with the motif in the

---

406. Baring, Anne and Jules Cashford. *The Myth of the Goddess: Evolution of an Image.* London: Arkana/Penguin Books, 1991, 42.

407. Pennick, Nigel. *Sacred Landscapes.* London: Thames & Hudson, 1996, 62.

408. http://web.ukonline.co.uk/paradigm/discoverframe.html.

409. Grant, Campbell. *Rock Art of the American Indian.* New York: Promontory Press, 1967, 66.

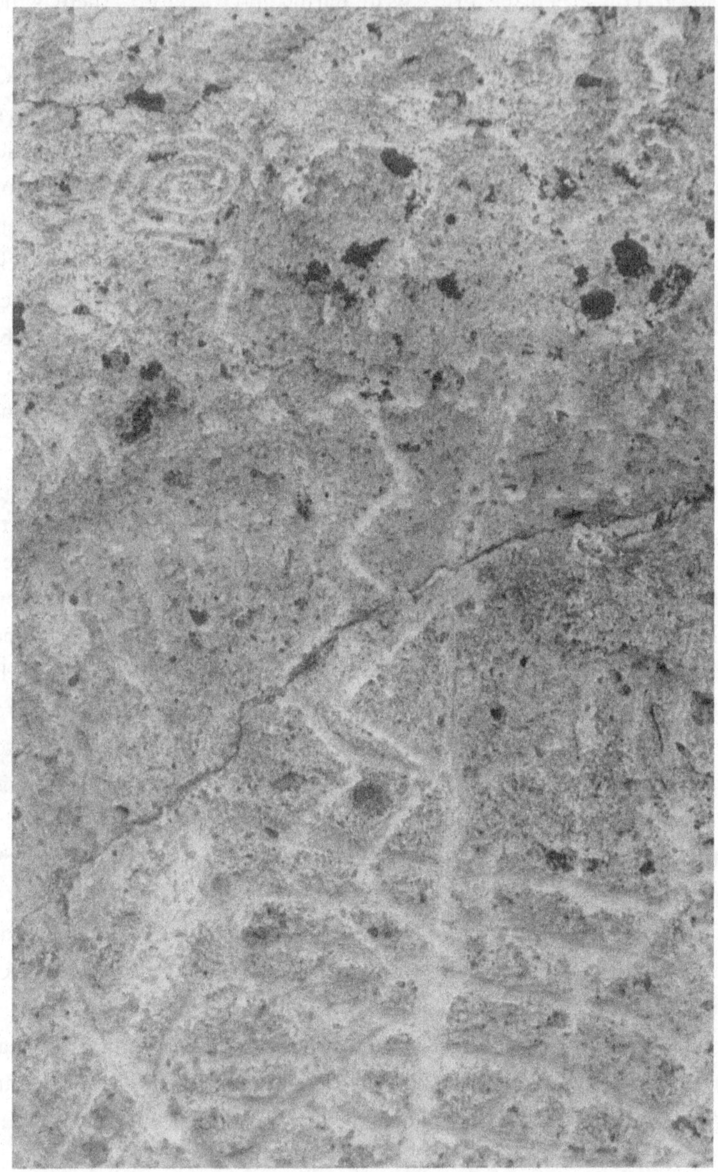

Paiute Spiral Rock Art Similar to a Nazca Design

Old World, transported these designs to North America in the early 1600s. Others believe that the Native Americans may have received it through prehis-

The Labyrinth at Tintagel's Rocky Valley

toric trade contacts; still others feel that such explanations are doubtful and that the Hopi people and other tribes of Arizona and elsewhere more likely did develop this motif independently — the mystery is, how?

Mazes, like the labyrinth, appear in rock art. The maze, according to Webster's Dictionary, is "a confusing, intricate network of winding pathways...such a network with one or more blind alleys." The labyrinth, on the other hand, is "an intricate network of winding passages hard to follow without losing one's way." The distinction is difficult to see, but while the two may appear to be identical, they are, in reality, different structures. The definition implies that, although it is difficult, the labyrinth can be traveled through to reach the other side, while the maze only leads the walker to one internal location.

Hopi Circular Maze

In rock art these are important distinctions. The labyrinth symbolizes the journey of the spirit along a difficult route which, if accomplished, leads to the spirit world or the deity. The maze, on the other hand, leads one along a difficult path which, if accomplished, allows the individual to reach a central point, which is within the spirit — a vision quest. An excellent representation of the maze appears on a large boulder in Riverside County, near Hemet, California, called the Maze Rock. Some have suggested that a hidden spiral can be seen within the maze design — perhaps an indication that finding one's internal spiritual core will lead onward to the creative force.

Other mazes appear in a few Southern California locations and early speculation suggested that the mazes showed a link with the Cliff Dwellers of Arizona. No information has been found to disprove this theory. [410] Two of them, as previously discussed, are also associated with unusual "ringing" or

The Maze Rock, Riverside County, California

"bell" stones. Mazes and labyrinths were known to figure into initiation-fertility ceremonies for girls in California, as shown in the photo below. The questions about the cup marks posed above can be applied to the spiral and labyrinth patterns as well.

THE POWER OF ROCK ART

Early Americans and other indigenous cultures around the world clearly believed in the power of rock art. It was a way to express visions, to provide pro-

410. Knight, Lavinia C. "Bell Rock and Indian Maze Rock of Orange County" in *Pacific Coast Archaeological Society Quarterly*, Vol. 15, No. 2, April 1979, 25-32.

Maze Designs made by Young Initiates in Southern California

tection and warning, to ensure fertility, and to bring on rain and snow and dry periods. It also could be used for less than honorable reasons.

As shamans could bring the rain, they could also stop it by creating symbols on stone. Travis Hudson and Ernest Underhay wrote of one such occurrence, as told by the Chumash Indians:

> A long time ago, a great famine was created by an astrologer who painted several figures on stone of men and women who were bleeding from the mouth and falling down. This "evil" astrologer took the stone and went into the hills to expose it to the sun. He then gave prayers for sickness, and his efforts were rewarded. No rain came for the next five years, and many people died from hunger. Fortunately for the people, a group of sorcerers found out about the painting. They saved the surviving people from death by tossing the stone into a body of water. The remedy apparently worked, for it soon began to rain.[411]

The universal application of certain rock art motifs brings us back again to the question of why they are, in fact, found universally. Do we assume independent creation to meet a specific need? Do we assume that some worldwide interaction had occurred thousands of years ago to bring these symbols to most every culture? Alternatively, do we assume that somehow humans as a species all shared something as abstract and arcane as a set of symbols and a sense of what they might represent, that has only recently disappeared with the advent of writing? One group of astronomical symbols painted on California rocks begs for explanation. One, classified as site CA-TUL-80, is almost identical to an ancient Egyptian drawing of the boat of Sokaris, God of the Necropolis from a papyrus, known as the Book of the Dead, dated to 1420 BCE. Another from site CA-MNT-253 is almost identical to a symbol from the Codex Nuttall 67 from Mesoamerica. While researchers state that these drawings "must have been made recently,"[412] they do "contain archaic American Indian elements beside the derived elements." [413] What "recent" means is not elucidated but if they were, in fact, made by Native Americans prior to their acculturation into mainstream American society, they must have been created with a common link to a specific item.

The symbol from CA-MNT-253 most likely does have Mesoamerican influence, which should not be a surprise when you think that the destruction of Mesoamerican empires by the Spanish resulted in the forced migration of countless Indians. At this site a stone was also found that was shaped like a mushroom that, again, is similar to mushroom shaped stones from Tabasco, Mexico and Highland Guatemala.

---

411. Hudson, Travis and Ernest Underhay. *Crystals in the Sky: An Intellectual Odyssey Involving Chumash Astronomy, Cosmology and Rock Art*. Socorro: Ballena Press Anthropological Papers #10, 36.

412. Mayer, Dorothy. "Sky Games in California Petroglyphs" in *Visions of the Sky: Archaeological and Ethnological Studies of California Indian Astronomy*. Salinas: Coyote Press—Coyote Press Archives of California Prehistory Number 16, 1988, 67.

413. Ibid.

Chapter 11. The Gods of Stone

All people are animist, to some degree. We see the power of wind and rain, lightening and thunder, and realize that we are insignificant objects in a much larger and fearsomely powerful universe. Tornados seem to have intelligence, or will, as they dance around some structures only to destroy others nearby. Rocks have been imbued with spirit by many cultures. In some areas of the world, stones are thought to represent individual gods. In Native American lore the "core of the universe" is Rock. To the Omaha, the Rock holds all of the powers of the universe and "is the steadfast center of the world, untouched by wind and change, immovable, enduring through all things."[414] The Rock both creates and destroys. The Count D'Alviella reminds us that a pyramid-shaped stone at Paphos represented Aphrodite.[415] Hermes is another Greek god who was represented in stone — in fact, Hermes was known as the "god of stones." The winged-footed courier of Mount Olympus, Hermes was also the god of shepherds, literature, weights and measures, athletics, and land travel. He was also a phallic god and thus his image was carved on pillars, which are symbolic phalluses, used to mark roads and boundaries. The pillars had the head of Hermes carved at the top and his phallus carved toward the base of the stone. The word *Hermes* is from the ancient Greek *herma*, which means a cairn or standing stone. Because the image of the god in pillar form was so ingrained in Greek society the

414. Alexander, Hartley Burr. *The World's Rim: Great Mysteries of the North American Indians.* Mineola: Dover Publications, Inc. 1999, 48

415. D'Alviella, Count Goblet. *The Migration of Symbols.* New York: University Books, 1956, 184.

word took on a dual meaning. Hermes was also responsible for guiding the souls of the dead on their journey to the afterworld, a fitting task for such a god.

Reading Wallis Budge's book *Cleopatra's Needles*, we see how ancient the practice of linking the sacred and the divine to stone is. He wrote, "the earliest axe-heads, whether single or double, were made of flint or stone, and it is a significant fact that the hieroglyph for 'god' represents a stone axe-head tied to a short handle. The spirit in the stone aided the efforts of the man wielding the axe, and, presumably, absorbed the blood of the man whom it slew." [416]

The representation of gods by standing stones is probably one of the oldest continuously used motifs in religion. While many times the symbolism is communicated as a male representation, due to the phallic image, it was not always so. "The pillar," remarks E.O. James, "was not exclusively the aniconic image of a male god...since it often has been the abode of a goddess like the asherah...." [417]

MacKenzie relates that Isis "was the standing-stone which was visited at certain phases of the moon by women who prayed for offspring. In the Scoto-Irish legend, the Caillech, after a period of spring storms, transforms herself into 'a gray stone looking over the sea.' In India, goats are sacrificed to the stone of the goddess Durga, which stands below a sacred tree....The original Zeus was evidently worshipped as a stone pillar — the pillar which enclosed his spirit..." [418] All of this suggests that the association of the god, or gods, of creation and fertility and life with stone date back to times beyond our science to comprehend.

Standing stones have also been believed to be the abodes of other nature spirits. In India, stone pillars and standing stones were normally erected under sacred trees, and the tree spirit is said to live in the stone during certain times of the year.

Inyan

According to the lore of the Lakota Sioux, Inyan is the Spirit of the Rock and creator of the world. As Andrews wrote, Inyan "was the spirit of the earth

---

416. Budge, E.A. Wallis. *Cleopatra's Needles and Other Egyptian Obelisks.* London: Religious Tract Society, 1926, 4.

417. James, E.O. *The Cult of the Mother-Goddess.* New York: Barnes & Noble Books, 1994, 133.

418. MacKenzie, Donald A. *Crete & Pre-Hellenic Myths and Legends.* London: Senate, 1995, 184

that lived in the rocks, and the Lakota invoked him more than any other deity. They made sacrifices to him, which usually consisted of pieces of skin left for their great god on oddly shaped stones." [419]

Inyan, or Iyan, was similar to other savior gods in that he sacrificed himself to create good. The Lakota creation story states:

> Iyan, the rock, existed in a void; it was dark and lonely there. Iyan wished to create something other, so that he would not be lonely and so that he could have power over something other than himself. He pierced himself, and his blood, which was blue, flowed out until he was shriveled, hard, and powerless. What came from him formed ... (Mother Earth)....The energy given up by the rock, now hard and powerless, is Taku Skan Skan, that which moves all things. This power is now diffused into the female earth, the male sky, and the waters. [420]

Sioux mythology places Inyan's home in the Black Hills in the Inyan Kara Mountain. "Inyan Kara" means "stone-made." The Black Hills, says the legend, "was the dwelling place of the 'Great Spirit' who had set aside the area as a temporary resting place for the spirits of the departed braves...it is said that when Indians entered the vicinity of Inyan Kara, they would hang offerings on the rocks and trees to appease the thunder gods who were responsible for the mysterious rumblings heard during the calmest days and nights. When Whites first discovered Inyan Kara they also mentioned the rumblings, which have been attributed to the escape of hydrogen from underground beds of burning coal." [421]

Part of the lore of Inyan Kara is that of a large stone forest. In the early 1800s, trapper James Clyman repeated to a St. Louis reporter a story told to him by mountaineer Moses Harris. Harris had told him that he has seen the forest, "whare the tree branches leaves and all were perfect and the small birds sitting on them with their mouths open singing at the time of their transformation to stone." [422]

The attempts of the US Government to take possession of the Black Hills and Inyan Kara in the 1870s resulted in the Battle of Little Big Horn.

Inyan is also known as Stone Boy. Stone Boy was the son of a young virgin Indian girl who had placed a white pebble (the pebble is "living stone," Stone

419. St. Pierre, Mark and Tilda Long Soldier. *Walking in the Sacred Manner: Healers, Dreamers, and Pipe Carriers—Medicine Women of the Plains Indians.* New York: Touchstone Books, 1995, 36.

420. Andrews, Tamra. *A Dictionary of Nature Myths.* Oxford: Oxford University Press, 1998, 101.

421. Untitled/undated request for Designation of Historic Places summary for Inyan Kara Mountain in Crook County, Wyoming Statement of Significance, page 3.

422. *Ibid.*, page 4.

Boy's father) in her mouth one day to keep thirst away. She fell asleep and swallowed the pebble, which impregnated her. Soon, she gave birth to a baby boy with skin of stone. This story is similar to that of other gods who are born as a result of their mothers ingesting small stones and other inanimate objects.

Grandfather Rock

Like the Sioux, the Arikara believe the creator of life is stone. The Arikara reportedly kept two sacred objects on the east side of the entryway to their medicine lodges. One was a stone pillar, the other an evergreen tree. The stone stood for "unchanging," the tree for the renewal of life. During festivals, the stone was painted red and covered with a red cloth, red being the color of life. The stone was called "Grandfather" and was lord of the mountains and all that rested under them; he was also the substance of Time. Anthropologist Hartley Alexander wrote of the Rock:

> In him lies authority; he is the avenger; he constructs and destroys....[423]

Kane, the "Rolling Stone" God of Hawaii

Kane is usually associated with water and creation. Kane is given credit for the waterfalls, springs and freshwater pools of the Hawaiian Islands, but another aspect of Kane is that of God of stones. He appears to humans in dreams, not in the form of a stone but with the body of a man and a head of stone. Farmers invoke him to bless their fields, and warriors to make their weapons as strong as rocks.

Altars to Kane consisted of conical stones anywhere from one foot to eight feet in height. The stone was planted in a family enclosure and situated with ti plants. The family would pray at the stone and ask for forgiveness in case they had broken any taboos. According to Martha Beckwith, who researched the folklore of Hawaii, "the place for setting up the stone and the offering to be made were revealed in a dream...the stone itself was sprinkled with water or with coconut oil and covered with a piece of bark cloth during the ceremony."[424]

---

423. Alexander, *op. cit.*, 43.

424. Beckwith, Martha. *Hawaiian Mythology*. Honolulu: University of Hawaii Press, 1970, 47.

This practice is similar to that of the New Guinea tribes, discussed earlier, who covered their sacred stones in bast.

Kane was not the only God of Stones. Games of sport were always played under the guidance of a god, who was chosen before the games commenced. Beckworth wrote, "to secure a god to preside over games, large stones were selected and wrapped in tapa, and ceremonies were performed over such a stone....Chiefs and priests worshipped these rocks and poured awa [425] over them as representative of the god." [426]

These special, sacred stones are regarded as such because the Hawaiians and other animists see a connection between them and their ancestors; these stones are gods.

And, as I have said before, the ancient perception of an interconnectedness between stones and water appears universal. The Hawaiians worshipped some stones as fish gods and Kane, the God of Stone, was also the God of Water — the supreme God of Hawaii.

Other Hawaiian stone gods are plentiful, as well. Many are simply unworked stone, described by Sir Peter H. Buck, former director of the Bishop Museum in Honolulu, as "disappointing as works of art." Buck cautions, though, that "it should be remembered that it was not the workmanship but the prayers and offerings which gave a material object power (mana) and converted it into a god, no matter what the form. Thus any individual could make a stone god for himself; and the manufacture of gods, particularly by fishermen, continued for some time after the acceptance of Christianity." [427] This is an important aspect of many indigenous religions. "God" is viewed as a power, which may be transferred to an object of veneration by prayers and offerings. This does not demean the god; in fact, it makes it even more awesome and powerful, because of the individual's total belief in it.

Examples of Hawaiian stone gods include a 3.2-inch stone which came to light in 1885. It was owned by an elderly fisherman, who kept the stone wrapped in tapa. According to Buck, he "prayed to it to bring him an abundant supply of fish." [428] Queen Emma is reported to have cherished a "dull water-worn beach stone" that she kept wrapped in tapa and sealed in a special casket. Many of the

425. Awa is a narcotic drink regarded as the drink of the Gods.

426. Beckwith, *op. cit.* 88.

427. Buck, Sir Peter H. *Arts and Crafts of Hawaii: XI Religion.* Bernice P. Bishop Museum Special Publication 45. Honolulu: Bishop Museum Press, 1964, 495.

428. *Ibid.*, 496.

stone gods of Hawaii are fish-gods. One unusual fish god is a stone, 7' 8" long, that was kept out in the open at Puuepa, Kohala; it has natural shark-like features.

Other worked-stone gods in human form became stone gods only after specific rituals were conducted. Many of these were hidden after the arrival of Christianity in caves, swamps, buried or placed in cairns. Buck noted "it was an accepted teaching that if offerings were not made from time to time to the symbols of the gods, the gods punished the family for its neglect, usually by afflicting it with sickness." [429] Many families that had converted to Christianity and still had these stone gods in their possession either destroyed them or donated them to the museum in an effort to rid them of the gods "malign" influence.

Ethnologist Gorgon MacGregor, in his field notes taken in 1932, wrote:

> In regard to the worship of stones, there is a rock in the bush at Kalvaka, called Tui Lopi, which was considered a god of that place. People who were going into the bush to collect julia, an ornamental fern, or sasa also an ornamental plant, always laid a leaf on this stone and asked Tui Lopi to protect them on their trip and keep them from falling over any stones in the way. The tupu'a is said to be covered with sasa and julia.
>
> A tupu'a is something everlasting or permanent and a thing that looks like something living. All stones are regarded as tupu'a. [430]

Oceanic cultures, as well as Native American, traditionally say that all creation and life originated from the sacred stone. This also applies to Mesoamerican cultures. The pre-Columbian Ixtepejanos in Oxaca, Mexico worshipped a small oracular stone, which they adorned with green feathers. According to ethnographic records, it was carried to hilltop temples where blood sacrifice was given to it through self-mortification. Those who could not offer their own blood would sacrifice turkeys and dogs and wash the stone in that blood. Marriage ceremonies were also conducted in front of this idol. [431]

There are many examples of megalithic monuments that researchers perceive to represent the personal gods worshipped by individuals and groups but there are also many examples of this veneration continuing into fairly modern times. The account of the "Pagan idol" from the Irish island of Inniskea mentioned earlier is typical of these individual accounts. Similar to the Inniskea idol

---

429. *Ibid.*, 498.

430. http://www.hawaii.edu/oceanic/rotuma/os/MacGregor/McReligionStones.html.

431. Kearney, Michael. *The Winds of Ixtepeji: World View and Society in a Zapotec Town.* New York: Holt, Rinehart and Winston Case Studies in Cultural Anthropology, 1972, 28.

that was clothed in flannel is another stone figure that was unearthed by a farmer in County Cork. Today, according to Nigel Pennick, it "is revered as the 'god stone'. It is treated as an aniconic image and dressed at certain times of the year."[432]

Shiva's Lingam Stones

While not really a "god" of stones, Shiva is represented in sacred stones taken from the River Narmada, in central-western India. The Narmada is one of the seven sacred Hindu sites of pilgrimage in India. Believed to be the most sacred icon of ancient and modern India, these particular stones, ranging in size from one inch to as large as six feet, are endlessly tumbled by the river current, which makes them rounded and polished. Their striations and coloring are peculiar to the region. Even a pebble from these stones is believed to be an incarnation of the God Shiva and is regarded as symbolic of his supreme creative powers. The stones are often placed in special shrines dedicated to the Lord Shiva and are symbolic of his fertile powers. The Shiva Lingams are only accessible during the dry season and are only harvested from the river by select families that are trained in recognizing them. The stones symbolize not only male fertility but also the feminine creative energy. In Hindu tradition, the lingam is regarded as the shape of the soul and is associated with the Fifth Chakra. The stones are not only regarded as energy generators, but also as healers.

The Ben Stone

The Ben Stone was a cult stone depicted as a short, thick obelisk and represented by the Benu bird in Egypt. The word *benu* is derived from the verb *weben*, which means "to rise." According to Richard Wilkinson, "the Benu bird was said to have flown over the waters of Nun before the original creation....the bird finally came to rest on a rock at which point its cry broke the primeval silence and was said to have determined what was and what was not to be in the unfolding creation." [433]

---

432. Pennick, Nigel. *Celtic Sacred Landscapes.* London: Thames and Hudson, 1996, 53.
433. Wilkinson, Richard H. *The Complete Gods and Goddesses of Ancient Egypt.* New York: Thames & Hudson 2003, 212.

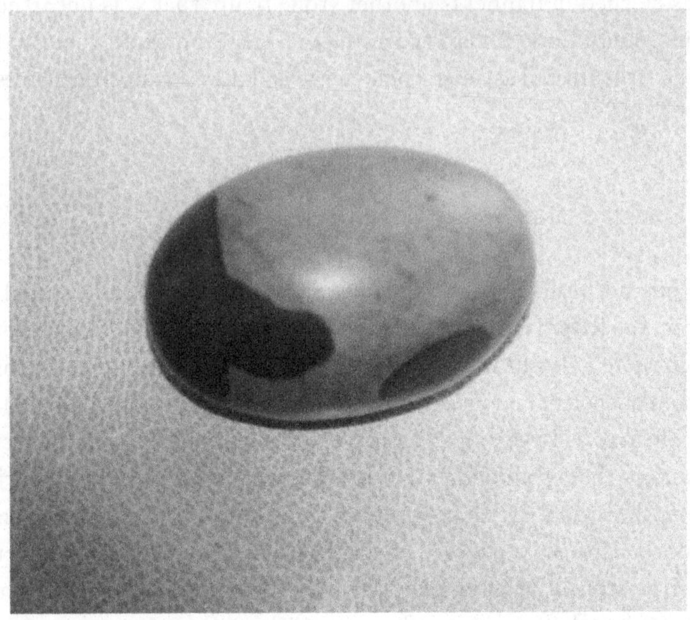

A Sacred Shiva Lingam Stone

The Ben Stone was the abode of the Sun Spirit, later called Ra. In fact, the Benu bird came to be seen as the incarnation of Ra and the heart of Osiris, the god of renewal. The origins of the Ben Stone, however, lie farther back in time than the tradition of the adoration of the Benu bird. The Benu bird was also known as the Phoenix in later mythology — the magical bird that arose from the all-consuming ashes every 500 years. The lore of the Benu bird was so widely spread that legends of the Phoenix became important aspects of Chinese, Greek and Arabic mythology. The Ben Stone was designed to be the site for human sacrifices, which were carried out on the east side of the stone. Channels were carved into the rock to allow the blood to run off into alabaster jars. The sacrifices were to the Sun God whose spirit was believed to reside in the stone, at least periodically.

The structure of the stone suggests that the upper part of it was regarded as the abode of the Sun God in the heavens. The construction of later Egyptian obelisks was most likely inspired by the Ben Stone. Budge suggests that the stone was originally volcanic or of meteoric origin, like the Black Stone of Ka'abah. He also notes that, "as Ra was eternal, the obelisk symbolized stability and permanence, and all the powers of rebirth, and virility, and fertility and creative force which he (as the Sun god) possessed."[434]

The Thunder God

The Thunder gods of the Greeks and Romans were perhaps the first of those that would become known to future generations as the classical gods. Jupiter Lapis is a lightning god, a god who came from the heavens as a meteor. The Romans erected monuments where lightning struck, which the populace were forbidden to touch. Charles Blinkenberg wrote, "the most solemn oath was that sworn by Jupiter Lapis...The sacred stone was used when the fetiales[435] took the oath and made sacrifice upon the formation of an allegiance with a foreign power. Such an alliance...received its highest sanction from the lightning god himself."[436] Stones "from heaven" are seen throughout history as "lifeless stone with living heavenly fire"[437] that are not only associated with the gods but become gods themselves.

The World of Stone Giants

Legends of a giant race of stone men are found worldwide. Many of these tales may be the results of stories told to explain unusual landscape features or how the world was created. For the most part, these giants were a fearsome group, not averse to eating the local population when they got hungry. They also were a playful group, tossing huge boulders in games of ball. Folklore also indicates that many of the megalithic tombs and dolmen are "Giant's Tombs."

A large number of these stories are about giants who were created from rock or who look like rock — or have a bad habit of throwing huge stones around to rearrange the landscape. Such tales are as common in Scandinavian and British folklore and mythology as they are in Native American lore. The

434. Budge *op. cit.*, 21.

435. "Fetiales" was a college of Roman priests that acted as guardians of the public faith. They normally were entrusted with resolving disputes involving foreign states.

436. Blinkenberg, Charles. *The Thunderweapon in Religion and Folklore: A Study in Comparative Archaeology*. Cambridge: Cambridge University Press, 1911, 31.

437. Alexander, Hartley Burr. *The World's Rim: The Mysteries of the North American Indians.* Mineola: Dover Publications Inc., 1999, 53.

widespread inclusion of these stories in our mythic encyclopedia suggests to some that humans have a kind of racial memory, or it may be due to the sharing of ideas during the prehistoric age, before the migrations that distributed humans across the continents; or, for some other reason, the ideas simply came independently to people everywhere as they addressed the unknown and mystical world.

On a modest hill near Lelant, Cornwall, called Trencrom Hill, are the remains of an ancient Iron Age stone fortification. Legend has it that a race of giants lived there who spent their time heaving huge boulders back and forth; they are supposed to have buried a rich treasure in the hill. On a gorgeous sunny day, the hill offers a commanding view; one can see St. Michael's Mount from the top. One of the boulders that legend says was tossed by the giants has the giant's finger-images pressed into the stone — it was under this stone that the treasure is said to rest — protected by the spirits of the giants or other Faery folk. Jennifer Westwood wrote that some time ago, perhaps 200 years, a man who thought he knew where the treasure was went to the hill and began to dig. Suddenly, "a great storm arose, and by the lightning's glare he saw swarms of spriggans (the ghostly spirits) coming out of the rocks. They looked 'ugly as if they would eat him,' and got bigger as they approached."[438] The terrified man ran home, hid in his bed for days, and was unable to work for sometime thereafter.

In Native American mythology, stories about giants are much rarer than stories about the Little People. Likewise, the number of giants in these stories is few compared to the legions of Faery beings in other Native American lore. The giants in these stories are usually less than friendly. The Iroquois tell of an invasion of stony-skinned cannibal giants who came from the west. Most giants in Native Indian mythology are cannibals, eating all in their path.

As mentioned earlier, the Cherokee speak of the Spear-Finger, a huge woman with skin that is like stone. In 1900, anthropologist James Mooney wrote of this creature:

> Long, long ago...there dwelt in the mountains a terrible ogress, woman monster, whose food was human livers. She could take on any shape or appearance to suit her purposes, but in her right form she looked very much like an old woman, excepting that her whole body was covered with a skin as hard as a rock and no weapon could wound or penetrate..."[439]

---

438. Westwood, Jennifer. *Albion: A Guide to Legendary Britain.* London: Paladin Books, 1987, 38.

Trencrom Hill's Stone, Complete with Finger Prints

Like other giants she had supernatural powers over stone and could carry or throw huge boulders or "cement them together by merely striking one against another." [440] The Creek Indians had a similar legend about "The Big Rock Man."

In Scandinavian lore, giants were flesh and blood — but if the rays of the sun caught them, they would instantly turn to stone, much in the same way as the Night Trolls in Iceland. Similarly, the Callanish Standing Stones on the Western Isles of Scotland, according to legend, were originally giants that were turned to stone by St. Kieran when they refused to adopt Christianity.

Folklorist John Rhys notes that a huge giant that supposedly lived on the Isle of Man was responsible for throwing five huge stones over several miles from a mountain called Cronk yn Irree Laa. "I have seen," he remarks, "the marks of his huge hands impressed on the top of two massive monoliths." [441]

---

439. Rhys, John. *Celtic Folklore: Welsh and Manx, Vol. 1.* New York: Gordon Press, 1974, 285.

440. Mooney, James. *Myths of the Cherokee.* New York: Dover Publications, Inc. 316-317.

441. *Ibid.*

The Stone "Godlings" of Nepal

The Magar tribe, living in the mountain pastureland of Nepal, is the remnants of an ancient migration of Mongolians into the area hundreds or thousands of years ago. Part of the Magar religious universe are the supernatural "godlings" that, in exchange for being worshipped, sacrificed to, and taken care of, provide the basic necessities of life for the Magar people. The godlings are nature spirits who, they say, control the weather, health, and reproduction of the land and the forces of nature for the humans living in their midst. All of these godlings are capable of both good and evil and exhibit many human characteristics. In fact, the Magars believe that the godlings are the transformed spirits of their dead ancestors.

Godlings cannot be seen but are known to be present due to things that happen or do not happen in Magar society. Godlings are represented by stones and are believed to reside in certain stones. As part of the sacrificial ceremonies, a stone is wrapped in string, which constitutes its clothing. The stone is surrounded by flowers and incense and fed through animal sacrifice or through the offering of rice, flour, butter and milk. In one instance, a man was taken ill and the shaman lapsed into a state of possession. A godling spoke through the shaman, saying, "Yes, I am giving him this illness. I am in a stone at the edge of Dev Bahadur's rice field. The stone is marked with three clefts. Bring the stone...and build a temple. Every three years all you people must sacrifice five living things there..." [442] The godling also instructed the people that when sacrifices were made, a particular musical group must also attend and play music and dance.

The shaman and villagers found the stone and built a small temple at the spot where several paths cross in the village," similar to the omphalos stones in other locations. Reportedly, the man who was ill recovered and the villagers have been making sacrifices, along with singing and dancing ever since. Individual shrines for godlings are erected in family homes and villages and are often accompanied by bells, carved posts and colored cloth. These shrines generally take the form of stone enclosures set up in woods or under a large banyan tree. As ethnologist Hitchcock noted, "whether it is land, crops, water, fertility in animals, or health, the ultimate meaning to the Magars of the...godlings and their

442. Hitchcock, John T. *The Magars of Banyan Hill.* New York: Holt, Rinehart and Winston Case Studies in Cultural Anthropology, 1966, 31.

blood spattered shrines is that one pays with death for the gift of life." [443] We see once more that sacred stones are linked to life and the fertility of the land and the well-being of the humans that reside with them.

While we customarily equate the belief in living inanimate objects to prehistoric cultures, these few illustrations of worldwide beliefs involving living and intelligent stone, in historic times, shows us that humans today have continued to link their psyches to an ancient system of religious beliefs.

443. *Ibid.*, 34.

Afterword. The Importance of Sacred Stones In Contemporary Society

Would we, as an "advanced" culture, have believed 50 years ago that the United States and the industrial world would continue to erect megaliths as memorials, as parts of church landscapes, as public monuments in our parks? Would we have thought, as we became preoccupied with Sputnik and the thought of space travel and UFOs that not only our culture would continue to erect these monuments but also that we would raise standing stones that were designed to mimic those of Stonehenge and the obelisks of Egypt? Would we have been surprised to know that individuals today would continue to erect cairns and construct labyrinths in an attempt to harmonize with nature?

Far from creating a world only of metals and plastics people continue to value stone, a symbol of permanency, as a symbol of things that are larger than life itself, and as emblems of an ancient history that recedes too far back in time for the average person to possibly begin to comprehend.

Bob Trubshaw wrote, "collective memories are socially constructed. Their permanence is dependent on their emotional importance." [444] The mythology and folklore of megalithic sites continue to appeal to the human mind. While many of the myths and legends described in this volume have little basis in our perceptions of fact or reality, in another sense they create their own, separate reality. "Time" exists in the universe, but in mythology it is without meaning and

---

444. Trubshaw, Bob. "Continuity in archaeology and folklore" in 3rd *Stone* April-June 1999, 7.

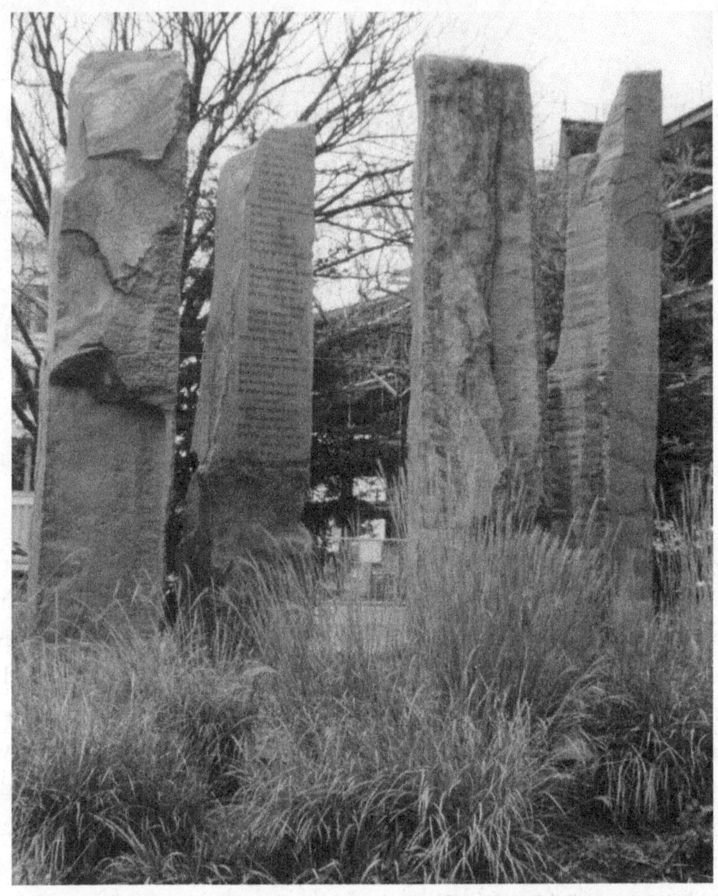

Modern day monoliths as part of an office building landscape

can best be compared to the Australian Aborigine's "Dream time" — a time that is neither here and now nor in the past — a fluid dimension that subtly alters one experience into another and adds a feeling of importance to being in a certain space at a certain "time." Our society, like all others throughout history, needs to feel that there is more to the world and our existence than the mundane reality that we experience, and we are happy to read meaning into everything. Most of the sites discussed in this book have a reputation that contributes to the visitor's sense of something beyond the ordinary. Whether it is due to our sense of mystery about how such enormous formations were created, our awe of the overwhelming forces of nature, the cherished sense of a connection to our most ancient ancestors, or the physical properties of these places — a feeling arises that we are in the presence of something beyond our understanding, even when obviously human-made objects are a part of the observed landscape. This feeling sometimes includes a sense of a special presence, an awareness of our connection with all humanity or with the universe at large, with things that go beyond our own individual self.

When I state in this book that ancient traditions have continued into contemporary times, it should not be construed to mean that I believe that the same tradition or ritual that was observed in Neolithic times can still be found in a rural village in Yorkshire or New Hampshire. However, as mankind seeks to understand what it is to be human, where we come from, what we are, how we relate to the rest of the universe and why, it is important to examine the many universal myths and usages associated with sacred sites and beliefs. Obviously, the cultures are different as are the various technologies that were used in their building, refinement, or utilization. However, for some reason, certain types of stones and certain types of places were selected again and again by various civilizations at various times, and certain other traditions evolved according to the same basic template.

There is no dispute that many of the surviving megaliths of today have been used by different people, for similar reasons. Stone sites dating back to Pagan times have been used by Christians to promote their cause as well as to "convert" the local populace. Many of the stories about sites that had a mythic theme were changed by these later people into stories about Christian saints. The stories are subtly changed, but the underlying theme is maintained. The possibilities are endless. W. Winwood Reade wrote of the Cathedral of Chartres, that has its ancient roots in Druid blood,

> At the close of service in the cathedral, no one leaves the church without kneeling and saying a short prayer before a small pillar or stone — without polish, base or capital — placed in a niche, and much worn on one side by the kisses of the devout....It was said to be a miraculous stone, and that its miracles were performed at the intercession of the Virgin Mary. [445]

This pillar, of course, is not based in Christian history or tradition but is a continuation of Pagan, pre-Christian traditions. While we do not know the original purpose of the stone, it has left its mark upon contemporary people who feel that it still beckons to them in a deep and primeval manner.

---

445. Reade, W. Winwood. *The Veil of Isis or Mysteries of the Druids*. North Hollywood: Newcastle Publishing Company, 1992, 230-231.

A recent discovery of ancient cities, wiped out in a 400-foot tidal wave up to 17,000 years ago, provides more food for thought. Civilizations have come and gone for untold centuries.[446] Archaeological discoveries have placed humankind in various locations across the Americas from between 20,000 and 40,000 years ago,[447] underscoring the serious possibility of prolonged and worldwide cultural exchanges. Worldwide trade provided a means for exchanging stories as well as goods, and religious ideas as well. The wheel was discovered more than once! Undoubtedly, many folkways and folktales do have a common source, but others were lost and then re-invented in the rebirth of culture, time and again, in the cycle of warfare, natural disasters, cultural evolution and re-evolution that makes up history.

In some places around the world, special stones are given public recognition. The Museum of Stones situated on the outskirts of Minsk, in Belarus, provides a place for people to learn about special stones and the folklore associated with them. The importance of their permanency is understood.

We continue to create myth and our own sacred space. The creation of dozens of stone cairns in the Sacramento River and in the sacred Wintu site of Panther Meadows, as well as the continued use of megalithic sites for contemporary rituals, speaks to our continued need to do so. It is not that folklore represents reality — and why should it, for what is "reality" but a perception? History changes often and it is always changed by the new victor. What is important is that folklore is important to the one who reads, hears, or participates in it.

By deriving meaning from these stones in our own way, we add to their heritage. The fact that so many people from so many different ages and locations do find that an internal need is satisfied by these places of power and mystery is enough, even if the "truth" is somewhat less than what scientists and historians hope to establish. The definition of truth, like those of time and reality, are fluid and changing. Emanuel Swedenborg, the 18th century Swedish philosopher, said, "by a stone is signified truth." [448] That we try to create our own truth through ancient means speaks eloquently of modern culture's need to connect both physically and spiritually with the unknown, to ensure a viable future — and a meaningful past.

---

446. "Submerged city may be older than Mesopotamia," *Hindustan Times*, December 4, 2003.

447. Espinoza-Ar, Amy. "Forty-Thousand Year Old Tools?" in *American Archaeology*, Vol. 7 No. 4 Winter 2003-04, pgs 48-49.

448. Gaskell, G.A. *Dictionary of All Scriptures and Myths*. New York: Avenel Books, 1981, 722.

APPENDIX: A MEGALITH TIMELINE

The following timeline illustrates when some of the major megalithic sites and events occurred in relationship to other cultures and environmental events such as the glaciations. It is unfortunate that dates for stone monuments are tenuous at best and lacking altogether in many instances.

25,000-10,000 BCE	5000-4000 BCE	3900-2500 BCE	2400-1000 BCE	100-1500 CE
End of the **Pleistocene Ice Age**; glaciers cover Canada, the upper Midwest and northern New England, Great Britain and much of Northern Europe. This glacier lasted from 115,000 years ago until at least 10,000 years before the common era. Paleo-Indians arrive in North America through a variety of ways, including over the land bridge in the Bering Strait and by small boats from Europe. San Dieguito Paleo-Indians in what is now San Diego County, California fashion 400-foot long stone alignments in the desert as well as hundreds of rock cairns.	Early Neolithic Creation of the Ben Stone in Egypt First true pyramid constructed for King Sneferu in Egypt Dolmen are built in Western Europe Cup-marked stones made by ancestors of the Miwok Indians at Chaw'se (Jackson, California) Unusual "cog-stones" crafted (Orange County, California)	Late Neolithic Avebury constructed, Stonehenge finished in its current form (England) West Kennet Long Barrow constructed (England) Megalithic temple-tomb built at New Grange (Ireland) Great Pyramid of Egypt built	Early Bronze Age - Middle Bronze Age Construction of the Rollright Stone circle (England) Creation of the statue of Memnon (Egypt); Cleopatra's Needles erected at Heliopolis Rise of the Olmec civilization in Central America Creation of South American pyramids The London Stone created, approx. 1000 BCE Labyrinths carved at Rocky Valley, Tintagel, approx. 1400 BCE	Rise and destruction of the Mayan, Aztec and Toltec civilizations in Central America and the Incas in South America The Kensington Stone perhaps carved by Scandinavian travelers to Minnesota, approx. 1020 CE Stone of Scone brought to Scone, Scotland by the first king of the Picts and Scots in 843 CE Tintagel castle built, approx. 1068 CE (Cornwall) The Homol'ovi settlements (Arizona) abandoned, approx. 1400 CE

Selected Bibliography

Adams, E. Charles. "Homol'ovi: An Ancestral Hopi Place" in *Archaeology Southwest*, Vol. 14, Number 4, Fall 2000, 1-3.

Alexander, Hartley Burr. *The World's Rim: Great Mysteries of the North American Indians.* Mineola: Dover Publications, Inc. 1999, (originally published 1967).

Alexander, Marc. *A Companion to the Folklore, Myths & Customs of Britain.* Gloucestershire: Sutton Publishing Limited 2002.

Andersen, Johannes C. *Myths and Legends of the Polynesians.* Rutland: Charles E. Tuttle Company 1969.

Andrews, Tamra. *A Dictionary of Nature Myths.* Oxford: Oxford University Press 1998.

Anon. "Our Hagiology," in *Blackwood's Edinburgh Magazine*, Vol. 82, October 1857, 454.

Ashe, Geoffrey. *Arthurian Britain.* Glastonbury: Gothic Image Publications 1997.

Atalie, Princess. *The Earth Speaks.* New York: Fleming H. Revell Company 1940.

Avi-Yonah, Michael. *Archaeology of the Holy Land.* Jerusalem: Keter Publishing House Jerusalem Ltd 1974.

Baring, Anne and Jules Cashford. *The Myth of the Goddess: Evolution of an Image.* London: Arkana/Penguin Books, 1993.

Beckwith, Martha. *Hawaiian Mythology.* Honolulu: University of Hawaii Press 1970.

Begole, Robert S. "Archaeological Phenomena in the California Desert," in *Pacific Coast Archaeological Society Quarterly, Vol. 10, No. 2, April 1974*, 59.

Bernal, Ignacio, trans. by Doris Heyden and Fernando Horcasitas. *The Olmec World.* Berkeley: University of California Press 1969.

Billson, Charles J. *Vestiges of Paganism in Leicestershire.* Loughborough: Heart of Albion Press 1994 (originally published 1911).

Black, William George. "Folk Medicine: A Chapter in the History of Culture." London: *Publications of the Folk-Lore Society #12,* 1883.

Blinkenberg, Charles. *The Thunderweapon in Religion and Folklore: A Study in Comparative Archaeology*. Cambridge: Cambridge University Press 1911.

Bonwick, James. *Irish Druids and Old Irish Religions.* New York: Barnes and Noble Books 1986 (Originally published 1894).

Bord, Janet and Colin. *Mysterious Britain: Ancient Secrets of Britain and Ireland.* London: Thorsons 1972.

Bourke, John G. *Apache Medicine-Men.* New York: Dover Publications, Inc. 1993 (Originally published 1892).

Bouteiller, Marcelle. *Medicine populaire: d'hier et d'aujourd'hui*. Paris 1966.

Briggs, Katharine. *British Folktales.* New York: Pantheon Books 1977.

Broadhurst, Paul. *Tintagel and the Arthurian Mythos.* Launceston: Pendragon Press 1992.

Brockman, Norbert C. *Encyclopedia of Sacred Places.* New York: Oxford University Press 1997.

Buck, Sir Peter H. *Arts and Crafts of Hawaii: XI Religion.* Bernice P. Bishop Museum Special Publication 45. Honolulu: Bishop Museum Press 1964.

Budge, E.A. Wallis. *Cleopatra's Needles and Other Egyptian Obelisks.* London: Religious Tract Society 1926.

Burgess, Colin. *The Age of Stonehenge.* Edison: Castle Books 2003.

Burkert, Walter. *Ancient Mystery Cults.* Cambridge: Harvard University Press 1987.

Burl, Aubrey. *Prehistoric Averbury.* New Haven: Yale University Press 1979.

Burl, Aubrey. *Rings of Stone: The Prehistoric stone circles of Britain and Ireland.* New Haven: Ticknor & Fields 1979.

Burl, Aubrey. *Megalithic Brittany.* New York: Thames and Hudson Inc., 1985.

Burl, Aubrey. *A Guide to the Stone Circles of Britain, Ireland and Brittany.* New Haven: Yale University Press 1995.

Bury, J.B. *A History of Greece to the Death of Alexander the Great.* New York: The Modern Library, n.d.

Bushnell, G.H.S. *Ancient Peoples and Places: Peru.* Lima: Libreria ABC Bookstore, SA 1963.

Clewlow, Jr., C. William & Mary Ellen Wheeling. *Rock Art: An Introductory Recording Manual for California and the Great Basin.* Los Angeles: Institute of Archaeology, University of California 1978.

Clifford, Richard J. *The Cosmic Mountain in Canaan and the Old Testament.* Harvard Semitic Monographs Volume 4. Cambridge: Harvard University Press 1972.

Courtney, R.A. *Cornwall's Holy Wells: Their Pagan Origins.* Penzance: Oakmagic Publications 1997. A reprint of the 1916 edition published by Beare & Son, Penzance.

Cowan, David & Chris Arnold. *Ley Lines and Earth Energies.* Kempton: Adventures Unlimited Press 2003.

Cumont, Franz. *Oriental Religions in Roman Paganism.* New York: Dover Publications 1956 (Originally published in French in 1911).

Curtin, Roland G. "The Medical Superstitions of Precious Stones, Including Notes on the Therapeutics of other Stones." *Bulletin of the American Academy of Medicine*, 8 (December 1907), 444-494.

D'Alviella, Count Goblet. *The Migration of Symbols.* New York: University Books 1956.

Dames, Michael. *The Avebury Cycle.* New York: Thames and Hudson Inc. 1977.

de Camp, L. Sprague and Catherine C. de Camp. *Ancient Ruins: The Past Uncovered.* New York: Barnes & Noble Books 1992.

De Lys, Claudia. *A Treasury of American Superstitions.* New York: The Philosophical Library 1948.

Devereux, Paul. *Places of Power.* London: Blandford 1990.

Devereux, Paul. *Symbolic Landscapes.* Glastonbury: Gothic Image Publications 1992.

Devereux, Paul. *Earth Memory: Sacred Sites—Doorways into Earth's Mysteries.* St. Paul: Llewellyn Publications 1992.

Edmonds, Margot and Ella E. Clark. *Voices of the Winds: Native American Legends.* New York: Facts on File 1989.

Eliade, Mircea. *Cosmos and History: The Myth of the Eternal Return.* New York: Harper & Row Publishers 1959.

Eliade, Mircea. *The Sacred & The Profane: The Nature of Religion.* San Diego: Harcourt Brace & Company 1959.

Eliade, Mircea. *Shamanism: Archaic Techniques of Ecstasy.* Princeton University Press/ Bollingen Foundation 1972.

Elsasser, A.B. *Indians of Sequoia and Kings Canyon.* Three Rivers: Sequoia Natural History Association 1962.

Erdogu, Rabia. "A major new megalithic complex in Europe," in *Antiquity*, Vol. 77, Number 297, September 2003.

Evans, E. Estyn. *Irish Folk Ways.* Mineola: Dover Books 2000 (Originally published 1957).

Evans-Wentz, W.Y. *The Fairy-Faith in Celtic Countries.* Mineola: Dover Publications 2002 (Originally published 1911).

Fink, Gary. "Some Rock Art Sites in San Diego County" in *Pacific Coast Archaeological Society Quarterly*, Vol. 15, No. 2, April 1979, pgs 61-69.

Fogel, Edwin Miller. "Beliefs and Superstitions of the Pennsylvania Germans" in *Americana Germanica* (Philadelphia), 18 (1915), 268.

Fort, Charles. *New Lands*. New York: Boni & Liveright 1923.

Francis, Evelyn. *Avebury*. Powys: Wooden Books Ltd. 2000.

Frazer, Sir James. *The Magic Art and the Evolution of Kings, Vol 1*. London: Macmillan & Co. Ltd. 1955.

Frazer, Sir James. *The Golden Bough: A Study in Magic and Religion*. Hertfordhsire: Wordsworth Editions Ltd. 1993.

Gaskell, G.A. *Dictionary of All Scriptures and Myths*. New York: Avenel Books 1981.

Gerald of Wales. *The History and Topogaphy of Ireland*. London: Penguin Books 1982.

Gould, Rupert T. *Enigmas*. New York: University Books 1965.

Grant, Campbell. *Rock Art of the American Indian*. New York: Promontory Press 1967.

Green, Miranda J. *The World of the Druids*. London: Thames and Hudson Ltd. 1997.

Greenspoon, Leonard J. "Between Alexandria and Antioch: Jews and Judaism in the Hellenistic Period," in *The Oxford History of the Biblical World*, ed. by Michael D. Coogan. Oxford: Oxford University Press 1998.

Griffyn, Sally. *Sacred Journeys: Stone Circles & Pagan Paths*. London: Kyle Cathie Limited 2000.

Grinsell, L. V. "Witchcraft at some Prehistoric Sites" in *The Witch in History*, ed. by Venetia Newall. New York: Barnes & Noble Books 1996.

Hadingham, Evan. *Lines to the Mountain Gods: Nazca and the Mysteries of Peru*. New York: Random House 1987.

Hallendy, Norman. *Inuksuit: Silent Messengers of the Arctic*. London: British Museum Press 2000.

Hand, Wayland D. *Magical Medicine*. Berkeley: University of California Press 1980.

Harpur, James. *The Atlas of Sacred Places: Meeting Points of Heaven and Earth*. New York: Henry Holt and Company, Inc. 1994

Heizer, Robert F. "Sacred Rain Rocks of Northern California," in *Reports of the University of California Archaeological Survey, No. 20*, March 16, 1953.

Heizer, Robert F. and Adan E. Treganza. *Mines and Quarries of the Indians of California*. Ramona: Ballena Press 1972.

Hitchcock, John T. *The Magars of Banyan Hill*. New York: Holt, Rinehart and Winston Case Studies in Cultural Anthropology 1966.

Hudson, Travis and Ernest Underhay. *Crystals in the Sky: An Intellectual Odyssey Involving Chumash Astronomy, Cosmology and Rock Art*. Socorro: Ballena Press Anthropological Papers #10 1978.

Hutton, Ronald. *The Pagan Religions of the Ancient British Isles: Their Nature and Legacy*. Oxford: Blackwell Publishers Ltd. 1993.

Imbrogno, Philip & Marianne Horrigan. *Celtic Mysteries in New England.* St. Paul: Llewellyn Publications 2000.

Irwin, Charles N. "A Material Representation of a Sacred Tradition," in *The Journal of California Anthropology*, Summer 1978, Vol.5, No.1, pgs 90-95.

James, E.O. *The Cult of the Mother-Goddess.* New York: Barnes & Noble Books 1994.

Johnson, W. Fletcher. *Life of Sitting Bull and History of the Indian War of 1890-'91.* Edgewood Publishing Company Publishers 1891.

Johnston, Bernice Eastman. *California's Gabrielino Indians.* Los Angeles: Southwest Museum 1962.

Jones, David E. *Sanapia: Comanche Medicine Woman.* New York: Holt, Rinehart and Winston Case Studies in Cultural Anthropology 1972.

Joussaume, Roger. *Dolmens for the Dead: Megalith-Building throughout the World.* Ithaca: Cornell University Press 1988.

Kearney, Michael. *The Winds of Ixtepeji: World View and Society in a Zapotec Town.* New York: Holt, Rinehart and Winston Case Studies in Cultural Anthropology 1972.

Kehoe, Alice B. and Thomas F. Kehoe. *Solstice-Aligned Boulder Configurations in Saskatchewan.* Canadian Ethnology Service Paper No. 48. Ottawa: National Museums of Canada 1979.

Kennedy, Conan. *Ancient Ireland: The User's Guide—An Exploration of Ireland's Pre-Christian Monuments, Mythology and Magic, Ritual and Folklore.* Killala: Morrigan Books 1997.

Kieckhefer, Richard. *Magic in the Middle Ages.* Cambridge: Cambridge University Press 1989.

Knaak, Manfred. *The Forgotten Artists: Indians of Anza-Borrego and Their Rock Art.* Borrego Springs: Anza-Borrego Desert Natural History Association 1988.

Knight, Lavinia C. "Bell Rock and Indian Maze Rock of Orange County" in *Pacific Coast Archaeological Society Quarterly* Vol. 15, No. 2, April 1979, pgs 25-32.

Koerper, Henry C. and Roger D. Mason. "A Red Ochre Cogged Stone From Orange County" in *Pacific Coast Archaeological Society Quarterly*, Vol. 34, Number 1, Winter 1998, pgs 59-72.

Kroeber, A.L. *Handbook of the Indians of California.* New York: Dover Publications Inc. 1976.

Kunz, George Frederick. *The Curious Lore of Precious Stones.* New York: Dover Publications, Inc. 1971 (Originally published 1913).

Lalayan, E. "Veranda: Family Customs" in *Ethnographic Review* #2 (1897), 113-186.

Lamont-Brown, Raymond. *Scottish Folklore.* Edinburgh: Birlinn Limited 1996.

Landsverk, O.G. *Ancient Norse Messages on American Stones.* Glendale: Norseman Press 1969.

Leland, Charles G. *Etruscan Roman Remains.* Blaine: Phoenix Publishing (originally published 1892).

Lenik, Edward J. "Sacred Places and Power Spots: Native American Rock Art at Middleborough, Massachusetts" in *Rock Art of the Eastern Woodlands: American Rock Art Research Associations Occasional Paper 2.* San Miguel: American Rock Art Research Association 1996.

Levi, Jerome Meyer. "Wii'pay: The Living Rocks—Ethnographic Notes on Crystal Magic Among Some California Yumans," in *The Journal of California Anthropology*, Summer 1978, Vol.5, No.1, pgs 42-52.

Livingstone, Sheila. *Scottish Customs.* New York: Barnes & Noble Books 1996.

Logan, Patrick. *The Holy Wells of Ireland.* Buckinghamshire: Colin Smythe 1980.

Lowie, Robert H. *Indians of the Plains.* Garden City: The Natural History Press 1963.

MacCulloch, J.A. *The Religion of the Celts.* Mineola: Dover Publications, Inc. 2003 (Originally published 1911).

Mack, Carol K. and Dinah Mack. *A Field Guide to Demons, Fairies, Fallen Angels, and Other Subversive Spirits.* New York: Owl Books 1998.

MacKenzie, Donald A. *Crete & Pre-Hellenic Myths and Legends.* London: Senate 1995 (originally published 1917).

Maringer, Johannes. *The Gods of Prehistoric Man.* London: The Phoenix Press 2002.

Mayer, Dorothy. "Sky Games in California Petroglyphs" in *Visions of the Sky: Archaeological and Ethnological Studies of California Indian Astronomy.* Salinas: Coyote Press—Coyote Press Archives of California Prehistory Number 16 1988, pgs 41-76.

McGowan, Charlotte. *Ceremonial Fertility Sites in Southern California*: San Diego Museum Papers No. 14. San Diego: San Diego Museum of Man 1982.

McLaren, Colin, translator. *The Aberdeen Beastiary.* Aberdeen: Aberdeen University Library MS 24 1995.

McDaniel, Walton Brooks. "The Medical and Magical Significance in Ancient Medicine of Things Connected with Reproduction and Its Organs," in *Journal of the History of Medicine, 3 (1948)*, 525-546.

Meaden, Terence. *Stonehenge: The Secret of the Solstice.* London: Souvenir Press Ltd. 1997.

Merrifield, Ralph. *The Archaeology of Ritual and Magic.* New York: New Amsterdam Books 1987.

Michell, John. *Megalithomania.* Ithaca: Cornell University Press 1982.

Michell, John. *Sacred England.* Glastonbury: Gothic Image Publications 1996.

Miller, Mary and Karl Taube. *An Illustrated Dictionary of the Gods and Symbols of Ancient Mexico and the Maya.* New York: Thames and Hudson 1997.

Mohen, Jean-Pierre. *Prehistoric Art: The Mythical Birth of Humanity.* Paris: Pierre Terrail 2002.

Molyneaux, Brian Leigh. *The Sacred Earth.* Boston: Little, Brown and Company 1995.

Mooney, James. *Myths of the Cherokee.* New York: Dover Publications, Inc. 1995 (originally published 1900).

Mulvaney, D.J. *The Prehistory of Australia.* New York: Frederick A. Praeger, Publishers 1969.

Nimmo, John. *Identity of the Religions Called Druidical and Hebrew: Demonstrated From the Nature and Objects of their Worship.* London: University of London Literary and Philosophical Society 1829.

Nixon, Lance, interviewer. Native American Folklore Interviews Collection OGL #1260, June 25, 1992: Alvina Alberts. Grand Forks: Elwyn B. Robinson Department of Special Collections, Chester Fritz Library, University of North Dakota.

Ó Nualláin, Seán. *Stone Circles in Ireland.* Dublin: Country House 1995, 45.

Opler, Morris Edward. *An Apache Life-Way: The Economic, Social, and Religious Institutions of the Chiricahua Indians.* Chicago: University of Chicago Press 1941.

Ó Riordáin, Seán P. *Antiquities of the Irish Countryside.* London: Methuen & Co. Ltd.1979.

Paul, Tom. "Hammonasset Line," a talk given at the Spring 2001 NEARA meeting. Text available at *www.neara.org/PAUL/Hammonasset02.htm.*

Penard, A.P. and T.E. Penard. "Popular Notions Pertaining to Primitive Stone Artifacts in Surinam," in *Journal of American Folklore*, 30 (1917), 251-261.

Pennick, Nigel. *Celtic Sacred Landscapes.* London: Thames and Hudson 1996.

Pepper, Elizabeth & John Wilcock. *Magical and Mystical Sites: Europe and the British Isles.* Grand Rapids: Phanes Press 2000.

Peterson, Frederick. *Ancient Mexico: An Introduction to the Pre-Hispanic Cultures.* New York: Capricorn Books 1962.

Powers, William K. *Oglala Religion.* Lincoln: The University of Nebraska Press 1975.

Puckett, Newbell Niles. *Popular Beliefs and Superstitions: A Compendium of American Folklore from the Ohio Collection of Newbell Niles Puckett*, ed.by Wayland D. Hand. Boston: G K Hall & Co 1981.

Radford, Edwin and Mona A. *Encyclopaedia of Superstitions.* New York: The Philosophical Library 1949.

Rands, Robert L. "Some Manifestations of Water in Mesoamerican Art," *Anthropological Papers, No. 48.* Washington: Smithsonian Institution Bureau of American Ethnology. Bulletin 157 1955.

Rappoport, Angelo S. *Myth and Legend of Ancient Israel: Vol. 1.* New York: Ktav Publishing House Inc. 1966.

Reade, W. Winwood. *The Veil of Isis, or Mysteries of the Druids.* North Hollywood: Newcastle Publishing Company 1992.

Rhys, John. *Celtic Folklore: Welsh and Manx.* Vol. 1. New York: Gordon Press 1974 (Originally published 1900).

Rickard, Bob and John Michell. *Unexplained Phenomena: Mysteries and Curiosities of Science, Folklore and Superstition.* London: Rough Guides, Ltd. 2000.

Rogers, Malcolm J. *Ancient Hunters of the Far West.* San Diego: Union-Tribune Publishing Company 1966.

Ross, Anne. *Folklore of the Scottish Highland.* Glouchestershire: Tempus Publishing Inc. 2000.

Rudgley, Richard. *The Lost Civilizations of the Stone Age.* New York: The Free Press 1999

Sauter, John and Bruce Johnson. *Tillamook Indians of the Oregon Coast.* Portland: Binfords & Mort, Publishers 1974.

Scarre, Chris & Paul Raux. "A new decorated menhir," in *Antiquity*, Vol. 74, Number 286, December 2000, pgs 757-8.

Schick, Kathy D. and Nicholas Toth. *Making Silent Stones Speak: Human Evolution and the Dawn of Technology*. New York: Simon & Schuster 1993.

Schulz, Paul E. *Indians of Lassen.* Mineral: Loomis Museum Association 1988.

Service, Alastair & Jean Bradbery. *Megaliths and Their Mysteries: A Guide to the Standing Stones of Europe.* New York: Macmillan Publishing Company 1979.

Shoushen, Jin. *Beijing Legends.* Beijing: Panda Books 1982.

Silverberg, Robert. *Mound Builders of Ancient America: The Archaeology of a Myth.* Greenwich: New York Graphic Society Ltd. 1968.

Simpson, Jacqueline. *Icelandic Folktales and Legends.* Berkeley: University of California Press 1972.

Simpson, Jacqueline, trans. *Legends of Icelandic Magicians.* Cambridge: D.S. Brewer Ltd for The Folklore Society 1975.

Smith, William Ramsay. *Aborigine Myths and Legends.* London: Senate 1996 (Originally published 1930).

Songling, Pu. *Selected Tales of Liaozhai.* Beijing: Panda Books 1981.

Spence, Lewis. *Legends and Romances of Brittany.* Mineola: Dover Publications, Inc. 1997.

Spence, Lewis. *The Magic Arts in Celtic Britain.* Mineola: Dover Publications, Inc. 1999.

Spier, Leslie. *Yuman Tribes of the Gila River.* New York: Dover Publications Inc., 1978 (Originally published 1933).

Squire, Charles. *Celtic Myths & Legends.* New York: Portland House, 1997.

St. Pierre, Mark and Tilda Long Soldier. *Walking in the Sacred Manner: Healers, Dreamers, and Pipe Carriers—Medicine Women of the Plains Indians.* New York: Touchstone Books 1995.

Storaker, Joh. Th. "Naturrigerne I den Norske Folketro" in *Norsk Folkeminnelag No 18.* Oslo, 1928, 12.

Storaker, Joh. Th. "Sygdom og Forgjo/relse I den Norske Folketero" in *Norsk Folkeminnelag No. 20*. Oslo, 1932, 31.

Straffon, Cheryl. *The Earth Goddess: Celtic and Pagan Legacy of the Landscape*. London: Blandford 1997.

Tennent, Sir J. Emerson. *Notes and Queries*, Vol. V, No. 119, Saturday, February 7, 1852, 121.

Thomsen, Marie-Louise. "Witchcraft and Magic in Ancient Mesopotamia," in *Witchcraft and Magic in Europe: Biblical and Pagan Societies*. Edited by Bengt Ankarloo and Stuart Clark. Philadelphia: University of Pennsylvania Press 2001.

True, D.L., C.W. Meighan & Harvey Crew. *Archaeological Investigations at Molpa, San Diego County, California*. University of California Publications in Anthropology, Volume 11, Berkeley: University of California Press 1974.

Trupe, Beverly S., John M. Rafter, and Wilson G. Turner. "Ring of Pictured Stones: Astronomical Connotations of a Rock Art Site in the Eastern Mojave Desert" in *Visions of the Sky: Archaeological and Ethnological Studies of California Indian Astronomy*, Salinas: Coyote Press—Coyote Press Archives of California Prehistory Number 16 1988, pgs 153-171.

Turner, Mark. *Folklore & Mysteries of the Cotswolds*. London: Robert Hale Limited 1993.

Tvauri, Andres. "Cup-Marked Stones in Estonia" in *Folklore*, vol. 11, October 1999. Tartu: Institute of the Estonian Language, pgs 113-169.

Wakefield, J.D. *Legendary Landscapes: Secrets of Ancient Wiltshire Revealed*. Marlborough: Nod Press 1999.

Walker, Barbara G. *The Women's Dictionary of Symbols and Sacred Objects*. Edison: Castle Books 1988.

Walker, James R., ed by Elaine A. Jahner. *Lakota Myth*. Lincoln: University of Nebraska Press, 1983.

Walker, James R. *Lakota Belief and Ritual*. Lincoln: University of Nebraska Press 1991.

Watson, Lyall. *The Nature of Things: The Secret Life of Inanimate Objects*. Rochester: Destiny Books 1992.

Wedel, Waldo R. "Archaeological Materials from the Vicinity of Mobridge, South Dakota," *Anthropological Papers, No. 45*. Washington: Smithsonian Institution Bureau of American Ethnology. Bulletin 157 1955.

Westervelt, William D. *Hawaiian Legends of Volcanoes*. Tokyo: Charles E. Tuttle Company 1963.

Westwood, Jennifer. *Albion: A Guide to Legendary Britain*. London: Paladin/Grafton Books 1985.

Whitley, David S. *A Guide to Rock Art Sites: Southern California and Southern Nevada*. Missoula: Mountain Press Publishing Company 1996.

Whitley, David S. *The Art of the Shaman: Rock Art of California.* Salt Lake City: The University of Utah Press 2000.

Wilbert, Johannes. *Yupa Folktales.* Los Angeles: Latin American Center, University of California Los Angeles 1974.

Wilde, Lady. *Irish Cures, Mystic Charms & Superstitions.* New York: Sterling Publishing Co., Inc. 1991.

Wilde, Lynn Webster. *On the Trail of the Women Warriors: The Amazons in Myth and History.* Uncorrected advance copy. New York: St. Martin's Press 1999.

Wilkinson, Richard H. *The Complete Gods and Goddesses of Ancient Egypt.* New York: Thames & Hudson 2003.

Zigmond, Maurice L. "The Supernatural World of the Kawaiisu," in *Flowers of the Wind: Papers on Ritual, Myth, and Symbolism in California and the Southwest.* ed. by Thomas C, Blackburn. Socorro: Ballena Press 1977, 59-95.

Zigmond, Maurice L. *Kawaiisu Mythology: An Oral Tradition of South-Central California.* Ballena Press Anthropological Papers No. 18. Menlo Park: Ballena Press 1980.

Index